Red Balloons

Published by Halcyon Publishing

First published 2023

ISBN: 978-1-9196240-7-5

Cover design: Steve Leard
Cover photograph: Graham Holland
Layout: Rob MacDonald
Edited by Adam Bushby & Rob MacDonald

Printed & bound by:
CMP (UK) Limited
G3 The Fulcrum
Vantage Way
Poole
Dorset
BH12 4NU

If I could find a souvenir
Just to prove the world was here
And here is a red balloon
I think of you, and let it go

Nena, '99 Red Balloons'

This book is for me.

Me, when I'm 75.
Slippers on.
Feet up.
Me.

About the author

Liam Walsh lives in his home town of Witney, Oxfordshire, with his family and their dog.

He has attended over a thousand Swindon Town games and has seen them play against every club in the top four divisions. He boasts a 59.7% win rate, although it doesn't always feel like that.

Some optimistically declared his 2021 running endeavour in London to be his *first* marathon. In the same spirit, this is Liam's first book.

Contents

Prologue

1993

April

I took the call from my friend Andy. I was in Mum and Dad's kitchen, the phone in the corner between the boiler and the door. This wasn't the time to perch on the high stool.

Nick had been shot dead.

In Brazil, and no, there weren't many details. He was in the jungle, it might have been random, it might have been crossfire. It was a million miles from here and the words, the details hardly mattered, Nick had died. It was April 1993, we were old student mates, now scattered across the globe in the two years since leaving Swansea. Our ties loosening, our connections fading as we found new ways, new possibilities and new beginnings.

And this numb, bright spring morning, very much an ending.

***

A couple of weeks later, we celebrated Nick's life, in the Manchester streets he loved to share with us, mourning his passing. We sent him off knowing he'd packed more living into twenty-three years than many of us might manage in eighty-three. He was, always, the literal life and soul: the only reason there was a party. He wasn't quite my best mate, but heck, he was an almighty mate. We'd met, bonded, I guess, initially through a loose network of the second generation Irish in Swansea. We had the Pogues and Jack

Charlton and a shared melancholic wrestle with a dual identity, the songs, the romance, the history, and the wild nature of Ireland. There was nothing cool about this in the late eighties — the country was economically poor, resolutely Catholic, defined by the troubles in the north. The Celtic tiger had yet to awaken, never mind roar.

Our Irishness with English accents was not a badge of honour in Wales. Swansea, a rainy, isolated, enchanting, windy, hilly, fiercely proud city had a ferry to the west and Ireland, and a motorway and railway line to the east and England. For us, literally between the two, the city straddled these identities. Living and occasionally studying in a bay we called home between the fading steelworks of Port Talbot and the breathtaking natural majesty of the Gower — living in Swansea — felt comforting, felt just right.

These were student days, and there were an awful lot of 'pound a pint' offers to navigate. And Nick was more generous with his navigating skills and easy-going sociability than anyone else. He was just as hospitable on his home territory and visits to Manchester would always include visits to the Withington Ale House and many more. He had a magnetic charm, had worked matchdays at Manchester City while supporting United. These were the days that my team, Swindon Town, could play City off the park at Maine Road, yet lose, with the soreness of another unlucky defeat eased by the prospect of the evening to come through trawling the hostelries of Rusholme, Fallowfield and Withington.

Music was ever-present for us, and while Nick extolled the virtues of a local Manchester band called the Stone Roses, Grant, another friend, earnestly implored us to support a supposedly upcoming group of Swansea students called the Manic Street Preachers. That two of them, Nicky and Richey, were studying Politics with me, did nothing to convince: if they weren't yet in *NME* or *Melody Maker*, I didn't care. They looked outlandishly garish and far removed from my staple spiky American rock of the Pixies, or meat-and-two-veg indie of the Wedding Present. Besides, they lived in the student village at Hendrefoilan, and nobody cool came from that way.

It might have been a quiet friend loudly championing, but I wasn't interested.

My 'thanks but no thanks' to the Manics wasn't to last for too long, but that's for later.

***

It's all a long time ago now, but the coming together of that old student friendship group for Nick's memorial service, funeral, burial, final goodbye has stayed with me. Maybe it was our final goodbye too, the full stop on our student years before we crept into grown-up life and towards lawnmowers and mortgages. I met Jackie at a pub on the outskirts of Oxford and we drove north. Best mates, drifted apart, brought back together in these cruellest of circumstances: a heady emotional whirl of being excited to see and catch up with each other, while gasping for breath and understanding as to why we had to be doing this, making this horrible, fantastic journey together, crying. We found our B&B and our mates, Andy, Mark, Helen, and plenty of others too.

There was a choking desperation of emotion and noise and terror, of what's the plan, we're late, oh this is so terrible, it's brilliant to see you, I hate this. Thing is, we'd all travelled, and we were now tense, running late for the evening memorial service. We dumped cars on verges of freshly cut April grass and ran in.

It was a vast, solemn, beautiful, brutal, service. The space around the silence, the grief, the sheer number of people, the words, every lilt, the dramatic Catholicism, the friends around me, the unpreparedness, the memories, the colour — church golds and silvers and reflections and tricks of light, the tiredness — sent my head spinning, reeling. I felt sick, dizzy, terrified.

It was never-ending.

Afterwards, we drank and drank and drank on the basis that it was what Nick would have wanted. It's what we wanted. We had a curry on the Rusholme mile and drank some more, he'd have wanted that. Our evening turned glorious. We laughed and shared, sang and drank some more. In the midst of it all, we agreed it was the perfect send off. We were all best friends again. Yeah, we are missing Nick but whose round is it now? Of course, it was the worst of times, but right now, as we giggled the night away, hugged our 'best friends forever' promises and talked ourselves hoarse, eventually to sleep, right there and then it was just an astonishing evening, the best of times.

In the morning, it was the worst of times. I had a crushing headache, a hangover the likes of which I had not had before or probably since. I endured the funeral service with — a phrase I have since come to understand — a hundred drummers in my head. As I trembled and withered, my fingernails were jabbed tightly into my legs through my trousers, saving me from collapse and public shame. Fighting tears of internal regret, the self-loathing that I felt like this — while Nick was cold, still, dead in that box, feeling nothing, ever again, eternal — it knew no bounds.

Nick was buried a couple of miles away, at the enormous Southern Cemetery. I can still feel the gulping relief at the chill fresh air and the sense of freedom in escaping the claustrophobic tightness of the packed out church. Here, my mate was being buried at twenty-three, and my immediate feeling in that moment was sheer, selfish, hideous relief: I was still standing, and I hadn't thrown up in the church.

I'll come back, I know I will, and Nick mate, I promise, next time it'll be more about you.

Blessed relief was soon manifested in the hair of the dog at the Irish Club on Mauldeth Road. The raucous reunion of the previous night was now a shared recognition of the need for some food, some reflection and maybe just one more for the road. It wasn't long since we had celebrated Nick's 21st here, I could still sense his speech in faded photographs, the new, garish shirt that I wore, the dances we danced. And through it all, I'd needed my football fix: while the others caught up in the Ale House, I stood, a neutral on the Kippax terrace and watched Manchester City draw 0-0 with Millwall.

So, once that quiet reflection and reluctant last pint was done, we said the goodbyes of those ready to hit the road. We said our sad farewells to the family, toasted and cherished our rediscovered best friendships, made vague plans for the future, weekend festivals, summer travels, football.

There'd always be football …

I've barely seen any of them since.

Other than Andy, who also supports Swindon Town. Inspired by Glenn Hoddle, we are a month away from reaching the newly-formed Premier League. Driven by the savage injustice of 1990's demotion, we're going to make it to the top division for the first time in our history. This coming Sunday we play West Ham, the penultimate league game before the playoffs. Somehow, I've missed just five games home or away all season, and as the rain clears over Morrissey's fabled cemetery gates in southern Manchester, I already have other priorities and the season's denouement to anticipate.

Mark drove me east, across the Pennines, to drop me with my girlfriend Kate and her family in Sheffield.

***

Fourteen years later, Kate and I have three children, Niamh, Euan and Patrick. This time, I'm driving, west over the Pennines, bleak, forbidding and foreboding, shrouded in dull mist, they're daring us to stop and explore at our peril. I drive on, from Sheffield to Manchester with Euan.

We're going to find Nick.

Actually, we're going to watch Swindon away at Stockport County, but the cemetery is only a goal kick or three away so it's high time I made good on my promise to return. Yeah, we used to play Manchester City, but this is a big game. I know it's the fourth division, but we're top and they're on a run. And I have children, Euan now old enough to feel this passion and to share these days. Patrick will lovingly follow his lead. Patrick is two, he will see Swindon for the first time in a month or so, be terrified by the mascot Rockin' Robin as we beat Mansfield and almost get promoted. Niamh, the eldest, has already had her fleeting football phase; now she has horses to ride and show jumps to imagine.

One day, I promise Euan, Swindon will rise again, and we'll pack our dreams and see them valiantly battle against City and United once more. Or even Stoke or Blackburn. Today though, first things first, it's Stockport County.

I'd made my promise, I'd be back to see Nick.

***

For Morrissey, it was a dreaded sunny day. For us, it's raining at the Southern Cemetery.

So we go inside and we gravely read the stones.
All those people, all those lives, where are they now?

Euan and I walk and walk, searching for his grave. It's massive, it's huge, it's impossible, the more we look, the bigger the cemetery gets. It's daunting, it's sprawling, it's growing before us, stretching further over the Manchester suburbs with every desperate step. In my head, the path was so clear. Again and again, I tried reimagining those simple few steps from the funeral. Unforgettable steps, surely?

He is just here!

But he's not. He's not here, or here, or there or there. Euan is patient, then impatient, then wet, then quiet. I'm grumpy.

At this rate Dad, we'll miss the kick-off. Dad, Dad! Please!

We won't miss the kick-off. We don't ever miss the kick-off. We cut things fine; I can be late for anything else, anywhere else. But we won't miss the kick-off. I'm desolate.

Come on Euan, we're going. Nick can wait for another time.

We don't miss the kick-off. But listless Swindon are stuffed 3-0 by a hungry Stockport and their fans celebrate like they've been promoted, just for breaking a record of clean sheets or something.

It's galling, and I feel like I've let Nick down.

They weren't promoted, and ultimately, we were, and come May we celebrated like we'd broken a record of clean sheets or something. Stockport have had a torrid time since, sinking deeper into financial ruin and non-league obscurity. But they too, at last, are recovering. In a footballing sense, I hope they continue their journey back towards league football and perhaps they'll get to stuff us three zip again, and to enjoy it accordingly.

Six hundred or so Swindon fans grumble, shuffle, moan into the cold damp air onto cold, stale coaches, or towards the train, or retracing steps to cars. Long journeys home. Lower-league fans doing what we do, thinking it'll be better next week. There's always next week.

We head back for Sheffield. My eyes sting. It hasn't been a good day.

***

Years later, I'm working in Manchester and I have the luxury of an overnight stop.

I park in the lay-by, take some deep breaths, and once more enter through those vast cemetery gates and look for Nick. This calm evening, I find his grave within five minutes. Everything is familiar and vast and incomprehensible all at the same time. I gather my thoughts, talk to Nick awhile, relight happy memories. I smile a rueful melancholic smile and walk back to my car.

I should have brought some flowers.

There's a memorial tree too, at Swansea University. It's a lot easier to find. I visit each time I'm there, never often enough. Never a proper reunion, never long enough, I pay a quiet visit and reflect. I'll think of the time Nick fell flat on his back with a full pint and never spilt a drop, of wild nights and cruel hangovers. I'll think of his permanent grin, the joy he enriched us with.

But honestly, do I think of the impact Nick's death had on those closest to him? Wonder how his family are doing?

No, not really, I haven't thought of Nick's family, their lives and their pain. My relationship with Nick is stuck of course in that intense period cut devastatingly short in 1993. Do his family or even those old friends know that I still care? That I occasionally talk to his tree and visit his grave?

No.

I've just left them to live and hopefully recover their lives. And when I do see those friends, do we talk through what happened and how we coped, how we felt, how we remember? Do we talk about Nick?

How we adored him?

No.

The tree has grown well in the mild climate. It's a couple of hundred yards from the sea, guaranteeing frequent lashings of rain. Nature helping nature. It's lived longer than Nick now.

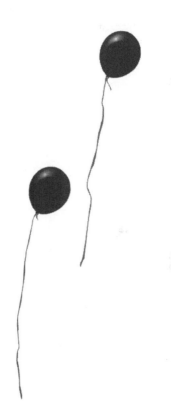

2019

July

Another League Two season awaits.

I've had a fairly typical football-supporting life. An only child, born three days after Swindon won the League Cup in 1969, I followed my Dad and Mum, uncle Jasper, old friends, new friends. I caught the bug, lived the obsession. Swindon. Town. Football. Club. We went everywhere together, to Carlisle and Newcastle and Brighton and Plymouth, and most points in between. We cheered together and moaned together, from the bottom tier to the Premier League and back again.

So, for me when the time came, following this parenting model was obvious enough. And I had three children to refine my approach with. First, Niamh, born with the Town top of what's now the Championship and seemingly destined for a return to the Premier League. Niamh was happy for an occasional day out and Dad time, but her obsession was saved for horses. She particularly enjoyed watching the sun set beyond the Town End, yellow then orange, gently disappearing beyond the horizon, a world beyond Swindon, a world beyond ours. There was an early season League Cup game against Brentford, made sweeter if only because it went to extra time and penalties, and meant a late night. I knew her footballing race was run when she excitedly asked whether the police horses deployed pre-match to control Millwall fans would be doing show jumping on the pitch after the game. They didn't, and she never came back.

When her brother Euan was born, the team promptly went on a record-breaking twenty-game streak without a win. His path was different, fortunate possibly to be afforded his first taste through hospitality, he's never looked back. When Swindon were in financial ruin, and the end of our world felt nigh, explaining that to an eight-year-old Euan felt the hardest task imaginable.

Finally, there was Patrick. He made his County Ground debut for that potential promotion clincher aged two, a planning and logistical masterpiece I'll forever be proud of, only marred by the traumatic effect that meeting Rockin' Robin had on the toddler. Patrick followed his brother's lead, grew slowly into the hand-me-down shirts, demanded his own, recreated the goals as he held my hand walking along Shrivenham Road back to the car and developed his own love for the club.

Together, we enjoyed and endured the modest joys and just around the corner disappointments of a pretty average club through a succession of owners and managers. Whether Wise or Sturrock, Wilson or Di Canio, we did our bit, each game, each hope and each despair tightening our ties to the club, and imperceptibly, to each other.

Recent seasons had been grim: turgid Flitcroft fare, then the befuddling meanderings of Phil Brown's team. And still we went, out of a sense of habit, of loyalty, of defiance, as the crowds and moans around us turned into empty and silent seats. We went because we had a fiercely competitive family prediction league to fulfil. We went because we just did. Sometimes, we didn't seem to agree on much, sometimes we put more effort into getting there than the players gave on the pitch, sometimes it was simply dull, insipid, and miserable — but it was our precious misery.

***

Dad hadn't been at his best through the last summer, the extent of which became clear when he was less keen on attending pre-season friendlies. When he did, we joked that his characteristic *get up, your mum's watching* calling card to injury feigning opponents seemed rustier than usual on its first summer outing, as we watched yet another brand new Town XI tentatively tiptoe through a friendly. Clearly, he wasn't yet match fit.

Summer has a lot to be commended for. Not least, the countdown to the day in late June when the fixtures for the new season are released, and we can start to look forward to winter. The shape of the season will be cast before us, an almighty download of details and optimism and hope and some certainty. Whatever life throws at us, this time, Swindon will be at home to Cambridge on Boxing Day and finish the season at Macclesfield. As usual, the scheduling will be mean, and we'll be on holiday for the first home game. Frankly, there's not much buzz to be had out of a League Two schedule, more than anything it's a sad indictment of how far we've fallen: you can only judge a boxer by the mediocrity of his opponents. Still, this is the time to muster some enthusiasm and hey, I can't help but pondering ... early season successive away games at Exeter, Cheltenham, Leyton Orient ... decent and popular away days each, now if only the Town could get on a roll ... mmm, this could be fun.

Before that though, there's the pre-season friendlies, and we all know that pre-season starts at Swindon Supermarine. So, winter starts, more or less, in the first week of July. And each year, Patrick, Euan and I literally count down those days, hours, minutes, seconds to leaves falling, winter starting, big coats on and life starting all over again.

The journey to Supermarine itself is a rehearsal for the real thing. Witney to Burford, smiling at the beautiful view of the Windrush valley to the right: the gateway to the Cotswolds and its rich golden honey of gentle limestone undulations. To the left, a crumbling dry-stone wall untouched in generations. On past the golf course, where in time-honoured tradition, we offer our score predictions. Patrick will dutifully capture them on his phone, reminding us of the league table, picking out trends ... Dad, you've said 1-1 four games on the trot. It's a glimpse into our psychology, our expectations ... and rationale. It's semi-competitive and at the end of the season, Grampy wins.

Now, do we do it for friendlies?

We can't remember but yeah, surely, we usually win this one comfortably enough. Four? Five? New striker, who knows? What about the trialists?

It's turning to winter in our heads, but the good folk flocking to the glorious Thames at picture-postcard Lechlade still think it's midsummer. We'll crawl through, acknowledging the field of swans and campers next to them, and on towards Highworth, up on the hill before us. Another season has turned, and still no progress on the proposed training ground to our right. We'll talk about Lee Power, Swindon's owner, his racehorses and our mutual connection through him, uncle Maurice back home in Waterford, Ireland. Each year, we'll marginally improve our impressions of him.

Well Shawwwwn, listen, we ain't got no bladdy manney but we're gonna give it a roight go this year.

Power's motives, methods and means have long been debated by Town fans. He was to come out less than favourably at a court judgement into long-standing and ongoing legal considerations regarding the clubs ownership structure in 2020. But there and then, in summer 2019, we just wanted him, old school Cockney accent or not, to help Richie Wellens put a decent team on the pitch.

Once we're atop the hill and through the lights at Highworth, past the chippy we'll stop at in the rush to make Tuesday night games, we're virtually at Supermarine. It is pretty busy and I'll end up doing some dodgy reversing onto a grass verge too close to a junction. It's not the best location and I'll look awkwardly at the car, possibly shuffle it to and fro some more, then leave it, just leave it Liam, and walk a few hundred yards to the turnstiles.

There is always a peculiar mood and sound to that queue and it is a queue that knows this is the year: chirpy, relaxed and buoyant. This is no ordinary football queue. It moves quickly and there is a satisfying click through as we pay our cash, buy a programme, look at the beautiful field of dreams before us.

Our heroes are lower-league footballers and while their earnings are modest enough, the difference in physique compared to their very much part-time hosts is striking. Up close, this view we only get in preseason confirms they are finely tuned professional athletes. We pin our emotions and expectations recklessly and unrealistically upon them. For the next ten months, every mistake will be pilloried, every success exaggerated. We'll forget there's a man before the squad number, our own perceptions and dreams foisted and projected onto them. Is our season going to be in ruins if we only beat them by three today? It was six last time and we know how that turned out: rubbish. Yes, definitely. We'll hypothesise and overthink and argue but jeez, we should be putting seven or eight past these.

Dad will try out his familiar jest when an opposition player hits the deck a little too willingly. This year he sounds hoarse, and his timing is awry. Fair play though Dad, none of us are quite on it yet — I don't even know who our number 11 is.

On the way home, there's a sharp and serious appraisal of the trialists, the boys Googling in the back for added detail, updates, will they keep him? Who else might we get in before Tuesday? We'll have different, precious, opinions. Sometimes, we'll agree to disagree. Sometimes, we'll just disagree. We're a family and we're talking to each other. It's all pored over with care and meaning. We will offer no unanimity on that new away kit. I don't even know what colour it's supposed to be.

"Dad, you couldn't even park the car properly."

"Can we go to the next game at Melksham Dad?"

Football is back.

This July though, is different.

I didn't know anything was different. Because it wasn't obvious.
But it soon would be.

***

Dad's chest complaints were as unresolved as they were
undiagnosed. He was a fit, proud, active man and this wasn't in
itself, a dramatic worry. He'd beaten two heart attacks, prostate
cancer, was hardy from a childhood in Ireland sharing shoes, so a
little local difficulty with his chest would be just that. He continued
to maintain his garden, and ours, with ferocious bursts of activity.
His strength to do so would shame me, nearly thirty years younger,
and countless others too.

A few years earlier, just before his 70th birthday and mindful
perhaps of his heart and cancer issues, we had a reunion of sorts
of the boys' football team he managed for many years. It was a
barnstorming night in the Elm Tree, a renewal of old acquaintances
and a reminder of old stories. He managed us from primary
school to the verge of adulthood and nurtured one of the finest
young football teams in Oxfordshire. And here we were laughing
and crying and drinking as if we'd never have a chance again.
There is a simply beautiful photo that captures the moment.
Men, tipsy, friends, happy.

It was the last picture taken of Marcus, our brightest light.
Six weeks later, after his wife Michele had delivered a most
extraordinary eulogy, we stood in the Elm Tree again, remembering
his life, recalling those stories, that night, that beautiful picture, in
disbelief this time. Kev was there, obviously solemn, his usual grin
and cheekiness gone, gutted that he'd missed our night out and
his last chance to laugh with his boyhood best mate. I wondered
again at Michele's speech: she'd only recently lost her son, and now
her husband. Amid the sheer grief and the wailing on a boiling
day, just where on earth does that guttural human strength and
capability, that dignity, come from?

Now, it's summer 2019 and Lea, another old team-mate from
Dad's team has died. My oldest friend Rob had messaged me with

the sad news, and later, recalling the estate where Marcus, Lea, Kevin and I had grown up, quipped in typical dark humour:

Beware you Burwell boys — if I were you or Kevin, I'd be checking my life insurance.

A month later, Kevin died too.

Rob is an immense character who seems to have taken on the unfortunate role of bearer of bad news. Each time I feel and share his fresh, raw hurt, reeling with him again.

Kev was a good player, he always was. Over the years, we would trade Oxford and Swindon insults, in a pantomime way, and always with a flash of a smile, mixing competitive local rivalry with friendship and respect. Kev's service in the Bampton church which stars in Downton Abbey, was attended by hundreds. Mainly men, men of every trade, men who saw the futility in singing or pretending to. During the hymns, it was eerily, sensationally quiet, and consequently, incredibly moving. One of his friends remembered him at the service as *loving Arsenal, hating Swindon*. It drew plenty of smirks, but I recoiled somewhat — why remember anyone for what they hated?

I stood outside with Dad, other teammates, numb, nodding and quietly greeting so many familiar faces. Three of Dad's beloved team have died, barely reaching fifty and I look at him, aghast, broken but more than anything, bewildered. It isn't supposed to be like this.

I'm flanked by Rob and Murph, the two giant characters from our childhood team, and many social occasions and a beautiful photo in the Elm Tree since. They are big lads now and I felt tiny between them. Murph had joined our young team and his Dad Mick was a vibrant, jovial foil for my Dad. They got on so well, for another forty years, a proud man from Crossmaglen in Armagh and a proud man from Waterford, opposite ends of Ireland, with the same Celtic heart and soul. Our Gaelic sporting interests contrasted, complemented, and never met, the Orchard county and the Déise, football and hurling, parallel tracks. That roaring pride, those hearty laughs, that friendship sustained and was most traditionally nourished each St Patrick's Day, as our families came together to toast what bound us, to be alive. Of course, there was always another pint of Guinness, another silly hat and another year celebrating with Hullabelloo and 'Weelya Weelya Walya' and 'Kelly the Boy from Killane' and a rowdy Athenry. And sometimes what passes, later in the evening, for dancing, or at least allowing the feeling, the Irishness and community and the songs to flow through us. Mick died after a very short illness just a couple of years ago, and I felt those ties and deep connections shake and loosen. It felt too close to home.

And now, in the rising heat of a July Monday morning after Kev's funeral service, we stood in the churchyard, shuffling and pointless in this scheme of things. Cars were parked haphazardly in that rushed and abandoned way, birds busied themselves around us, darting in and out of still-thickening summer hedgerow. There were no surprise Japanese tourists, converging in the churchyard, snapping every angle, as there had been here at my Aunt Janet's premature funeral to break the awkwardness.

No, I didn't think there'd be a turn out quite like this.

Yeah, you'd have some team from the lads here today.

Nice to see you mate, but not in these circumstances hey.

It wasn't supposed to be like this.

Dad didn't come back for the reception at the Snooker Club.

***

Dad's appointments kept on coming. Mum would always accompany him. But so too did the pain, the chest pain with no apparent cause. He would send me a quick text, matter of fact, and they'd update me honestly afterwards.

My right lung is distorted, keyhole investigation for biopsy to be arranged. Enjoy your day xx

Just a series of breathing tests, carried out by a very quiet young fellow, no chat x

On a sunny Sunday evening, Dad had an appointment in Banbury. The only other time I had been to the Horton hospital was with Euan, again on a Sunday night, nine years earlier, as he struggled in the aftermath of swine flu. It was horribly grim, a prescription of codeine to offer, apparently, relief. Some brutal relief that was. While that was a dark autumnal late night, this was entirely different. Just me, Mum and Dad. The way we'd always been, the three of us together. We didn't need to talk, to worry about what was coming, to share, or maybe even have anxieties. We had the new Bruce Springsteen album to listen to, we had the summer sun, we had each other.

As we left Witney, Bruce sang of hitch-hiking on his own journey:

I'm hitch-hikin' all day long
Got what I can carry and my song
I'm a rolling stone just rolling on
Catch me now 'cause tomorrow I'll be gone.

The Cotswolds, magnificent in the early evening light, open up as we pass Charlbury towards Enstone, a dreamy, wide-open landscape to match Bruce's travels and adventures. There's the Saltway medieval road, there's a village I've never explored to my right, there's the Evenlode valley, relaxed in its splendour. I've travelled this road a hundred, five hundred times, its twists and turns I know so well. I've taken this road all those times, but never like this.

Here in the canyons above Sunset, the desert don't give up the fight
A coyote with someone's Chihuahua in its teeth skitters 'cross my veranda in the night
Some lost sheep from Oklahoma sips her Mojito down at the Whiskey Bar
Smiles and says she thinks she remembers me from that commercial with the credit card.

On we go, towards and soon past the village of Great Tew, which would do the usual idyllic, quintessential charming platitudes a disservice. This weekend, it's home to the Cornbury Festival,

Niamh is attending, and we strain for any sight or festival sound, later tonight to be the Beach Boys. It feels surreal, as we drive these familiar, quiet local roads, our roads, this fine evening, to imagine the vibrant life, the thousands of revelling tourists, contained just a couple of fields away. But we won't be constrained, Bruce won't be constrained. All we see are hedges, and green, and the weathered stone of a farm outbuilding here and there. All we need is the road ahead, wherever that may take us, and the next song. We drive on, in magical, utterly contained peace and Bruce aside, silence. Before Banbury, there's Bloxham, and the mellow accompaniment gets better and better: he's 'Chasin' Wild Horses', he's twenty-five hundred miles away from where he wants to be in 'Sundown', drifting from bar to bar.

It's a golden, perfect moment, punctured by the Banbury outskirts and housing estates, by abrupt arrival at the hospital. And maybe it's a jolt, a shock back into the real world, a real world where Dad is ill, and nobody quite knows why. The hospital is eerily quiet, its old corridors over-adorned with communication, blazing messages about this, that and everything else. There are no people, yet it's so busy that it's hard to actually work out where to go. It feels improbable that there are going to be any hidden teams of NHS heroes working here, and more improbable still that we'll locate them. When we eventually do find our destination, there's calm, the welcome is warm and the service prompt; the appointment itself takes less time than it did to find it. There'll be results soon and follow-up appointments arranged and we're back in the car before we know it.

I drive a different way home, Adderbury, Deddington on, on towards Bladon. Again, it's a stunning drive as the light begins to fade. For miles, we are transfixed by a magnificent hot air balloon, literally taking all our thoughts and attentions. These are different moments though, the earlier magic spell has been broken. The hospital offered a stark, cool wake-up call. The imagery of that balloon, drifting gracefully towards its resting place, suggests a reality that I am neither prepared for nor ready to contemplate.

Not yet.

Springsteen checks into the musty smell of wilted flowers and lazy afternoon flowers at the 'Moonlight Motel'.

August

Pre-season had simply fizzed along. Swindon were away at Scunthorpe to start the season. I was not entirely popular with Euan and Patrick for electing to pack suitcases rather than aim for the M1 and M18, despite an utterly abject outing there a few years previously. A dishevelled and disheartened Swindon team were 4-0 down at half-time. Although later, as the sun set over the expansive flatlands, there was a simply stunning murmuration of starlings. It was nature's way of saving the day, and with the open road ahead of us, of course, we looked forward to the next match and the next week.

But instead, as I delved for swimming shorts, I wistfully remembered an opening day boys' road trip for Euan, Patrick and I, Carlisle away, via Liverpool and Manchester from two years prior. Swindon won and raised hopes for a season that eventually, typically, unravelled and ended with barely a whimper. Still buzzing from the Brunton Park experience and three points, the next day, Patrick and I went to the Community Shield at Wembley. There were countless identikit thousands of Arsenal and Chelsea fans, they'd done this a thousand times before, bored with a new season before it started. Two weeks later, we were fulfilling dreams in the San Siro, watching Inter against Fiorentina, my heart beating in a long-lost time of Italia '90: Schillaci, 'Nessun Dorma', Gazza, David O'Leary, Alan McLoughlin.

For Patrick, Swindon winning away at Carlisle, with his Dad, with his brother, was the one that counted. It had been an impossibly special time, and as I delved for passports, I resolved that there would be plenty more memories to make.

Even without us, Swindon won at Scunthorpe. Maybe this would be our year?

***

Suitcases appropriately packed, we had a family holiday just south of Barcelona. With Niamh and Euan hitting their twenties, we knew the probability of us having the five of us together was something to treasure, and boy, it was. Vilanova i la Geltrú, August 2019: the vivid colour and cracks of sounds of a proud, defiantly Catalonian traditional town at fiesta time. The fierce heat, the maze of narrow streets, its majestic ramblas, even its extraordinary storm.

Still, old habits, own passions, die hard. We watched Swindon's games on the iFollow subscription service. Some sensible people like to boycott the pretty pointless Leasing.com Trophy; we paid to watch our reserves play and lose to a Chelsea U21 team. We cared less about the result than the opportunity to see some new and fringe players, and earnestly discussed their merits and failings. We sulked through a family meal in a friendly restaurant near the beach as we tracked Swindon being unceremoniously dumped out of the League Cup at Colchester. It's what holidays are for. For tomorrow, we can go to the Camp Nou, do the tour, sit in the dugouts, wander, and wonder in awe. Somehow, it's the same game.

***

It's the same game that soon sees us on the road to away games at Exeter and Cheltenham, full of bright, early season optimism, shared by increasing numbers of fellow supporters. Sorry Patrick, it's an early start for the trip down the M5 to Exeter. While Euan is conveniently living en route in Bristol, Patrick hadn't factored in my need to complete a parkrun. So, I join nearly four hundred others in Eastville Park enjoying this wonderful Saturday morning 5k ritual.

Soon, I'm showered and we're on the M5 south, looking out for and spotting other Swindon cars heading on the same three points mission. We get tense and restless as traffic slows, excitement giving way to some apprehension, just how long can this take. Eventually we're there, parked where I'd planned, halfway between the ground and the city centre. I don't know the place at all well, other than it's a city worth seeing, of old world charm and affluence, and we still have time to quickly take in the sites. We're here to storm your citadel. Which perhaps explains why we're soon in Burger King: this army will not march on empty stomachs.

Three sumptuous feasts later, Coca Cola'd up and having used the code for the loos, we're back on our way. We do march on, that particular purposeful stride of away fans in a remote city, we're not just here to loot the cathedral, we're here for the points. The cathedral does look magnificent, but unfortunately, with time also marching, we don't have time to loot it, so we take a few pictures instead. We peer at the local peculiarities as we walk around the stadium, a new stand which very much takes second priority to the railway line, and once inside, the largest terrace still in use in the country. I take a picture of my two sons watching the warm-up. It's already been a long day, but it's a contented, expectant, happy one.

The pulsating game ebbs and flows to a draw, and rather unexpectedly, we find ourselves top of the fledgling league. Well over a thousand Town fans have travelled for this moment, this time that we get to sing *WE ARE TOP OF THE LEAGUE*, and we sing it on and on and on, for we appreciate it may be some time before we get the chance again. However, possibly, there is something stirring here. There's a steel allied to flair in the team and a fanbase palpably desperate for something to dream for. There is a swagger in our walk back to the car, a chirpiness all around us.

This is what football does.

That evening, we sailed back up the M5, dropping Euan in Bristol, listening to the Charlie Austin interview on the fabulous Loathed Strangers podcast. Listening to Charlie invokes a fierce spirit that our club can instil hope, that we can have expectations. I can't wait to get back, to have a pint with Dad, and to tell him all about our magic day. After that pint, and perhaps several others, we confirm that while it's only 17th August, we do believe, and declare, that we are destined for richly deserved, Richie Wellens-driven promotion.

September

On the first Tuesday in September, I'm nearly home from work, a routine forty-five-minute commute, when everything changes. I'm looking forward to a quick cup of tea and then getting changed and set for running club.

Kate calls. We need to go straight to Mum and Dad's. Five minutes later, I pick her up, and already it doesn't feel right.

Dad has been diagnosed with mesothelioma. This is not, as Prince would have it, a big disease with a little name. This is a big disease with a big name. So big, that I never, ever, get my tongue round it.

More importantly, it's terminal. That much I understand.

We're calm, rational and peaceful. It's an asbestos-caused cancer, and there's a foreboding stack of shiny booklets to read. The stuff that has been troubling Dad, interrupting his sleep, preventing him from shouting coherently at referees, is killing him. There are options and leaflets and hugs and a cup of tea and more appointments to arrange. 'The One Show' chirps earnestly to itself. There are breaths to take and there's sitting down to be done.

It's literally killing him.

It's not a relief, but it's now a direction. I have a walk through the town we love so well. I walk alone, aimlessly but subconsciously, and soon find my running group warming down. They're chatty, friendly, high after exercise and while they don't know it, or why, an enormous comfort blanket of normal life going on. As they complete their stretches, I talk to Chris, everyday stuff, see you Saturday at parkrun, and with a sinking heart as I quickly jolt back into my new normal life, I walk back home.

Niamh is a student in Sheffield, Euan a student in Bristol. Patrick is upstairs on the PlayStation. We don't know what to tell them, or how.

***

A few days later, Patrick and I pose for pictures at Hanborough station. I'm wearing a Swindon polo, which he widely, repeatedly, and probably fairly, ridicules. It's been bottom of the bottom drawer ever since. This train has already travelled through the heart of the Cotswolds, Great Malvern, Worcester, Honeybourne, Evesham, Charlbury, and while another sell-out away following are starting their journeys, we're the only two starting here. Euan is booked on the Megabus from Bristol, a ridiculously early start following a late-night working finish. It sounds to me like a perfect recipe for a Plan B. Once we're safely through Oxford though, I check his location and Euan is well on his way down the M4. I get a little London away day buzz: he's made it after four hours sleep, it's his away day buzz too.

The passenger in front is a loud Australian woman, and she's been having quite the time of it lately. Does he really like her? He really doesn't, but that's ok because she doesn't really like him either. But really maybe she does like him. I'm less sure than her as we go through Didcot, and in turn she's less sure than me by the time we get to Reading. Unfortunately, unexpectedly, this service terminates here, and we have to join a different service, on a different platform, to continue the service to London Paddington. We move quickly, but not quickly enough to sit close enough to Australian Woman, and so never get the chance to become even more engrossed and confused. For Patrick though, this is Opportunity Central, and he spends the rest of the journey, much of the day, and some of the weekend mocking, mercilessly, perfecting her every tone, intonation, and intention. It's our in joke, ours, and ours alone.

Euan is waiting at Paddington, bleary-eyed and having walked via Victoria and The Mall. We do enjoy some urban exploring but I tell him that's unnecessary this time. There are other arrivals in red and white at the station, but we take the short walk to Lancaster Gate, then the Central Line all the way out to Leyton. We cross the High Road and peer out over the Olympic Park. We can't see much, but we can feel everything: the pride of 2012, majestic, inspirational, unforgettable days and achievements. And that was just building the temporary McDonald's.

As ever, I'd enjoyed researching, imagining our day out, our travelling and meeting options, a pub or two perhaps. In the event, having bypassed the Coaldrops Yard option around King's Cross, we're soon in the Leyton Technical. It's the old town hall, now passing excellent muster as a traditional East End boozer, with an abundance of beers to choose from. I know this because it takes bloody ages to get served, and I change my mind about fifteen times. The bar is crammed with boisterous Swindon fans; families, friends, noisily enjoying a capital day out. With another pint comes increased optimism, and thus our promotion is all but confirmed an hour before kick-off. We meet our friends Andy and Jill, and Andy sneaks out to partake in a work conference call. These systems implementations don't implement themselves you know. Andy misses a pint in the noble call of duty, Jill asks how my Dad is. Patrick is now comfortable in the pub environment, enjoying the sights and songs whereas just a year ago he'd have tugged at my arm for fresh air and to get to the ground. Euan is in the queue for another pint and refreshing that bleariness by the minute.

Suddenly, it's nearly 2:45pm and we're back on the High Road, Andy wants a catch-up pint somewhere but it's too late. We go

through the motions of looking for another pub, but Brisbane
Road and kick-off beckons. After forty-five gloriously one-sided
minutes, it's Leyton Orient 0-3 Swindon Town. Merriment and
giddiness abounds. I find and chat to other smiling faces under the
old wooden stand; do Premier League fans get this rush? I'm sure
they do, but the lower-league experience, such that it still exists, at
traditional locations like this between two fantastically mediocre
clubs, community institutions both, is unique. Clubs, that's what
we are.

Clubs. I text my Dad:

What a half!!!

The second half is a parade, we serenade our new hero, Lloyd
Isgrove, to the tune of Spandau Ballet's 'Gold', and waltz our
way to another victory. After all the noise, the passion, the colour,
the journey home is a blessed quiet one. There are no obvious
Australian women wondering what Saturday night will be.
Kate picks us up from Hanborough. It's been a perfect day.

***

Later in September, rare circumstances meant I was alone at the
County Ground an hour or so before an evening game. It was a still
night, with the first fresh feeling of autumn in the air. I walked and
reflected on how much our matchday rituals have been a constant,
game by game, year on year for, literally, decades. I became acutely
aware, in the moment, of change. As I wandered streets I'd never
seen, peered at shops I'd never noticed, ate chips from a newly
discovered delight, felt matchday slowly creep into life around me,
I knew that my life was changing too. I felt a melancholic awe at
the mighty privilege I'd had, forty-five years of sharing a football
supporting life with my Dad. My mind raced back and forth, being
that four-year-old terrified of the steepling steps into the rattling
old Shrivenham Road stand, tightly gripping his hand for fear
of falling through the gaps. To the afternoon I had an interview
in Warwick, and we just looked at each other and drove to the

evening game ... at Ipswich. A sentimental energy pulsed through me; enough overwhelming feelings and sensations and memories to be able to fill a book in five minutes. At just how bloody lucky I was to be able to do this with my own boys too.

In time, they had set out on their own memorable adventures, to Grimsby, to Oldham, towards lifetime commitment. You can understand how happy that made me, proud father mission accomplished, thank you boys, so very much.

I did my best to attend Dad's appointments.

The prognosis was that he had nine to twelve months to live. It gave the desperation of the season — that Swindon must, *must* be promoted — an immediate, acute focus.

So it was a relief of peculiar sorts when he had been diagnosed with mesothelioma — I was now understanding, through the glossy leaflets and Kate's internet research, that it was a particularly brutal cancer. While the long-term prognosis was not good, it was something to work with. We could take the positives and move on, one day at a time. Of course, our family team would stick together, roll our sleeves up and do whatever we needed to. But we knew there was a fair chance this would be his last season.

I've never been the most medically minded and have always found it easier to focus on the practicals. I'll drop off, pick up, sort the car park, ensure there's food and drink somewhere. I trust the medical professionals and am utterly in awe of their expertise, dedication and measure. I don't quite get those who have the energy to argue or demand second opinions. And here I am again, marvelling at the detail, the precision in the descriptions, the warmth. This week, our noble government has been disingenuous, dishonest and vague. It seems a spiteful and cruel country, yet another hour with these heroes in the NHS is genuinely inspiring and life-affirming. And so is Dad. He understands what the next year may bring and radiates defiance and humour.

Of course I'm well doctor, I laid thirteen metre square of turf yesterday, don't you know.

This impresses his doctors. After a pause there is a hint of a possible option about exploring an early stage, no promises trial. My non-medically minded ears are tuned in to the guarded yet optimistic suggestion that this trial is the real deal. Yes, it will involve travel to and difficult surgery in London, but clearly, it's a pathway towards not only increasing short-term quality and expectation of life but tantalisingly, it could, could be the treatment to beat mesothelioma. True or not, that's what we heard, and once more we are renewed. The trial can run in conjunction with radiotherapy and chemotherapy, once the first two rounds, the simpler ones, are successfully negotiated.

I can start to think about next season, Dad shouting during preseason at Supermarine, and looking forward to the League One fixture list.

October

The first time I went to Tottenham was with my uncle Jasper in October 1981. So much is etched within me still; evocative childhood memories preserved through the sheer magnitude of the thrill that day. I remember the radio being full of tributes to the master Liverpool manager, Bill Shankly, who'd died that week. Kenny Dalglish adorned my bedroom wall; Shanks made it all possible.

With little fuss, we were parked, soon through the turnstiles and picked a spot on the Paxton Road terrace. We were plenty early enough, it was a calm, warm, autumn day, and as the crowd grew, there was still space to sit, and wait, on the terrace.

We waited, and waited, the rich blue ink of the programme smudging my fingers. Waiting some more, it felt as if the construction project of the vast, modernistic, hulking concrete of the West Stand to our right might even be completed before this game ever started. In an era of savage decay, when we allowed our precious Saturday monuments to slowly crumble until they became death traps, this, like its hulking new counterparts at Nottingham Forest and Wolves, was a daring, ostentatious hint of what the future might look like. To our left, the wondrous sight of the Shelf, iconic, bursting now as kick-off at last loomed. This is what the past looked like. Black and white pictures of the Lilywhites, a ball in the air and half of London in the background, Danny Blanchflower grinning. The noise and confidence and cries of the crowd, the roughness and contrast of this aggressive sounding accent: the County Ground this was not.

The players, players I imagined through a childhood of radio commentaries, stared at in Shoot, argued about on the school playground, occasionally glimpsed on TV, idolised, read about in the paper, there they were before me, and thirty-five thousand others, but mainly, they were there for me.

Clemence, Hughton, Miller, Roberts, Perryman, Ardiles, Galvin, Hazard, Hoddle, Archibald, Falco.

They were all there just for me.

I didn't need to be a Tottenham fan to appreciate, to be thrilled by some of the magic to behold here. The artistry of Ardiles, the majesty of Hoddle and Hazard, the industry of Galvin, bizarrely each would later represent the red and white of Swindon, with Ossie and Glenn also to be immortalised as sensational managers. I knew how lucky I was, and I knew I couldn't wait to share this at school on Monday.

At half time, enthusiastic traders roamed the terraces selling roasted peanuts to lucky punters, and I was transfixed. Spurs cantered to a comfortable 3-0 win, the match itself curiously devoid of character or drama. We waited and watched some more. The West Stand still hadn't been completed, the game over, the East Stand quickly emptied. Discarded cups and papers and peanut packets were strewn around our feet. Did the size of the crowd make the experience less personal? Maybe it wasn't just for me after all?

I loved it, but was confused by it. I had to come back, but simultaneously Swindon had won away today, and I couldn't wait to be at the County Ground for next week's Third Division visit of Carlisle. Luckily, Jasper felt the same, and even more luckily, he still does.

I'd got the big-time bug though. Spurs became my second team. Sorry Liverpool, special as all those European Cups and

League Championships and King Kenny posters were, I'd had an authentic taste of Tottenham, and it wasn't going away. Hoddle and Ardiles became my idols. I was thrilled by their FA Cup wins, their style, their 'glory, glory' history.

That bug, it was there to stay. Swindon continued their descent, to the bottom half of Division Four and league crowds of less than two thousand. We were there. Tottenham though, freewheeled joyously, too inconsistent to ever win the league, saving their best for the cups. We were particularly drawn to the knockout thrill of these, hypnotised by the glamour, heady anticipation, and giddy attacking football. Embracing new fan engagement technology, I'd phone Clubcall, scribbling down the ticket information being relayed by recorded announcement down the line. I can still hear the clear, authoritative voice now — in a couple of days' time, he'd surely be the same guy opening the envelope containing my ticket application and a cheque from Mum. He'd consider it, nod respectfully and make my dreams come true by putting some tickets in my self-addressed envelope and sending it back.

The wait was interminable.

Sometimes, it became unbearable, my envelope returned with a photocopied 'we're sorry, this match is over-subscribed, thank you for your support' and Mum's uncashed cheque. So back to the radio, gloomy, but dreaming still, hearing the sounds, imagining, feeling. Sometimes, as I picked the envelope off the mat, I could tell, it looked thicker, meaningful, fulfilling. This way we went to some fabulous European games — Bayern Munich a couple of times, Barcelona too. The atmosphere, the floodlights, the sense of occasion, the smell, the roasted peanuts; this was football, this was life. By now, once we'd navigated the endless traffic lights, roadworks, delays on the North Circular Road, we knew our way around enough to have a cleverly found regular parking spot. It would be a short walk to the tiny club shop on the corner of the High Road, a programme, and a peak at the trappings of fandom, through the street traders, in the crowd, with the crowd, being the crowd. Each time I entered White Hart Lane, wherever we stood or sat, I'd gasp and smile. It was a unique, glorious place to be. In the middle of it all, was a hallowed rectangle of green, where magic happened.

There was the time the indicators in Dad's car had packed up, but we went anyway, a white-knuckle ride to white hart dreams. There was the time Barcelona came to kick Spurs off the park, Graham Roberts took swift, sly retribution and ran seventy yards to hide from the crime scene. There was the time I saw Karl-Heinz Rummenigge play in real life for Bayern. Come Saturday, Swindon would host Tranmere Rovers. Tranmere Rovers! Again! Didn't we play them last week?

The nature of following Spurs changed as I grew older and went to uni. No longer reliant on Mum and Dad paying the Clubcall bills, I took independent trips. Phil and I travelled from Swansea to see Derby's Dean Saunders score twice on a lifeless, dispiriting afternoon. Saunders' Dad was our uni football team coach, a lovely man and eager for our reports and feedback. Immersed in fanzine culture, *The Spur* was essential, high-quality reading. Our game was changing. I went to away games too, one rare weekend 'home' travelling to see Swindon away at Stoke on the Saturday (Rob was wearing an outlandish white coat he'd bought in Ibiza. It didn't work in the Potteries. I never saw it again), then Tottenham at Sheffield Wednesday on the Sunday. It was live on telly. At the Baseball Ground once, the legendary Brian Clough, on TV punditry duty, eschewed the corner gantry and came and sat just in front of us with the travelling Spurs fans to watch the first half. Judging by the way he made his appearance, and his tottering to and fro, the hospitality in the television studio was possibly more generous than that afforded to the rank and file.

There was the time Matt and I splashed out and sat in the top tier of the West Stand, gobsmacked at the luxury, smirking and smug at our new-found status. It didn't last. Come the Premier League and all-seater stadiums, astronomical ticket prices, sell-out crowds and Klinsmann's swan diving, combined with Swindon's merry advance to the top flight, Spurs became a fading hobby, eventually just an interest. Still, an interest is an interest, and the lure of roasted peanuts never quite leaves. I occasionally worked in the area and would peer optimistically for a glimpse of the Lane, and savour a taste of those teenage years, waiting for the postman.

Mum's paternal family were, in the nineteenth century, Eastenders living around Leytonstone. We spent an evocative weekend, the five of us, plus Mum and Dad, exploring old addresses, wondering and wandering. Maybe, they'd have supported Tottenham, we vaguely hoped, pulling up outside the Lane mid-redevelopment to check on progress. The tiny club shop was by now a corporate megastore, filled with flashing screens and replica shirts and attractive leisure wear. This represents progress of course, but it wasn't ours. We left, resolving to be back, to visit this magnificent new arena, watching twenty-first century heroes, as swiftly as we could.

Euan and Patrick would get their chance before me.

***

Dad's first round of chemotherapy is something of a surprise — an anti-climatic disappointment. Most noticeably, he suffers awfully with hiccups, while the dose has other troubling impacts, some he shares, some less so. He's in constant contact with the medical experts, mentors, our crutches now. I imagine them experimenting and tweaking and testing like Willy Wonka, and this reassured me. Next time, they assert, they'll get it right, the dose can be modified, or improved. Either way, he braved it with dignity and humility.

In between times, Kate took Mum and Dad on the train to London, to discuss his probable participation in that pioneering trial. While there were no promises — and we're told that half those taking part will be given placebos — it felt that there were enough nods and winks and meaningful silences that this could, most literally, be life-changing. Rather than a prognosis of months to live, this offered a tantalising glimpse of years, maybe even plenty of them. Dad has convinced them of his general fitness, his turf laying par excellence, and though there are hurdles ahead, at least he's bought a ticket for this lottery.

Throughout the day, I get updates of varying levels of excitement: a smooth train journey into Marylebone, a treasured catch-up with friends from Mediterranean Irish dancing holidays at London Bridge, all on track as they book in at the hospital. I smiled as I thought of last month's train journey to London with Patrick, of the Australian woman with the stories and his mimicry. I smiled too thinking of the memories those Irish music and dancing holidays have created, the 3am text updates I'd get, the stories of late night revelry with famous names, the county parades ... and the week's holiday they'd need to recover from each fleadh in the sunshine. Now though, they're making their way back, and I can look forward to hearing of next steps with the promising-sounding mesothelioma trial over a nice cup of tea.

But there's a problem.

There's an emergency on the line and the train back is stuck, just outside Wembley for hours. Hours. The more I stare at Find My Friends, the less the train moves. I get an occasional update from Kate — good spirits, bored, restless, hey we've had an optimistic day, will we ever move. I pace around the kitchen and feel the earlier optimism drain away around me. The more I stare at the kettle, the more it gnarls back at me. It's practically midnight before they're finally back, shattered.

In the grey dim light of the coming autumn day, optimism is restored by breakfast. There's the revolutionary trial for Dad to look forward to, we're already looking at pencilling in surgery dates around Christmas. How do we work that around Swindon games? Cambridge at home, Port Vale away? And before that, there'll be a more effective and less painfully disruptive round of chemotherapy.

November

And so the season's arc was set: Mum and Dad would attend the very occasional home game, me and the boys would do those plus plenty of aways, the team would canter towards that destined triumphant championship. Indeed, after years of grim, underachieving mediocrity, the team, the club had come alive. If desperation alone could win titles, Swindon would have been promoted by Christmas. Still, in the real world things were dandy enough and of course we were top of the league throughout. While empty vessels wittered about Brexit, we made all the noise across the country. Our away days were incredibly special: bumping into Exeter cathedral, singing on Leyton High Road, climbing the hill at Forest Green, getting a parking fine at Cheltenham ... we kept winning, and we kept coming home to dutifully report to Mum and Dad, that yes, this team, this adventure was the real deal. Our private sense of destiny was being fulfilled.

It had been a long day for me too. I left work in Swindon late and didn't enjoy the cat's eyes and relentless oncoming traffic on the slog of the A420 drive. I was tired, apprehensive when I arrived to collect them from the Churchill Hospital, where Dad was having the second round of his chemotherapy treatment. I didn't know what to expect and I wanted to be sat at home, nodding off on the sofa.

I was greeted with the best sort of shock.

Dad was absolutely buzzing — yes, it's been a long day, but we've met a builder from Swindon and someone else who knows someone and this other couple too. It took nearly another hour to get back home, but Mum and Dad both gabbled excitedly all the way. I am completely energised — who would have thought chemotherapy could be so much fun! But if anyone could find a social substitute for the pub in an unlikely place, it would be Mum and Dad.

Otherwise, as Swindon gave us joy, Dad's chemotherapy offered cautious hope, November brought a tour of local schools as Patrick considered his sixth form choices. I was proud that he was open to exploring new options — different subjects, a new school maybe, friendship groups to develop. So we toured open evenings at Burford, Henry Box, Wood Green, sitting through the presentations, talking to teachers, meeting students. It was delightful that he'd grown in confidence enough to explore, and even if he was most likely to stick, he was taking this opportunity to twist seriously.

For me, it was always a chance to catch up with my acquaintances, familiar and long lost. We'd joke that these evenings were the highlights of our social lives, the only chance we got to see each other. I could sit in my old school hall at Wood Green, allow my mind to drift back over thirty years, to admire how much had changed and to delight in how much hadn't. History, Geography, Sociology: Patrick's humanities path was emerging, and our third proud parent round of A-Level mentoring, nurturing and encouraging was just months away. Kate and I both felt a pang too, a sense of time moving quickly on, of all three children completing their mandatory schooling adventures. Still, as he looked forward to potentially life-defining choices, each evening Patrick would stand for the start of *I'm A Celebrity … Get Me Out Of Here* and act out the opening introduction moves just as he did every year. A morsel of innocent childhood then, and how we loved him for it.

***

Swindon have a shocking recent record in the FA Cup, humbled in the last ten years or so by ooh, Histon, Macclesfield (twice), Eastleigh, Woking ... even when we had an exciting side on an upward curve we lost 5-0 against a woeful Cheltenham team. Now, it's First Round Proper time again and we're back in the Cotswolds, at Cheltenham again. This is more keenly fought, tight, tense and we should be winning. We really should be winning. It's 0-0 heading into injury time, and a replay. We've never even won at Whaddon Road, it's a lamentable record. As we ready for the exits, improbably we score, and Patrick leaps ecstatically from his seat at the back of the stand to tumble down the steps to join the celebrating throng at the front. Euan and I swiftly follow. It's an impromptu, glorious moment. We won't win the cup, but there is an enormous release of joy, of this is why we do this, of smiles and guttural noises.

An away win, in the FA Cup.

By the time we're back in our seats, Cheltenham have equalised. Straight from the kick-off, replay next week.

Come the return fixture a week on Tuesday, the County Ground is cold, sparse and quiet. The vibrant explosion of that Saturday is forgotten, and after we miss an early penalty, the fare is dull and predictable. We're sat in the peace and quiet of the upper reaches of the Don Rogers stand, keeping an eye on the occasional action and looking out to the north. Towards the railway line and Stratton and beyond, to Honda and beyond some more. In an hour or so, with please, no extra time, I'll drive home in that direction, have a cup of tea, go to bed, then get up, tired, drive back to Swindon to work. Around us, some groans, some kids eating crisps, hundreds of empty red seats.

And a cat.

A cat! Right at the top of the stand too, it's ginger and much like us, not sure what it's doing there. It skulks around, feline-muttering about the so-called magic of the cup, it crouches still for photos, and while we have a corner, hitting the first man again and wasted, it disappears. It's not much of a game, and long after, 'ginger' is the main talking point of the evening, the photo edited and chuckled over. We lose 1-0, and trudging miserably back towards the car, feel a tiny bit daft for our premature and exuberant celebrations on Saturday. But only a tiny bit: you know what, you have to enjoy these moments when they come along. It was part football panto, our performative touch of theatre, and part an entirely genuine rush. This is why football matters: magic in fleeting, taunting, gold-dust, authentic form.

We had looked forward to the next away game — Salford, a new team, a new ground — since the fixtures were published. For me, it offered a chance to re-establish a somewhat rare and cherished achievement. An achievement in the admittedly limited sense of being a football fan, for I hadn't swum the channel, inspired peace among warring nations or invented a hangover cure. I had, though, seen Swindon play against every club in the Premier and Football League. From Accrington to Arsenal, Grimsby to Chelsea, I could tick them all off. Salford's recent promotion had temporarily ruined that, so of course, I'd be taking the first opportunity to put things right.

On the way to pick up Euan from the train station, Patrick surprised me. I knew that he didn't like, say, 'Danny Nedelko' by Idles, because he never tired of telling me. So this once, for him, I turned BBC6 Music off. It was his turn. His musical tastes were, let's say, evolving and he loved to roam YouTube searching for the songs the fans of different clubs sang, searching for the soul of being a fan. He adored Jamie Webster, who'd taken an immensely popular folk twist on so many Liverpool songs.

We've conquered all of Europe
We're never going to stop
From Paris down to Turkey
We've won the fucking lot
Bob Paisley and Bill Shankly

The Fields of Anfield Road
We are loyal supporters
And we come from Liverpool
Allez, Allez, Allez
Allez, Allez, Allez
Allez, Allez, Allez
Allez, Allez, Allez

This refrain regaled us everywhere, as did 'Poor Scouser Tommy', and more lately Hibernian's fans take on the Proclaimers classic 'Sunshine On Leith'. Oh Hampden Park, 21st May, 2016, what have you given us?! It was the first time that Hibs had won the Scottish Cup since 1902 — an incredible drought for one of the country's biggest clubs, and the fans celebrated with a most glorious rendition of an anthem written by their own, about their own. And now, this timeless ballad was roared with the passion a century's worth of frustrations and near misses had fuelled.

Patrick immersed himself in it.

Of course, it was no shock that his interest and ears had taken a Celtic twist, and then moved on towards Hibernian, but it was still a surprise when he started playing Irish rebel songs. Music had awakened in him a new sense of belonging and identity and this was another away game we'd start with belting out 'Come out Ye Black and Tans', 'Go Home British Soldiers' and 'On The One Road'. I'd tell him about all the times I've seen the Pogues, the Wolfe Tones and many more, a rite of passage, a coming of age I'd so lovingly shared with my Dad too.

So this was life coming full circle and as the Dubliners would have it: this circle will be unbroken. We were amused, entertained, bonded and of course a little nearer our own destination. Soon, we'd take refuge in Radio 5Live and more customary, respectable, benign match-day listening.

We left early. I had another Manchester pilgrimage to make. Sorry Nick, maybe next time for the cemetery. As a teenage Smiths fan, with romanticised visions of an always rainy, brutalist, harsh city, Salford Lads Club was the Mecca I'd never been to. This was the day, at fifty, I could finally re-enact the picture immortalised on the seminal 'The Queen Is Dead' album. These days Johnny Marr is rather more in vogue than the politically ostracised Morrissey, but thirty years' distant, this record, those songs meant the world to me. Here we were, turning sharply off the dual carriageway and onto an estate possibly preserved from the eighties that the Smiths so brutally and acutely documented. There were few cars, fewer pedestrians, all it needed were some youths kicking a can around to complete a dull, desolate scene. We found the club easily, and there, kicking a can around were the youths. It was indeed a dull, desolate scene. It was Coronation Street, Salford. Don't say I didn't warn you, Niamh would say.

I stood, posing Morrissey-like, about as awkward as it is possible for a middle-aged man reenacting an eighties album picture on a dull desolate estate, watched by a gang of youths kicking a can about, can look. They weren't bothered, they probably see about three of these sad idiots an hour. We didn't hang around for small talk. The pictures were pretty average.

The second reason for our earlier start was also special, and in retrospect, even more so. Despite a customary Mancunian shower, we were soon admiring the redeveloped west end and its swish apartments, premium brands, fountains in the right places. We were headed for and quickly engrossed in the Classic Football Shirts shop on Deansgate. We could have stayed there all day. Eventually, after much humming and an awful lot of ahhing, Patrick bought a vintage Hibs away shirt, while Euan and I reluctantly, indecisively just about kept our hands in our pockets. It was as much museum as shop, experience as transaction. At risk of never actually making it out to the stadium at Salford, we binned the idea of lunch, grabbed a meal deal and headed a couple of miles north.

It's a grim time. The nation is in the grip of an entirely hopeless, rancorous general election campaign. Empty promises, spiteful language and backward thinking abound as we sleepwalk towards isolationism and probably jousting competitions. A sell-out away end in Salford utterly confounds this reality. We live on our own island of hope and dreams and expectation. *We are Swindon, we're top of the league.*

It's a small but modern terrace in a small but modern Lego-style ground. It's ours for the afternoon. Our defenders command, our midfielders dictate and our strikers, well, Eoin Doyle, our Ginger Pele, take the glory. The final scoreline is 3-2, which doesn't reflect our dominance, but it's three points, we'll move on to the next one. Singing the songs of contentment, we drift from the ground, the crowd becoming groups, the groups becoming carloads as the floodlights, further away now, fade. Back slaps, bonhomie and cheery farewells, this has been another perfect away day.

December

For all the optimism after Dad's second round of chemotherapy, he hadn't progressed as planned. Every day, I'd text or phone from work, urging, willing improvement, some energy, anything to cling to. It wasn't coming. Hiccups, no appetite, minimal energy, little exercise, it was a repeating and difficult cycle. Every day, I'd urge them to use the mesothelioma support the hospital was offering. They did, sometimes the advice seemed conflicting, sometimes confusing. I was optimistic though. The experts knew better than us. We had to trust them. Dad had to improve, and then we could look forward to a life-changing trial, surgery ... and next season.

After a work trip to Dubai, I got off the bus at Oxford and Kate was waiting for me. The last time I'd been away, my pal Dunc accidentally drilled through the gas pipe while mending our fence, taking out the supply to the school (Kate's responsibility), the house (Kate's responsibility) and the neighbours (Kate's responsibility). It was a torrid time, with days of gas workers sitting with furrowed brows in various vans outside, before normality was restored.

So now what?

Well, she took my hand. Dad had been kept in hospital for forty-eight hours with a blood clot, presumed to be an unexpected and most unwelcome side effect of his chemotherapy.

They'd taken a difficult decision not to inform me while away.

Just a few hours earlier, I'd been cruising at thirty-five thousand feet, oblivious and content with the wistful melancholy of my listening playlist and Sally Rooney's mesmerising *Normal People*. If only, I thought earnestly, if only I could write one page as good as this, as I read and re-read the opening lines of a chapter. Different 'if only's' were playing out in the real world with my precious normal people.

He was now home, but would need an injection every day for the rest of his days. Only Kate was trained to deliver it. We drove straight to their house. Dad was characteristically calm, optimistic and gorgeous. He was grateful for the life-saving magnificence of our NHS. Mum was understandably squeamish but ready to learn her duty. Kate administered the injection as I looked away, admiring some of the Christmas cards already adorning the wall.

We went home. Jolted unceremoniously out of my flying melancholic contentment, I dumped my bags, hugged Patrick and put the kettle on.

Christmas itself came and went in a characteristic blur. Dad had revived somewhat and joined the five of us, Kate's parents Mick and Sue, uncle Jasper, cousin James and his wife Sofie for a traditional dinner. Despite his diminished powers he still won the impromptu family quiz that broke out. How did he know stuff about the Pacific island Guam, for instance? Is it a Pacific island? Don't ask me. And aside from deriding most pop music of the last fifty years, he was still the only one who knew who'd been the hideous Christmas number one in some otherwise best-forgotten year.

***

In those twilight days, waiting for Port Vale away, between Christmas and New Year, there was a wonderful catch up in the pub with Graham. He had an away game to look forward to as well — Oxford at Wimbledon — and we could share our respective teams' excellent progress without bitterness, or pointless banter. We were acting like grown-ups. We bumped into another childhood friend, Nigel, visiting Witney with his wife Jackie from their Galway home. Many years ago, Nigel would have seemed an unlikely candidate to become 'Irish' but now, glowing with tales of GAA, local characters and laid back living, it all made sense.

The next lunchtime, I was in a pub in Burslem, Stoke-on-Trent, fondly catching up with my old uni housemate Bunny. We'd seen each other just a handful of times in thirty years, almost always momentous for some reason or other, but it was an easy delight to reminisce and put the world to rights. There was the time he married Victoria (most helpfully sharing her name with Stoke City's home ground), and quite astonishingly it was during a test match; there was the time I called in when my uncle Pete died, and I didn't know which of the six Potteries towns I was actually waiting for him in; there was the time he came to watch Stoke at Swindon, and the second he closed the door to leave, Kate told me she was pregnant with Niamh. With Dad declining, I recalled an article that Bunny had written about his own father, who'd died suddenly on his way home from a Stoke City victory. It was the most beautiful, poignant father-son tribute I'd ever read.

I hope the tales he told were true, but if they weren't, we loved listening to them anyway: how he came back from Ajax so late that he and his mates simply went straight to Stoke's next game; or how he moved his wedding day to a Sunday to avoid playing in a cricket match; and how he got a lift home on the team bus (and drank ale with the players) after his transport conked out on the way home from Spurs in the seventies (all of those are definitely true!).

He told his tales time and again, but it didn't matter. Our group loved nursing a pint of 'Peddy' and watching the glint in his eye as he told them.

Proper Werther's Original stuff.

But strangely, what makes him unique is that he's just like any one of us.

Sounds daft that, yeah, but does anyone who doesn't follow their football club truly know what it means to belong to something so special? How can they ever replace taking their kid to watch their city's football club? How do they ever feel what we feel? Can their bond with their father ever be as emotionally watertight as ours is with our fathers who support the stripes?

I couldn't find a way to express to Dad what he meant to me, so I printed Bunny's words instead and gave them to him for Christmas.

Bunny, clearly a fine writer and editor of the Stoke City magazine *Duck*, was doing all the talking. Patrick and I were sipping a Coke, Euan enjoying a beer, as just over Bunny's left ear, Celtic were limping to a listless defeat against Rangers on the big screen. We heard all the latest Stoke City gossip before he dropped us off at the away end — here we were at the once intended Wembley of the North: Vale Park.

Port Vale v Swindon Town.

There was no grandeur now, this was a rotten old ground, the very beating heart and soul of the English football league. Within the first five joyless minutes, Ellis Iandolo had his season ended by the sort of wild, reckless challenge that were it not in the very early stages, in front of baying natives and a terribly lenient referee clearly still in the festive period, would have unquestionably been a straight red. It set the tone. The locals are rancorous, their team aggressive to reflect the spirit and expectations. It wasn't Christmas anymore. It's clear from the start they're up to roughen up and show these southern fancy Dans what proper football is. And they do. Their muscular, well-drilled passion grinds us into ineffective submission.

At half-time, I wander the concourse, grab a coffee and search for any familiar face to grumble to. I fail and instead end up admiring the dedication of fans of dozens of clubs over dozens of years to leave calling cards amidst the stench of the forbidding toilet facilities. How many years since this place, forgotten by the twenty-first century, has changed? And how many more until it will be? Some of our football grounds, the County Ground for sure, stand unmoved, loved and unloved, hopeful and despondent, for decades, generations, as the world outside shifts and shapes around progression, fashion and innovation. Alive for a couple of hours, every other Saturday, nine months a year, Vale Park lives its life tucked away in the dark of Burslem, in aching slow motion.

There's a stunning sunset somewhere over in the direction of Crewe, and it's better than watching this to be honest. When Keshi Anderson, thought fresh from a Boxing Day hat-trick against Cambridge a few days earlier, becomes tired from a rushed, overplayed return from injury and succumbs once again, we're effectively, or ineffectively, playing with ten, and losing 2-0. The locals' hostility gradually turns to confident mocking of the afflicted. We make a mental note that we'll be playing them at home in a few weeks, wait for the final whistle and can't get out of Stoke-on-Trent quickly enough. Soon enough, we're just three boys, analysis done, lost in the commentary of the match on the radio. Lost in the journey, a dark December night and the bright lights of fellow evening travellers on the M6. We'll have another game in a few days. We're looking forward to Burger King at Warwick services. Patrick will take ages configuring his at the self-service station, and he won't be having mayonnaise.

2020

January

New Year's Eve is different, it's difficult. The traditional highlight is our family quiz of the year, with each of us responsible for creating a round. It's mildly competitive, occasionally argumentative, fitfully informative, and then Dad wins. His improvement, such as there was, or that we wished or imagined, was marginal, after he'd rallied and joined us for Christmas Day and dinner. By New Year's Eve though, he was tucked up in bed, pained but willing Mum to join us for the ritual proceedings. That, she bravely did, but our collective lacked sparkle, if not Pringles. I drove her home after midnight, and kissed her and Dad goodnight, wishing them a happy new year as I wondered how happy it would be. Come the morning, I'd be a parkrun volunteer, delivering the first timer briefing, encouraging their new beginnings and seeking mine.

In the afternoon on New Year's Day, Kate and I were in Oxford, having a delightful walk to see Graham and Jemima and a friendly gathering in East Oxford. We parked on St Giles, its yellow stone colleges, living forever, refusing to mark the passing of time. Another year for these buildings? It's nothing. A decade? Pah! A century? Yeah, seen about eight of those. It's the same country, yet a different world to Burslem a couple of days ago. Broad Street, Radcliffe Camera, the High, and over Magdalen Bridge ... it was beautiful, a mix of tourist gazers and dreamers and local walkers and more dreamers. We can all dream can't we?

Swindon are away at Plymouth and need to show resolve, bouncebackability and some new year's intent. I'd hoped to go, it was many bank holidays hence that Dad had driven the never-ending M5 to a season-defining defeat. It's a long way back too. This time I'd painstakingly investigated train options, thought about Euan and Patrick going without me, on the train, on a supporters' coach — from Cheltenham, Oxford, Reading, Didcot, Bristol Parkway or Swindon — I knew the price of everything, and the value of ... everything too after all that research. Come the day, practicalities beat us, none of us went, there would be plenty more days out ahead.

So, happy in east Oxford, Kate and I enjoyed the contrast in the streets, the life and dynamic urban beat. Our company was bright too, I was merry in the company of friends old and acquaintances new, albeit easily distracted.

Oxford were losing!

And! Swindon were winning!

Patrick was sending clips on the phone. We admired the carpentry and the logic defying marvel of the cupboard under the stairs, and I explained who was who to Kate.

Oh no, Swindon are drawing, Plymouth have equalised but we're playing well. I had another sausage roll. The kitchen is really nice too. I'm so sorry to hear that my dear old mate Daisy has lost his mum, encouraged to hear his Dad is doing ok, tending gardens and mending houses for the rest of the village. Just as we're thanking our hosts, bidding our farewells and planning our see you soons, Swindon score.

Eoin Doyle, you beauty. You beauty! We headed for the Cowley Road, Swindon hung on and happy new year to you too. After floating home, I phoned Dad, he was up and buoyant too. Euan and Patrick are chanting, reimagining, being.

Happy new year.

***

Roll on 4th January, to Swindon's first home game of the year in a month which may define our season. Welcome to Bradford City, another club like us, ok rather grander than us, to have flirted with better times, now entrenched in the League Two dungeon. Faded glory, righteous sense of entitlement and expectation? Come this way. We're looking forward to it, even with a hint of nerves as we walk along Shrivenham Road, babbling about the team, scenarios, how many Bradford will bring.

Hey, is that the cat?

We spot a ginger cat. Is it the same one that visited us in that night game against Cheltenham a couple of months ago? I take a picture, which is inconclusive compared to the FA Cup cat. It's unlikely, we conclude, as we're still at least a quarter of a mile from the ground.

A week later, Swindon were at home again, this time to Crewe, more promotion contenders. Euan was back at uni, and we were late meeting him at the station. He was soaked in Bristol, and the rain has followed him east — we're all going to get drenched this time. He's really grumpy, but I can't help a smirk, he's just bought practically the same pair of Adidas Stan Smith trainers as me and he's going to hate it. Despite the rain, and despite Euan and Patrick desperate to just get to the ground, I have half an eye out for the cat ... and there it is! This time, it's shy, elusive, almost taunting. I guess it's just being a cat. Which is fine, because I'm just being me. That's why I followed it when it took cover under a white Ford Focus. And that's why I crawled, practically rubbing against the wheel trim to take whatever pictures I could of moggy. Patrick was mortified. What the hell was I doing, crawling on the road trying to take a picture of a cat? The pavement was busy, fans waiting at the traffic lights, ready to cross, wondering who that idiot was.

All part of the day's fun, I said.

I got the pictures I wanted, surely it was our cat, the FA Cup cat. I knew it. But why, how, did it come to be in the ground that night? Swindon won an absolutely enthralling game 3-1. This time our celebrations, noise, and passion, were meaningful. It was 11th January and the momentum was with us, champions in waiting, at last we could be proud of our club, our team, our players. It really felt that they were ours — Caddis, Doughty, Grant. They were doing this, literally, for us.

We skipped back to the car. *We are Swindon, we're top of the league.*

***

The next day, there was another picture to capture another moment. I was quite pleased with the photograph I'd taken. Looking west, from Mum and Dad's, the sun was setting out over Burford somewhere. A cold, blue January day was winding its way down, with low, vague, wispy clouds breaking the sky and the sun going down. The orange hue through the trees was striking, stark enough for me to pause, take a picture of the moment and try to edit it. The others were ready, impatient to walk home. The evening was drawing to a close, and I was happy.

Dad had seemed ok, in decent spirits, out of bed, trying to eat. Small victories and all that. As ever I could feel his resilience, marvel at his optimism and feel humbled by his grace and fortitude. Euan had walked with Kate and I to visit, and had an idea I loved and envied in equal measure.

Tottenham had a replay in the FA Cup against Middlesbrough on Tuesday and tickets were a tenner a pop.

It took me back to simpler times. We could make a late decision and rock up to Villa Park, Stamford Bridge, Loftus Road, Highbury, White Hart Lane, wherever, to watch a game as neutrals. And we did. And I would take everything in, the floodlights, the terraces, the songs, the walk around the ground. I would store the memories for a rainy day, and cherish every single one. The day we dropped my Mum and gran off visiting an elderly great aunt in an old folks' caravan park in Windsor and Dad and I went to see a Portsmouth procession towards promotion at Craven Cottage. The day he said, *fancy seeing Everton at Watford?* at about 1:30, and we were parked up, in, and on the open terrace when the teams ran out at 2:55. The Boxing Day morning we set off to watch Swindon at Aldershot, and after it was postponed shortly before we arrived, raced on to see West Ham at Tottenham. Ahh, White Hart Lane. So here was Euan suggesting he went to this sparkling new glory, glory version of that beautiful old ground. I'd been longing to go there, see it, feel it shimmering amidst the bustle and other world-ness of Tottenham High Road. It's a bit different to Witney. It's a suggestion, a spirit, a sense of adventure, a calling to be there I recognised in myself. *Of course it's a great idea, Euan.* And I'd love to be there, but y'know work and busy and maybe that spirit and calling and need is yours now.

He had one question.

Can Patrick come?

Patrick was sitting at home on the PlayStation, but there was only going to be one answer, yes it was a school night, yes it was the middle of January, yes, yes ... get tickets now and surprise him.

These are simpler ticket purchasing times. It took five minutes for Euan to be showing me exactly where their seats were located. My orientation had gone, is that where the Shelf should be? I remembered the tight streets behind the old stands, the squeeze and noise, the tension and giddiness, taking pictures in my mind for a story to be told. Now though, it was a story for Euan, for Patrick. They'd have pictures on their phones, but the pictures in their minds would be vivid, evocative, unforgettable too.

For me, it felt a little weird, I had spent years nurturing their love of football. It was me who bought the tickets, the programmes, the kits, the chips and now they were forging their own adventures, together.

Brothers, best mates. They didn't need me.

Nevertheless, I had my own need to be part of it, even if they didn't need me to. I messaged friends about the best way to do the journey on public transport. I didn't need to, I could have found the same answers in twenty minutes. But I wanted to be part of this too. I imagined the walk from Seven Sisters, I thought about the practicalities of Tottenham Hale, I wondered about bus rather than train. For me, this was normal, it was part of the excitement: I wouldn't be thinking too much about what formation Middlesbrough would be playing in. But I wanted to know how many fans they'd bring, what their journeys would be, their own excitement at being in London, where they would drink, what they'd sing, what they felt about being in the best, newest stadium in what, the world? The cheap tickets would mean this experience would be brand new for many of what, forty, fifty, sixty thousand people? And this, this is the starry-eyed wonder, the heart and soul of football. Tales to be told, memories cherished, repeated, embellished over time. And all those hopes, journeys, jokes, emotions would be brought together by a rectangle of green, a ball and some guys in white and some others proudly in red. Eventually, probably, Spurs would win a forgettable game played out by weakened teams, but that wouldn't much matter.

My friends replied. Rich in a single line, Ron in a single chapter, and both confirmed what I thought anyway.

Come Tuesday morning, I was characteristically rushing for a busy day for work. On Sunday, I was flying to Dubai for work with clients in Sharjah and there was too much to do. There were training courses to prepare, itineraries to finalise, money to sort, it was a mad few days ahead. Patrick was stirring in bed, soon he'd be doing his own rushing for a day at school before his trip to London.

I said: *have a great day, love you.*

Through the day, I fretted about the weather. Storm Brendan was determinedly, howlingly upon us, and I knew neither Euan nor Patrick would wrap up warm enough. Boys! I considered that walk along the High Road, twenty minutes? Half an hour? I checked the BBC weather forecast and the Met Office rain radar. They could be in for a soaking. Kate was taking them to the train station in Oxford, so I nagged her about nagging the boys about their coats. Some chance.

At work, we ran a practice training session ahead of the weekend trip. It was good fun, but not just rough around the edges, it was rough. I had plenty more prep to do and then I'd still be relying on charm and basically a game with hundreds of coloured sticky dots to get me through with clients I barely knew and in a culture I didn't understand. As the boys were heading for London, I felt envious of them and professionally uncomfortable as I packed up and headed for the car.

That discomfort was nothing compared to what was ahead. The journey home — I took the A361 rather than the A420 — was apocalyptic. The rain lashed, the wind whipped and howled, I gripped the steering wheel and clung on for precious life. I made it through Highworth, across the rising Thames at Lechlade and on, on towards Burford. I knew every twist, every corner, every nuance of this familiar road, yet tonight, tonight it terrified me. I thought of nothing, nothing other than concentrating on steering, on seeing and being. Eventually, mercifully, I was home. I took a deep breath before getting drenched merely walking from the car to the front door.

Within two minutes, with the kettle still yet to boil, I received a message telling me that tonight's running group had been cancelled due to the somewhat inclement weather. I was actually, in the moment, disappointed: it would have been one of those 'I was there' runs. A story of a foolhardy few, running because they could, and mainly, because they were stupid. A story to repeat and embellish over months and years to come. Yeah, my boys were making their own story, what about me? I checked their whereabouts, safely in the stadium well before kick-off, and now felt mightily relieved that I wasn't outside running. Once that option was taken from me, I made a cup of tea, ate a sausage sandwich and watched the Tottenham game on the telly.

Patrick sent me a text, with a picture (of course there was a picture) that said:

Somehow got these seats.

They weren't sitting high up on the corner, where they should have been. They were sitting in a plush looking area behind the dugouts. José Mourinho was pacing in the technical area, maybe 20m below them. The stadium lights fizzed like laser beams. There was that rectangle of green, of dreams. It was perfect. A couple of early Spurs goals had made it a routine game. At half-time, I replied:

Who's impressed you most? Telly giving Sanchez at the back some stick!

He didn't reply, maybe there were half-time refreshments or exploring to do. They would have gaped and gasped in awe in the concourses. Vale Park a couple of weeks ago wasn't like this, they'd have said. And there was a meandering second half to watch, tame and tepid save for a late Middlesbrough rally. They scored, surely a consolation, nobody needed extra time. Not me. The boys needed to be on the 23:09 out of Marylebone, and I needed to pick them up an hour later in Oxford. I needed to hear some of their tired tales, get home, get to sleep. I needed to be in Bath first thing. So I urged bad luck on the plucky underdogs, and wished that those Spurs reserves could cling on, ready to go again in the next round.

Maybe I'd get to go?

The final whistle blew and I instinctively headed back to the kettle. I checked the boys whereabouts, and they were already out of the stadium, already on Tottenham High Road, already marching south towards Seven Sisters and home. They'd been sensible, they had their stories, they'd seen enough and left before the end. I could feel their hearts beating with mine, that sensation, there's a train to catch, not a second to spare, a touch anxious maybe. Suddenly it was chill, dark, wet, another busy London day coming to its end. Headlights, buses, navigating unfamiliar road crossings.

A football crowd wanting the warm. Getting home was all that mattered now.

At home, sitting on the sofa, I was never far from checking their locations: sometimes visible, mainly deep underground on the

Victoria Line, through Finsbury Park, Kings Cross, now central London at last. They'd reached Oxford Circus in good time, now it looked like they'd opted to walk north through the grand wide avenues to Marylebone. They had time to spare, and were squeezing as much from their capital day as they could.

This was enough. Kate was reassured that Patrick's dodgy knee had held up, they were maybe fifteen minutes' walk from the train station. She went to bed, I'd watch the news, flick through my phone and later, head for the station to pick them up.

It was nearly 11, and they weren't at Marylebone. Boys, cutting it fine, because they could, and they did. It seemed their location didn't move, for five minutes, ten minutes ... now I was refreshing Find My Friends every minute. If they didn't make this train, the next one was a slow one, not due in Oxford until gone 1am. By the time I'd collected them, driven home, got to bed, relaxed into sleep it would be 2am at best.

I was not thrilled.

They were going to miss the train weren't they?

More time.

They were anchored on Gloucester Place, just a few minutes from the station. I wondered why they were walking that last bit. Goodness knows there were enough options, Kings Cross to Baker Street, or maybe even the Bakerloo line. My mind was racing with practical options and tube scenarios.

23:09 came and went.

I checked the live train times, it had left just a minute late.

It appeared that Euan and Patrick weren't on it, as their locations hadn't changed. I was a mixture of cross, confused and concerned. Momentarily, hope ... what if the location data had frozen?

Surely they were on the train, there was no reason they wouldn't be.

A minute or two and maybe a lifetime passed, then Kate came back downstairs.

She was on the phone. To ... Euan?

I gathered that Patrick had fallen, and I assumed it was his bloody knee again. I was gutted for him, and his operation couldn't come soon enough.

Would they make the next train? And now, now the tone changed and hushed, Kate was listening intently and that wasn't Euan's voice anymore.

Time stopped as I heard the voice say — *CPR*.

All I knew was that this was serious.

My fuddled brain didn't understand why CPR was needed if his knee was hurt. I didn't think, didn't pause to consider what CPR might actually mean.

I just understood, from Kate, that we needed to get to London, to find them, as soon as possible.

Still dressed for work, I went upstairs and put some jeans and my pink Fat Face hoodie on. I thought, who knows, we could be sitting in A&E for a while somewhere, best be comfortable.

Quiet, calm, dazed we took deep breaths, hugged and headed for the car.

Storm Brendan continued to rip and rage. Driving conditions remained horrific. I switched back into the same manic, gripping-the-steering-wheel-with-all-my-life mode I was in a few hours earlier.

Now, I felt sick too with fear and uncertainty.

Kate spoke to a doctor: we just needed to get to A&E at St Mary's Hospital in Paddington as soon as possible. How long would this take? They wanted to know. An hour and a quarter maybe? The wind and the rain were incessant and remorseless, so maybe longer. The storm felt like the end of the world, but this was a different end of the world that we were driving straight into. The drive took forever, the A40, first Eynsham then skirting north Oxford and at last on to the M40.

We were in silence.

There was no update from the hospital, no words to reassure us, no comfort, no crumbs. The weather battered and buffeted the car, my grip grew tighter, we just had to get there. The hill up into the Chilterns, past Wycombe, and Beaconsfield, still no update or crumbs. I zoned out of what was to come and focused on aiming the car over the M25 and the A40 again into London's outer reaches. Hillingdon, the Hoover building, Ruislip, the turn for Wembley, the north circular and the road to Tottenham, on towards White City. Familiar landmarks of countless capital trips, some memorable, some mundane. And new ones, ever brighter lights, changed junctions, retail parks, hotels. The world's greatest city, evolving, adapting, always beguiling.

A lifetime of memories flashed through me, London was changing before me.

At last, at last, the elevated Westway and a couple of turns and we were outside the hospital. All those times at Paddington station, and I never knew this hospital was right behind it. Fancy that, I thought. I paused on some double yellow, no, they were red lines at A&E. I was all for moving the car forward a little, or parking across the road, which looked more sensible.

It was 12:30am, deserted and Kate told me to just get out of the bloody car.

We hurtled up a ramp, running the short distance and into the A&E entrance. Literally two minutes ago, I was driving the car along the Westway, now, we were thrust into a small room. Me, Kate, a crumpled Euan and a serious looking lady, about to tell us that our precious Patrick, our youngest child, our brother, our best friend, had died.

First though, there was momentary awkwardness as to who would sit where, a couple of two-seater sofas meant we couldn't sit together. And how could we both hug Euan, while waiting to hear how Patrick was? The lady, the serious one, started ominously, they had done everything they could ... then she said something — the very best paramedics were on the scene to attend to Patrick almost immediately — and I felt my heart skip and soar with mighty relief.

Thank goodness for the very best paramedics.

Thank goodness they were there almost immediately.

How is he now? my brain pleaded, although my voice was silent and the question never asked, as the serious one was still talking.

She went on for one more crushing sentence, which started and ended with I'm so sorry.

Patrick went to a football game and never came home. Full of dreams, full of smiles, full of being fifteen, he had collapsed and died on Gloucester Place in Marylebone.

I was taken to a nearby room, and gently kissed his forehead. It was impossible. Eighteen hours earlier, I'd wished him a happy day, and now they were telling me that he was dead. That they'd performed CPR for over an hour, but there wasn't a flicker in all that time. That Euan had been brave and held him and hadn't left his side. But, however sorry they were, that was it.

How did they know? They didn't know Patrick. They didn't know his gift for tricks or his propensity for surprises. Why should this be different? Give him a couple of hours and he'll be moaning about not being ready for Maths at school.

We had phone calls to make, somehow. Kate had to phone Niamh at uni in Sheffield, and her own parents, and I to call mine. As I was ushered back towards That Room to make my call, I felt as if my heart was being ripped out through my rib cage and thrown at the sign imploring me to take a flu vaccine on the wall opposite. This time I was alone, and there were no seating dilemmas in this hateful, hurtful room. The clean, NHS regulation sofas were before me, it was the loneliest, emptiest, scariest moment.

How on earth do I do this?

I cannot imagine making or receiving anything more impossible, and I can still feel Mum's shock, bewildered heartbreak, incomprehension, sheer shattered silence at the end of the call.

If you're wondering what happens then, when your child has just died, out of the blue, and no one knows why, and it's the middle of the night in the most magnificent city in the world, and that world has just ended, and you're sitting in an austere hospital room … it's not much.

***

As a child, when I perceived the world to be flat I guess, linear and finite, I thought that there was an end to it; a load of countryside and then a huge, vast, slightly decaying brick wall. On the other side, I pictured tin cans, flat tyres, smelly, sodden mattresses, dead cats, burnt out grass, a dark foreboding sky, rotten teeth, a few rusty old cars, long-forgotten cartoon characters, all crumpled, barely recognisable with their vibrant TV show life squeezed out of them. And bones. Lots of bones. This was the end of the world. And this is where I was now, in St Mary's Hospital, Paddington, London.

Kate, Euan and I were all those things: crumpled, barely recognisable. The NHS team were of course caring, devastated with us, but ultimately, utterly inconsequential. They could give us leaflets, and weak tea, and a plastic bag with Patrick's belongings and phone numbers and a biscuit, but that was it. I went back and kissed him again.

There was nothing to stay for, and nothing to leave for.

We left, and London had changed. The storm had passed. But London! London! Why have you done this? The car was still parked on its double red lines — I thought — at least we don't have a parking ticket. We were just yards from the Westway, and pointing the car west, and hoping it would take us home. But through empty, wet one way streets, rubbish from the storm strewn around us, we couldn't navigate our way back to the A40. Around Edgware Road and Maida Vale and Hyde Park Corner. Along Gloucester Place — just there — that's where it happened, said Euan, almost incidentally. Around a roundabout for the second time, a stray taxi impatient with my middle of the night indecision and lane weaving. Take me home, London, please let me go.

But London wouldn't let me go. Patrick had just died, and here I was, irate and cross because I couldn't follow the right route.

We had no one to blame. It seemed peaceful. He'd had immediate treatment from paramedics and there was a hospital around the corner ... nothing could have been done differently and nothing could have saved Patrick. The angels had chosen him and his final whistle was blown, that was it.

There was and is no comfort for Euan in knowing he couldn't have done anything more. He held Patrick in his last moments. He had become an adult very suddenly in those seconds.

For us, there is comfort in knowing how happy Patrick was, and with the brother he loved and adored. For Patrick, the league table would be frozen from that night, Swindon Town: top, champions elect, in eternity.

***

There was nothing that could have prepared us for what was coming, and for that at least I'm grateful. For whatever shape or form such preparation would have come in, my heart, body, mind, soul would have violently rejected it. I could never have been ready.

We were home before dawn and lay, the three of us, crumpled, entangled on a corner of the sofa, a blanket over us and beaten. Here, the dog now had an opportunity to prove the fabled dog empathy, to understand, to be with us, to comfort. She had one job. She failed. Between us, for an hour or so, we dozed and perhaps we've never woken up.

Soon, it was a time for school and work. The world outside our windows shook into life as we recoiled from it. We shut the curtains, wailed, made tea, sent messages, and cried. Mum and Dad were soon with us to do the same, and Niamh, Mick and Sue took the first road out of Sheffield to do the same again. And as that wider world went about their usual business, we had to tell that wider world that they had to stop and to care for us.

We tried to communicate with nearest and dearest before sharing publicly.

I posted to Facebook:

We are heartbroken to let you know that last night our beautiful youngest son Patrick went to football and never came home.

He collapsed and died in London last night after happily watching the Tottenham game with his brother Euan. Despite the best efforts of public and paramedics carrying out cpr, he never came back — we're told it was sudden and pain free and peaceful x

The messages poured in, they were simply overwhelming. We knew, very quickly, that this wasn't 'just' our loss, it was also a shocking jolt to our beautiful community.

Darkness fell and with it, we had formalities at our local health centre to complete. There we sat, awaiting our turn, Kate and I, next to Dad and Mum, one after another traipsing in to see Dr Smith. Dad was clearly struggling, he looked miniature, ghostly, fading. The doctor prescribed him a trip to the hospital, forty-eight hours to drain fluid and restore some spirit and energy. That in itself, was a considerable relief: we needed him now like never before.

The next few days saw deliveries of flowers, cards, love, food, messages that I never thought possible. We broke cover late each night to march the streets, howl at the moon, and then try, try to find a way to sleep, and then, if we had to, wake up to the suffocating pain and do it all again. In the real world, Euan and I had a pressing dilemma too. Swindon were away at Newport on Saturday, and we'd only secured tickets because Patrick was Johnny on the spot, reminding me before they'd sold out the same day they'd gone on sale. We knew what Patrick would have wanted, and we knew, come the day, he'd be there with us. We had to do it.

Even so, there was a remarkable turn of events. I hadn't picked our tickets up, as I'd planned to pop to the club one lunchtime at work. Now, having missed the post, we'd have to make a special journey to Swindon. Well, that was Plan B. On the Thursday evening, I had a couple of alerts from friends Andy and Diddle to say that someone else had posted on a fan webpage that he'd most inadvertently picked up our tickets, and was somewhat unfortunately based in West Wiltshire, maybe ninety minutes drive from us. Of all the weeks, of all the times for some good old human ticket office error. So amidst the grief, the worrying about Dad still in hospital, the flowers, the sheer effort of staying alive every hour, I was enacting Plan C in order to rescue Plan B, liaising with a guy in Chippenham about collecting some tickets for the match on Saturday. He was good as gold, returning them to the ticket office, and late on Friday afternoon, Euan and I headed for the County Ground, listening to the latest Peter Crouch podcast, keeping a semblance of spirits chipper. We parked next to the magic roundabout, pulling up on Shrivenham Road; the green outside the Don Rogers stand was sodden and the trees bare.

There's always something odd, maybe disconcerting, maybe oddly thrilling, about being at the ground on a non-match day. There's nothing happening, there's an empty rectangle of green within, and for Euan and I, everything is happening. And so, the most emotional visit I've ever made to the club shop and ticket office, is a purely transactional one. I'm bursting with passion: my son has died, you've mucked the tickets up. I've driven nearly an hour to get here, we simply must go to the game on Saturday. Euan says — *if anything comes of this, I just hope the players, the management, the club, know how much this means to us.* It's a shared feeling of astonishing, driven intensity.

Whoever serves us knows none of this, none, and why on earth should they? The whole transaction takes perhaps twenty seconds of the virtually two-hour round trip. We walk back past the puddle on the Town End corner, and are in the car a minute later. There are three tickets: one for me, one for Euan and one for Patrick. Peter Crouch and his podcast sidekicks chirp on, we drive home, to more flowers, more cards, another generous food delivery. Plans B and C have succeeded. We will go to the game tomorrow.

There's that great quote from Arrigo Sacchi, who said: "Football is the most important of the least important things in life" and somehow Euan and I knew we had to go to the game at Newport.

It might be cathartic, it would be what he wanted, and we would meet my old friend Phil for remarkable, unforgettable comfort. Yet it was a cruelly brutal reminder of how life goes on around us. We stood, outsiders, alone, in tears, desperately missing Patrick as a dreadful match played out on a terrible pitch. The rancour, the stench and the abuse around us was offensive. Our precious team was bullied into meek defeat.

"Football comes in many shapes and sizes", I said, and we drove home.

***

The two days of recuperation in hospital for Dad turned into four, five, six and there weren't many encouraging noises made about the recuperation part. The shape of days became familiar. Survival at home, hospital with Mum. Kate worked miracles with managing the Patrick requirements with the relevant authorities and to ensure that there was food for all on the table. She was continuously liaising with our hospital support (miracle) worker. There was an interim post-mortem and a crushing sense already that there were no answers.

We each had three daily responsibilities. To eat, to sleep, to exercise. And each evening, we would talk to each other to ensure that we were on task. And we added to it. We must each find a positive from the day. Sometimes it was simply breathing, sometimes it was recognising the astonishing outpouring of love that was around us. It was protecting us, enabling us to eat, sleep, and breathe. Sometimes the tears nearly beat us all.

Graham had to dig deep into our decades deep well of friendship. I took an unfeasibly full box and bag of Patrick's favourite things for him to photograph at his studio about a mile from the hospital, with early thoughts of a display at a forthcoming memorial for Patrick yet to be organised. There was his school tie, a stone Kate had carried with her through pregnancy, Lightning McQueen from Cars, a Swindon scarf, his Touring England

board game, some Microstars, an empty box of Corn Flakes and
football shirts. About twenty football shirts. Plenty of Swindon;
home, away, third strips, good seasons, dreadful ones, new and
old. Each had a meaning of its own. These shirts were forever,
rarely recycled. And then: Ireland, England. Tower Hill, Freeland,
Henry Box. Benfica, Barcelona, Valencia. Hibernian. If Patrick
had spent approximately 40% of his life asleep, he must have spent
at least another 40% wearing a football shirt. Wearing them, he
lived his dreams.

I walked around the Churchill Hospital area. It was too damp
now for the meadow that I had determinedly, optimistically and a
little naively marched through as summer turned and the shades of
the leaves begged their own questions. How much more of summer
was there? Maybe, how much more of anything was there?
Now, in late January, there were no leaves. Instead, I explored
South Parks, Divinity Road, and Cowley Road. They all took on
a new familiar, nothing was the same any more. Niamh trawled
through Patrick's more recent school books and found a quote that
took our breath away.

I would like to be remembered for being funny and kind, and changing
people for the better.

His influential people, his inspirations were:

Mum, Dad, brother, sister.

Still the flowers came.

Dad wasn't getting better.

Seven days, eight, nine.

Euan and I visited on our way to watch Swindon against
Port Vale. It was less than a month since we'd been to Vale Park,
enjoying that catch up with Bunny, and now the return fixture,
this. Dad barely knew what day it was, never mind who we were
playing. We cried when the teams came out, but were soon raging
at the referee, shouting encouragement, being matchday normal.
There was an empty seat next to us and Swindon won 3-0.
The season was back on track.

I sent Dad a text:

Sleep well, and keep those three points safe tonight xxx

He didn't reply.

***

In our other existence, we'd set a date for Patrick's private cremation, and for a Memorial Service the following day. We'd arranged Graham's pictures of the football shirts into a heart (oh, how thrilled he'd have been to have his own brand identity, we solemnly joked), engaged another friend Rich in readiness for printing work, sifted through hundreds of pictures as our display for the memorial gathered momentum. We visited school, realising the enormous impact it was having far beyond our front door, and heard stories of how the news broke, of community sadness and more tears and shock.

And still, we had no answers as to why. As we'd been gently led to expect, the initial post-mortem was utterly inconclusive. No clues, never mind reasons, nothing. It was sudden, unexpected, presumed peaceful. Maybe it was those angels after all. And, gently again, we were informed that it would be months, *months*, before the full results.

Ten days, eleven, twelve.

Mum would spend most of the day with Dad, our own family angels usually taking her one way, and me covering the other. One evening I brought her, and her guardian angel sister Sonia back to Witney. The plan was that they'd eat together at Mum's. But first we'd have to call in to Sonia's to collect food. I was entirely shattered, exhausted with the enormity of everything, and short-tempered with the sisters' indecision and faffing about. I just needed to be at home. We called in at Sonia's. It took her five minutes to find the keys and another ten to shut the door after. We were nearly back at Mum's when she said — I've forgotten the food. Normal circumstances? Maybe not so much of an issue. These were not normal circumstances.

We returned, across town, to then go through the key and door rigmarole once more. This time, dinner came back triumphantly with us. Sonia sat in the back, cradling a saucepan of part boiled potatoes, still bubbling away in steaming water. It was a precious, priceless, exhaustion shattering, life-affirming moment, and we giggled all the way home.

Thirteen days, fourteen, fifteen.

Mum and I were taken to a room in the hospital, a small room, with a sofa and a tiny table. A few books, and tissues. I recognised this sort of room, and shivered. We met a lovely doctor with a charming smile who told us that Dad wasn't going to get better. There wasn't anything else they could do. Mum, most sweetly, disagreed, and begged to differ. You see, she explained, he's booked on a trial in London, we have an appointment in a couple of weeks. It's not part of the treatment here, so perhaps you don't know about that?

And then, in Mum's world, who knows? Successful surgery and a steady, determined, satisfying recovery. Walking by spring and dancing by summer. Swindon Supermarine and the start of pre-season. And everything could start again. But Mum, Mum ... *listen.*

The demeanour of those around us, the placement of the tissues, the weariness in Dad. They are talking hours, days at best, not seasons.

And for my part, the part of me not ready for more reality, was to search for solace in anything and everything else in the hospital. Which way the chairs were facing, the different routes I might drive home, securing a long term car park pass, choosing the right sandwich, finding the right crisps, admiring the artwork along the vast corridors, checking whether I'd got my daily steps, wondering who was visiting next. Distractions, distractions. I'd mindlessly scroll on my phone to follow the rest of the world when everything in the world was here in this tiny room.

My gorgeous friend Jimmy asked to visit. He was having what he'd describe as major surgery to fix a long-standing issue in his hand. To me, he was looking for a few weeks of easy respite from the motorway and work. Either way, it was fabulous to see him, and Dad actually perked up somewhat in his presence. *Small consolation for us*, I said, *here we are putting in the hard hours for little reward. You come in for five minutes and get a full blown conversation, some twinkles, humour.* Trying to keep Dad alert and interested as his consciousness faded, he had tried and tried to name all of Swindon's League Cup-winning team from 1969.

Downsborough.

Thomas.

Trollope.

Butler.

Burrows.

Harland.

Smart.

Smith.

Noble.

Rogers.

That was ten. Whichever order he recalled them in, he could only get to ten. The same ten. Try as he might, he couldn't recall the outside right, Don Heath.

Given that I was born just three days after that Wembley triumph, it's a date and occasion that's etched inexorably into my being, and now Dad was before me, his life draining away as he strained to recall who wore number seven on that spring day fifty-odd years ago. Jimmy fondly reminded me much later that Dad had said:

Liam, you're a very modern man

as I held his hand, kissed him, and told him I loved him (Dad, not Jimmy, I'm not that modern).

***

On Thursday 30th January, Patrick's school football team were playing in the County Cup final at Oxford City. His knee injury had cruelly curtailed his involvement in their cup run, but I knew he should have been there too. He was with them. The boys, his friends, knew that. He always will be. Kate and I walked slowly, hesitantly through the car park, almost pretending we didn't know the way in — subconsciously looking for any excuse not to do this. We stood, initially alone, under a small stand as the boys warmed up. Boys, many of whom I'd known since they first kicked a ball. Boys, at fifteen, sixteen, somewhere between childhood and whatever follows. Boys, who one by one came to quietly hug us. Boys who were all wearing sensitively thought and hastily sourced 'RIP Patrick' shirts. Boys who were about to win a County Cup final, and they'll never forget it. And I'll never forget that, and I'll never forget having to stand through a minute's silence for my own son. The boys were ready, they had a purpose. Their Teacher Coach greeted us too, unfortunately with an inadvertent *thanks for coming, I hope you have a nice day* — and yeah, we have rueful, fixed smiles for these times. Those parents there watching hugged us too, brought calm, heartfelt condolence and we edged back towards the car park.

We had no difficulties finding the way out, and left the boys to their glory and to bring the cup home.

If there was another positive, it was that the Oxford City ground was just a couple of miles from Dad's hospital. Bingo! The final could have been in Banbury or Bicester or wherever and we'd have had a slog across the county! So what fortune this felt, talk about killing two birds with one stone, we half joked. Dad was in and out of consciousness now, morphine taking the edge off his hacking, he was less delirious, more restful. He'd lost his cantankerous battle of throwing off sheets, breathing aids and the tangled multitude of wires. We had no idea how long this would last.

That afternoon I had a horrible 'should I stay or should I go' dilemma. I was reluctant to leave him, to leave Mum. I had to be there.

But equally, I felt a need to run, to run to be free and to be me.

An hour or so later, I'd twisted, rather than called stick. I crept in late to Witney Roadrunners pre-run brief, hid at the back, and without a plan, found myself running with Dan, of course I did. We ran up familiar streets, Station Lane, along Ducklington Lane and up through South Lawn, Curbridge Road, Smiths Estate, down Burford Road, past home, Mill Street, Bridge Street, Newland, Cogges Hill Road, down to Church Lane and the Farm Museum, over the bridges and back to the leisure centre. A touch under five miles and we chattered all the way.

It was a welcome, refreshing, happy run. I was so grateful for Dan's compassion and company. I was so glad that I'd called twist. The endorphins kicked in and I returned to the car, with a sense of runner's euphoria.

I had about a million missed calls and messages, and needed to be somewhere else.

Decisions, decisions.

Modern man I may be Dad, but you don't want to see me in fetching winter lycra leggings and a sweaty Adidas t-shirt. I went home, showered, and thankfully more suitably attired, pointed the car back towards the A40 and with Kate, went to say goodbye to Dad. He was alive, but his breathing was faint now. The grip on his hand, the hand that had guided me, taught me, held me, loved me, was weak. Kate and other relatives took charge of tea, of the rest of the world in the day room, while Mum and I sat, one either side of Dad.

Just the three of us.

I recalled the night we'd driven to Banbury, just us and Bruce Springsteen. I remembered such special, special times we'd had.

***

Tonight, it was us, and the songs of Christy Moore. Over and over again.

'Motherland'.

Motherland cradle me, close my eyes lullaby me to sleep,
Keep me safe, lie with me, stay beside me, don't go.

'Magic Nights In The Lobby Bar'.

'A Pair Of Brown Eyes' — with his eyes tight shut, peace coming, he managed a few words, in the faintest, mournful recognition.

And a rovin, a rovin, a rovin I'll go
For a pair of brown eyes

I looked at Mum, and her brown eyes, watching her love constant for sixty years slip quietly from her.

'Spancil Hill'. Oh Spancil Hill.

'Before The Deluge'. That night in Camden.

'Missing You'.

'The Reel In The Flickering Light'.

'Only Our Rivers Run Free'.

'Easter Snow'.

'Ride On'.

'Black Is The Colour'.

'Mandolin Mountain'.

My life is running through me,
And I'm satisfied,
The old songs keep calling me,
Calling in the night
Calling in the night

A more beautiful, peaceful, suitable sweep of the lushest lullabies I could not conceive. We'd never imagined or discussed or planned this moment, but Jesus, he'd have said, thank you for that.

What some songs to leave us on.

What some songs Dad.

I thought he'd hang on past midnight. Come 31st January, and come Britain's mournful day of destiny, leaving the European Union. Dad had argued, debated, opposed this monumentally ridiculous outcome with characteristic prickly passion, and some provocation too, it should be said. We could see him lying there, unconscious, nearly dead … knowing he was smiling, thinking *I'll show 'em — I'm not living a minute under any of these new British empire nationalistic notions.*

The early hours came, they went. Mum and I dozed fitfully, occasionally. Kate brought tea. The rest of this incredible hospital was silent, waiting, resting. Christy softly sang on and on. Dad's breathing slowed still more. The next day crept towards dawn and life as Dad crept towards his dusk and the opposite direction.

Please — we implored him — *please go and look after Patrick.*

It's your time now, Dad.

Eventually, at last, it was his time, it was nearly 7am, and ultimately it was our blessed relief. It had been a beautiful privilege, the peace we shared together that night, Mum and I had held his hands, each other's hands, we were lucky to be together.

There were phone calls to make, belongings to collect, hugs to hug, leaflets to put in pockets. It was rush hour now. I knew he'd do this, awkward sod. We could have been home in twenty-five minutes if he'd died an hour or two earlier. His purpose had unravelled desperately quickly though; it was just over a month since he'd won our Christmas quiz, two weeks since Patrick had died. I drove home and with the ring road congested it took a lot longer than twenty-five minutes.

I shared on Facebook:

Deep breath time friends …

This morning Mick Walsh — Husband, Dad, Grampy, Hero — passed away just as he lived: gently, gracefully, humbly with Mum and I holding his hands and the lullabies of Christy Moore to soothe him.

Ride on, see you.

He fought his cancer with all his heart, and is now free, with his treasured grandson Patrick, to send robins to us from above x

Ar dheis Dé go raibh a anam.

I've had better Januarys.

February

The day after, Swindon were at home to Exeter, first against second. The end of the transfer window had seen the glorious return of our prodigal talismen, Eoin Doyle and Jerry Yates. In a world utterly parallel to our real one, Euan and I had spent the preceding few days excitedly checking online ticket sales (yep, two left in DR4, they'll have to open the whole of the Arkells) so much that he had his account suspended as it was assumed he was a bot. It's what an obsession with football can do to you.

Utterly bizarrely, it was a thirteen thousand-plus crowd, our first sell-out for home fans in years and a gloriously vibrant riot of noise, colour, of life, hope. It felt extraordinary, like they'd all come for us. It *was* extraordinary. Forty-five years I've grasped at hope at the County Ground, and there have been so few occasions quite like this monumental gathering of optimism. It was absolutely the sort of day Patrick yearned for, deserved, yet wasn't here beside us for.

It was surreal and beautiful and heartbreakingly unbearable at the same time. We wept and sang and wept some more. The guy next to me casually remarked that it was a shame to have an empty seat on a day like today. Yeah, I said, my son's died and by the way, my Dad too. He was right, it was a shame. And soon, too soon, we were disagreeing about the linesman's decision. Swindon won, of course, 2-1, and it felt as if we'd won the Champions League.

And you know what? We had. Being top of Division Four is like that.

In between times, Mum was seventy-five. She'd have loved a party. Instead we sat staring at soggy sandwiches in a forlorn garden centre. I have no idea if we even managed to raise a glass. Sorry, Mum.

Over the last few years, attending various funerals and memorial services, I'd found myself wondering how I'd organise and cope when the time came for me to do so. I'd made mental notes. At the funeral of Marcus, my childhood football buddy, his wife Michele gave the most inspirational, natural speech imaginable from the depths of her grief. My mate John gave an equally courageous, gut-wrenching, part tribute, part men, just look after yourselves eulogy after Fish, another sporting comrade and friend of everyone, had died suddenly. We listened to the astonishing, agonising Jeff Buckley version of 'Hallelujah' at my young cousin Kelly's funeral. Just a couple of months ago, Rupert and his family had somehow conjured up and curated a stunningly affecting farewell to their father.

As an only child, it would be my responsibility, but hey, I'd have artistic and creative licence, and I would learn from those who'd had to go before me. I assumed, if they could do it, so could I, and that from somewhere I'd find my own courage and voice and be able to speak too. I assumed, I suppose, that I'd be doing it for Dad first. Well, I was only a couple of weeks out, but never in my reckonings did I consider I'd be saying farewell to my youngest child first.

We held a private cremation followed by a walk in the glorious sunshine and brisk breeze up White Horse Hill. Instead, we'd chosen a minimalist service, about as brief and brutal as it could have been. Kate, Niamh, Euan, me, Mum, grandma Sue, grandad Mike, Kate's brother Jim, flown in from Brisbane, and uncle Jasper. That was us.

Other than us being stood motionless, defeated, so long at the end that the Waterboys' classic 'Whole of the Moon' played cheerily and wistfully twice, I remember nothing.

Unicorns and cannonballs, palaces and piers
Trumpets, towers and tenements
Wide oceans full of tears
Flags, rags, ferryboats
Scimitars and scarves
Every precious dream and vision
Underneath the stars, yes, you climbed on the ladder
With the wind in your sails
You came like a comet
Blazing your trail too high
Too far
Too soon
You saw the whole of the moon

I wish I remembered even less.

There was a modicum of comfort in the defiance of the sun as we meandered up and around White Horse Hill. We could see for miles, distracted for a moment by the clump on the Cotswolds just beyond Burford. As ever, Brunel's train line remained a focal point. To the east, Didcot and Reading and London Paddington and all that. To the west, Swindon, Bristol, Cardiff, Swansea. How I loved that line, how much it had given me. It took minutes to trace a train from one end of the vale to the other, minutes in which I could try to switch off, try to pretend that all that mattered was keeping sight of a train miles away as it disappeared behind hedges, a line of oak trees, fields of haphazard shapes of every shade of green, lined with winter battered hedges, waiting again for spring. The very cut and curve and sheer eternity of this prehistoric landscape. Below us, carved into the chalk of this ancient hillside was the white horse itself, three thousand years older than any of us, however we felt.

Every time I see it I'm taken back to a Sunday morning A-level Geography field trip and how our teacher, Mr Bunting, wore his ambition for us in his heart. Reluctant seventeen year-olds were knocked up and rescued from their Sunday morning beds to join us, moaning, on the minibus to hell. We were huddled by the trig point, with no mercy from the wind and rain as Bunts rambled on about glaciers and corallian limestone ridges and sarsen stones. We hated it. Decades later, I still remember it, more fondly now of course. Character building, bonding, expectation setting, growing up. I'm jolted back to real life: Patrick will not get this. Patrick will not get his moments, howling storm or luscious calm. Nature has taken our nature.

We ambled back to the car park, sympathising with the National Trust guy trying to tempt the very occasional passers-by to engage. We drove the long way home because it took some more time up. Soon it would be dark again, and this day would be over.

The preparation for the public memorial service in the Corn Exchange had been frantic, intense and understandably fraught. We were in turns bewildered, overwhelmed, frightened, energised and scared. At last we were here, sat quietly, contemplative, stunned and listening as the entrance music began — including a couple of songs of Swindon's goal music — latterly Dave Clarke Five's 'Glad All Over' and more recently XTC's 'Senses Working Overtime', and our accidental anthem, Elvis Presley singing 'Can't Help Falling in Love'. There were a clutch of FIFA game classics, and then the plaintive tone of Frank Turner's 'Be More Kind':

In a world that has decided
That it's going to lose its mind
Be more kind, my friends
Try to be more kind

Silence.

The service started after we listened to the Waterboys, again. I daren't turn around. I didn't know who or what was behind me, but I knew hundreds of people had got my back. I concentrated on Stu controlling the music. Stu is skilled, experienced, familiar with late-night celebrations, heaving exuberant dance floors.

I'm not sure he'd had a gig like this before, and I didn't give him much choice this time. He had to do this. Don't mess up Stu, don't mess up. He played 'Whole of the Moon' just the once, and we were off.

Our celebrant was Zoe, and my goodness how we needed her. She began, addressing the vast numbers inside and outside the hall, by acknowledging that the shock of a young life lost is desperately difficult to bear. She implored us to think of, and find joy in his life and friendships.

Today is the day to focus on the kind, strong-willed and very funny person Patrick was. However well you knew Patrick or his family, you are all here because you played a part in his life. So to really start our special celebration of Patrick's life we are going to sing together. The song we are going to sing has been chosen, as after Patrick was born very quickly at home in Burford Road, he came into the world, screaming loudly and he continued to scream for some hours. To soothe his new-born son, Liam sang the following song to him over and over and it has remained a very special song in the family ever since.

Led by Catrin Russ, Patrick's music teacher, on piano, we sang 'What Shall We Do With The Drunken Sailor' — it was the first song he'd heard as a newborn, if my singing counts, and it was the only way we could begin. That said, I don't think I've ever heard it sung with less gusto: it felt awkward and perhaps inappropriate to expect people to sing. There couldn't have been a worse song that was so right to begin this ending.

I looked around the Corn Exchange. We'd chosen it because it had stood, grand and resolute in the centre of our town for over 150 years. It was the finest building we had, its beautiful Cotswold stone had endured everything, seen everything. When we came to thank our helpers, we counted forty-five heroes who had made this happen for us. We were, in turn, humbled and staggered by this response. The Witney Music Festival, Libfest and parkrun teams, each at the heart of our community, helping shoulder by shoulder in the building at the heart of our community.

Now it was my turn. I knew I had to say something, and I knew I had to say something early in the service or there would be no chance of standing up. At least I'd been able to plan the running order. Kate squeezed my hand and I lurched for the lectern.

I took a breath before I spoke. I could see faces ahead of me I'd not seen in thirty, forty years. I daren't look too far, or for too long. I had to say this.

Thank you to everyone for coming today. For every card, every hug, every message, every knock on the door, every smile and every tear.

We've needed them all and it's fair to say that Patrick would have loved the attention.

And what attention it's been. Whatever your connection — friend of Patrick, of Euan, of Niamh, of Kate, of mine — or unluckily perhaps a mix of all of us, or relative, thank you.

And whether we see you most days, or we've not heard from you in twenty years; whether you've crossed the street to be here, or flown across the oceans, a sincere and humble thank you for thinking of us, for supporting us, and for amazing us.

If there can be some good to come from this, please let us recognise and appreciate and nurture those friendships and connections.

So while today is about Patrick, it's also about you, and us, and what binds us together and I hope that you sing and laugh and smile, and later, talk, and remember and make new connections and hope and that together we can look forward to a sunny day tomorrow.

And that was that. I'd finished just before my voice broke with despair. The immense pride I felt in my son, family and community had taken hold.

Zoe continued with a tribute we'd asked her to read.

As we know, Patrick was born at home on the 27th May, 2004. From a really young age, Patrick always knew his own mind, his family had to smile when they said, "no-one could throw a paddy like Paddy". Surrounded by his laid-back family, he quickly mellowed as he became a young boy. Kate was a childminder in those days and so the family home was always filled with children to play with.

Patrick has always loved football, right from when he could sit and roll a ball back and forth. At just two years old, Patrick attended his first Swindon Town football match. This has been his football team ever since.

He attended Tower Hill Primary School and settled in well. Liam ran the U6 Tower Hill football team and Patrick was a good little player, although much more importantly, he absolutely loved being part of the team and developing his skills. He also formed important friendship bonds through football that led him to choose Henry Box as his secondary school. The football team developed strong bonds between players and parents and Saturdays were the highlight of Patrick's week. Whilst he loved being outdoors and sporty, he didn't take well to learning to ride a bike, and woe betide anyone who tried to 'help' him.

Patrick liked school, made academic achievements seem effortless and was known as a boy that would go out of his way to help you if he could. His friends from school have said that he really was one of the kindest and most genuine people you could meet, with the best sense of humour. He loved playing football for his school team and Freeland FC, until he suffered a football injury a couple of years ago. Despite his injury, Freeland continued to include Patrick, which he loved and appreciated and the family are very grateful for their support. He continued to support his friends from the side-lines and thoroughly enjoyed recovering enough to play a full part in the Henry Box School football tour to Portugal last year.

Travel was something he absolutely loved. Discovering new destinations on holiday, visiting his family in Sheffield or wonderful day trips to London — whether the Sky Garden, roaming the South Bank, wandering the West End, or the Imperial War Museum, the Olympic Park, Leyton Orient, Brentford, Wembley, Lord's, Greenwich, Charlton, Millwall or meeting the Wealdstone Raider. The family have very special memories of trips to see relations and roam beaches in Ireland and warmer times in Spain, funnily enough, usually within an hour of Barcelona. He certainly didn't like to be left behind, if any of his family were embarking on a trip away — New York or Belfast, Dungarvan or Dubai — if Patrick wasn't going he let all know about it. The family has a ticket wall at home, and on it are the up and coming days out. Patrick loved this and if you asked him what he would like for Christmas, he would ask for an experience.

At home he loved his weekly trips to coffee shops with his Mum. Saturdays were all about football and being a Swindon Town supporter, if that meant a trip to Carlisle or Grimsby or Oldham rather than Manchester United or Arsenal, so much the better. Playing on his PlayStation, talking (well, mainly shouting) to his friends online. Engaging in good natured banter with other football fans on Twitter. He had enough football shirts to clothe a small country. And every so often, we'd bag them up, and send them off to clothe a small country. And then replace them. It makes the family smile to think that somewhere in the world there are kids running around in an eclectic mix of his old Celtic, Liverpool, Lille, Waterford and of course Swindon shirts.

Watching British comedies, like Outnumbered, The Inbetweeners, Friday Night Dinners and This Country and simply just being with his family. He was politically curious and inquisitive, loved a good election debate and sometimes, when his parents thought he was playing with friends, could actually be found watching a political documentary or playing a politics manager game on his phone. He remained sensitive and loving. Kate said, he really was such an affectionate boy, he still loved a hug every day after school ... although he never did get to riding a bike!

The students of Henry Box, his friends, did us absolutely proud. 'Long Way Home' was sung by Sam and Georgina accompanied by Isabelle, and 'Après Un Rêve', played by Alex with Catrin again on piano.

The evening before, I read the contributions that our speakers had prepared. With one, I was taken back to my thoughts about Kev's funeral last July, and him 'hating Swindon' and it wasn't the way that I'd want to be defined. It certainly wasn't how I wanted Patrick to be defined. Tracey was his primary school head teacher. In my role as Chair of Governors, I'd appointed her as an outstanding national leader of education. And she was outstanding. We'd sat together, discussing wilfully obscure and forgotten Oxford bands like the Candyskins and Dustball who should've made it but didn't, as we awaited a visit from our MP and prime minister David Cameron. We'd been through a lot of tough times and Ofsted together, and good times and Ofsted together. Yet her piece for Patrick mentioned Oxford United and 'banter' and rivalry four or five times. That was her reality. It wasn't his. I edited the piece, made it more generic; not in Patrick's name, please.

Tracey said:

I am completely honoured to have been asked to speak about Patrick. I was his headteacher and fortunate to be his class teacher for a year.

Patrick was a joy to teach. Kind, caring, modest about his abilities and loved learning. He was bright and intelligent and always worked hard, helping others whenever he could along the way. He had a sharp sense of humour and certainly loved those Mondays after a Swindon win.

The tributes she read from his other teachers were touching and heartfelt too. She ended by saying:

And to finish with a quote from my son, who was good friends with Patrick and engaged in much banter with him. Alfie said 'I suppose I ought to stop hating Swindon now, out of respect for Patrick, but he wouldn't want that'.

Patrick didn't want anyone to hate anyone.

***

Next up was Brad, and I knew this was tough. Patrick loved being with the lads at Freeland, but was constrained by his literally never-ending knee injury at every twist and turn. It was, until 14th January, what I thought was heartbreaking. I couldn't face watching them when he wasn't playing, but the boys and especially Gary and Brad were inclusive, welcoming, patient and generous. It meant so so much to all of us, although it was equally unbearably difficult to accept. And once again, Brad stepped up when we needed him:

I've had the pleasure of running a kids football team for around five years now. One of the great things about this is helping develop a nice bunch of kids and interacting along the way with their parents. We've won leagues, had many remarkable games and been progressing throughout the seasons. I could look back and say we'd done alright. Of course, with these highs come lows as well. Part and parcel. The odd loss, player leaving, fallout with another coach etc. you can get over, but this week our club was hit with the lowest of lows.

I just wanted to say a few words in tribute to a lad I had come to know as a really lovely boy. Patrick has been with us for around three seasons now, but in this time he's been dogged by injury. He arrived on the recommendation of a couple of our lads who had been playing with him from way back. Luckily we had space in our squad and it was clear that, despite his small size, Patrick could play. He made his debut at Deddington but sadly only lasted a short while, going down with the knee injury that kept him out for a long time. During his time out, Patrick would come and watch our games, I'd look round and see him, quiet and polite, always a handshake and update on the injury.

Then came his return to training, under his Dad's advice, he'd do half an hour. Tentative at first, Patrick was soon flying round the pitch doing what he does, shining like a beacon with his heart and talent. The rehab would continue until he got the all clear. He was back. Fast forward to a cup final last year. We included him on the bench against Garden City and he probably expected not to play. With around twenty-five minutes left, I let him know he was coming on. His reaction will live with me forever. His face lit up and the smile was lovely. That's a beautiful thing coaching kids. Anyway, he went on and I genuinely felt a warm glow as he got into the game. Well, sadly, he only lasted two minutes when the knee went again. We as a team were all gutted for him. We lost to a last-minute goal but we were more choked that we'd lost the little man again. Cruel as all he wanted was to play with his mates.

This season we'd regularly see him on the touchline and the last time we spoke, Patrick had seemingly got to the bottom of his injury problems and looked to be coming back. As with all fifteen-year olds, he was bigger, the voice deeper and handshake firmer. It was a matter of time, no matter how much game time he'd missed, that he was coming back stronger than ever. Until this. No words can really describe what we all feel, just numb. I'll sign off by just saying personally I'll miss Patrick deeply. Not only playing, but normally there most match days with his little smile, watching his mates. Rest easy, the little man with the massive heart. It was a pleasure to meet you and your Dad. God bless and rest in peace. And kick a few balls up in heaven.

Brad folded with emotion, and the Corn Exchange held his hand. He was afforded a magnificent, deserved ovation, and then we had a song to sing.

Patrick had developed a keen awareness of the sense of community that football brings, far beyond Swindon Town. The spirit, the sight, the soul and the styles of fans.

And more than anything, the songs. It was always the songs, the sounds of the crowd. His Celtic soul led on to Hibernian, and to 'Sunshine On Leith', the favourite anthem of Hibs fans.

What a song to pick for your own Patrick, what a song.

The celebrant Zoe had advised we used it as reflection music, but Patrick wouldn't want that, and he didn't get that. We sang it as heartily as we could. It wasn't quite Hibs at Hampden in 2016, but it was ours.

Laura was next up. Poor Laura, I felt.

How on earth can you find the strength and courage to follow that? Yet she did, and I watched Laura walk to the stage, thinking how much she'd given our Witney community in a few blink-and-you've-missed-them years. How much she'd given our family, a South Yorkshire kindred spark for Kate, music star-stalking stories to cackle to, and now she was speaking, her voice cracking with emotion too.

Everyone here today has the joy of having a Walsh in their life. As individuals they are by turn kind, funny, clever and generous. As a family they radiate love. They have heart by the bucketload and are always quick to offer a helping hand in times of need, no matter how big or small the challenge. The fingerprints of their contribution are all over our town, from a library bus on a school playground to a smiling face at parkrun.

We all have our individual reasons to love Witney, but for all of us who have built our lives here, we know that it's our connection to each other that really counts. It counts when we are doing the fun stuff together, but perhaps it counts more when we come together with so much sadness, to share in loss and celebrate a life.

We will hold Patrick in our hearts and we won't allow the sadness to wipe away the joy of his life, or let the fear of painful emotion stop us from remembering him.

Together, we can wrap our collective arms around this family and say that we're here for them today, and for tomorrow and the many tough days that will follow. It will be difficult, and we won't always know the right thing to do or say, but we won't shy away from it, because the Walsh family have never shied away from giving what they can to us.

Becky, Patrick's class teacher, spoke of his kindness, of his good humour and cheeriness, of the reaction of his classmates and the rest of the school. For us, deep in the immediacy, it was beyond comprehension to think there was a parallel world of grief, and thought and tenderness. Yet Henry Box was its own special place.

Becky read from and with pupils, presented a gorgeous, lovingly crafted Book Of Memories. I know it's beautiful and I know the tributes are heartfelt and fabulous. I see it before me every day.

It's a year later, and I've never touched it.

We were nearly done now. It was nearly time to breathe.

Zoe stood again before Patrick's enormous heart of football shirts and read our 'Promises To Patrick', and these are with us every day still:

We will love and cherish you forever.

We may never understand why this happened but we hope to learn to accept it.

We will always be grateful for the 15 years we had together. They were a gift.

We will always be together as a family wherever we are.

We will always keep your memory alive.

Our lives will never be the same but we will live them to the full.

Zoe continued with closing words, reminding all of the difficult times ahead, reading 'Death Is Nothing At All' by Henry Scott Holland, summarising Patrick's life, love and spark. It was impossible, that it had come to this, and now, this was how the world had ended.

We sung, in some communal shape or form, 'You'll Never Walk Alone', and I was part consumed by a grief too vast and part inspired by this vast blanket of comfort that our community had drawn over us. This treasured, historic room fell silent and then tiptoed back to life as people shuffled, hazily towards the shock of

February evening air. There was a whirl of activity as our army of helpers transformed the room, chairs were moved, tables raised, refreshments prepared, the bar opened.

And the next couple of hours were possibly the most astonishing blur of my life. I hardly saw Kate or Niamh or Euan or Mum. It felt like I spoke to a thousand sympathetic beautiful people. I barely had a drink. I missed the food. Yet those two hours fed me for the next six months.

Eventually, much later, the evening ended quietly, warmly, softly in the Elm Tree. It was the only place it could have been.

***

And then there was Sally, I've not even mentioned Sally, mum's eldest, dear sister.

One of three sisters who'd lived in each other's pockets for seventy-five years, practically interchangeable. Old friends would bump into them in town, not sure which of the three they were greeting. Sally had had cancer longer than Dad, phoning him every day to check his symptoms, share her worries. It was tough, but she'd done OK. At Christmas though she was struggling, turning her nose up at her food, being uncharacteristically irritable. Now she was in hospital, not only was she in the same hospital as Dad, but the same ward. She was three rooms from where Dad had been when we went to visit her. The staff, the same fabulous staff, gave us double looks — I could feel them thinking *why are they back* and even *what cruel world of denial are they in if they're still trying to visit that poor man who died last week?*

We left Sally on Sunday, down in the dumps but grateful to see us, hoping she'd be out soon. We were thoroughly exhausted and dejected by the same corridors, always dreading those imposing heavy doors onto the ward. And an improving Sally, back at home, would give everyone a lift. Also, our car park permit was about to run out.

Come Thursday, I was shattered, with the events of the month catching up on me. I just wanted to lie down, close my eyes, and be somewhere else.

Mum though, she understood that her precious big sister was gravely ill.

I didn't; I thought she'd pull through, this time at least. I had a cup of tea with Mum, and she said, *I think we should go and visit Sally.* Mum knew how tired I was, and I knew Mum would never put upon me. We finished our tea, and we were back in the car. Two of Sally's daughters were at the hospital, with Sonia. Sally was sleeping peacefully. In the flash of an afternoon, her life was slipping away, desperately quickly. It was another devastatingly quick end to a long, loving lifetime. In the space of four brutal weeks my Mum had lost her grandson, her husband and her sister.

Like I said, she didn't want to put upon me, and she was there for her sister.

I don't remember the journey home.

That was a bleak time, but at least it was Valentine's Day the next day. I thought of my friends, Phil in South Wales and my old teammate Murph, celebrating their respective birthdays, and hoped the sun was shining for them.

***

The next week was filled with preparation for Dad's funeral. I was as determined as I could be to do it right for him. I met two treasured friends I'd asked to speak at his service, Rob from boyhood football days, Terry from a magical, poetic world of story and soul. They would both do Dad, and themselves proud. Rich at PrintReady was heroic again, as I indulged my control freakery, ensuring the same fonts, sizes, displays, same bloody everything as Patrick's, save for the words.

And you know what, they weren't so different either.

We waited at Mum's for the funeral directors to arrive, it would be a thirty-minute journey back to the crematorium, maybe forty in the Friday afternoon traffic.

We waited.

They were late. We paced, watching neighbours depart, while on and on we waited.

This was getting ridiculous.

Eventually, I called to see where they were.

They were waiting at our house, on the other side of the river, on the other side of town, and ten minutes closer to the crematorium. It's the sort of detail that's so easy to overlook when you're organising two funerals at once I suppose.

It was entirely my fault.

So now, we were actually going to be late, late for Dad's last journey. At least I was able to ask the driver of the hearse to step on it, which amused me more than him I think. We sat back, as the green fields rushed by, as all around us there was that sense of a weekend easing into being, people rushing home, oblivious.

Or as oblivious as you can be to a hearse doing seventy-five miles per hour on a country road.

As we arrived, we jumped out of the hearse as if rushing to make last orders in a pub at the edge of town. These were Dad's last orders, there were people everywhere, faces, memories, tears, blurs. A lot of blurs, we were bundled in and under way before we could draw breath. The message was clear — be quick! There's another one scheduled at five! Over the speakers, the Dubliners were already singing 'Will The Circle Be Unbroken', but not for long as we had to get on with it. Step on it! It was such a special song for me. Many years ago, Dad was doing his Christmas shopping, as usual on Christmas Eve. As usual, he also came back with a gift for himself, and as usual, it was another Dubliners compilation.

With each fresh compilation came the same songs arranged in a different order. And this gorgeous old gospel song crept into my soul. It was melancholic, rich and deeply evocative. In one of those festive rituals we all have, I've played it every Christmas Eve for about thirty years. Here it was, taking on new meaning, asking and pleading:

Will the circle be unbroken
By and by, Lord, by and by
There's a better home a-waiting
In the sky, Lord, in the sky

Brave Zoe was with us again, and she was talking at once:

This is indeed a very sad time for the Walsh family as it's only two weeks since we said a very heartfelt farewell to Mick's beloved grandson, Patrick, and in another week or so's time, will do so to Jean's sister Sally too … Mick was the calm patriarch of the family. The husband, father and grandfather who has been there for everyone, no matter what … Last summer, Mick started to suffer with his health, and by September he was diagnosed with mesothelioma, an asbestos-related cancer. However, no one was prepared for how quickly he was to deteriorate after Christmas. He never complained, he remained as active, as positive, as supportive as he could. With his dancing, his digging and his loving done, he sang a line or two of 'A Pair Of Brown Eyes' by the Pogues and died peacefully with Jean and Liam holding his hands.

It felt like I'd only just sat down. I was still caught in the rushing blur of our late arrival, not settled, not ready. But I had to stand, to speak, to say the words I needed to say, to be settled and to be ready. I said:

Dad was always there for me, and thank you, for being here, for us.

Ask me later about our Dublin night out that we read about in the Irish national newspapers the next day.

Or when he took me for an interview in Warwick and we ended up watching Swindon, three hours away, at Ipswich.

Or maybe that FA Cup replay we went to at West Ham, via another match. At Loughborough.

Or driving to Tottenham around the north circular and back one night without his indicators working.

You get the picture.

He was there in Genoa for David O'Leary's winning penalty for Ireland in Italia '90, he was there in Cardiff for Munster winning the European Cup. He was here, there and everywhere supporting Swindon, passing on his passion, whether we'd asked for it or not. He was there at Cheltenham racecourse, welcoming spring every year. He was there in Croke Park, for Waterford winning their first All-Ireland hurling semi-final in nearly fifty years.

The last game of football I played was for a veterans team at Clanfield on a cold winter's night. Huddled in the stand under the floodlights, there was a crowd of just two: my uncle Jasper, and Dad.

He was there.

And that was it, speaking actually helped me settle. I half wished I'd made a better job of it, but, but, I'd done it. On one side, Kate squeezed my hand, and the other, Mum did the same.

Meanwhile Zoe filled in the details:

Mick was born in Cappoquin in County Waterford, Ireland on the 4th April, 1942. His parents were Patrick and Margaret and he grew up alongside his older brothers, Maurice and Jack and his younger siblings, Jasper and Bernie. His hard-working parents were employed in service and as was typical of those days, he fondly told stories of hard times as children, often having to share everything including shoes.

His father died when he was young, soon after the family had relocated to England. They lived in Dorset, North Leach and Faringdon, before moving to Bampton, while continuing to enjoy long summers in Ireland. He joined the youth club and helped to run it. It was at the youth club that he met a young lady called Jean. Mick was seventeen and Jean was fourteen. It was the night of the fireworks! Kids were setting off fireworks all down the street, putting them through doors. Mick grabbed Jean saying, 'Come with me the Police are coming, I'll look after you.'

My, how he did.

Jean would watch him play football for Bampton Town. That led on to going to watch Swindon Town Football Club together, another lifelong passion. They enjoyed the following years of courtship together and with friends travelled to Blackpool, Brighton and Ireland where they had many great times.

Mick, brother-in-law Pete and Graeme used to travel to Glasgow to watch Scotland v England at Hampden Park every couple of years. One time, Mick and Pete managed to down a bottle of 100 Piper's Whiskey! Next day, shopping in a department store, they lost Mick. The lift doors opened and there was Mick in the lift, the doors shut again with Mick still inside. They finally caught up with him where he said: "I think I have a hundred pipers marching in my head".

From when Mick started work, he was known as a hard worker, and gained general building employment for some of the local firms.

In 1965, he and Jean were married in Carterton. They set up home together in a flat in Bampton for three years before moving to Witney. Mick started working at Smiths Industries and then went on to work for Morris Motors. After this he worked for a firm building swimming pools before making the brave decision to start his own glazed tiling business ... His van didn't even need signwriting as his peers and his customers knew him through his great reputation.

When Liam introduced Kate to his parents, he welcomed her into the family fold with open arms and I will now share a tribute that has been written by Kate:

"I first met Mick, my father-in-law, in 1991. In all the years I knew him, he was nothing but generous and kind. He was my DIY friend and put up and took down walls, extensions, shelves and pictures and put up with all my interior design phases over the years.

"When Liam knocked himself out playing football after Niamh was born, he drove us home from hospital at a snail's pace to protect our precious cargo.

"He was a fantastic grampy to our three children, even learning to ride a horse to keep up with Niamh, and supporting the boys through hundreds of football games. I will treasure memories of holidays, days out, meals out and roast dinners. I know that wherever he is, he is taking good care of Patrick and I am grateful for that."

Niamh had shared:

Wednesday afternoons with Grampy (and of course, with Granny too) were sacred. I'd finish school early, and Grampy would be there waiting, ready to whisk me away to Chestnut Close for one of his famous bacon sandwiches, a cup of tea and a packet of salt and vinegar Walkers. This lunch was better than any offered at the various cafés Grampy and I also frequented — Hilltop, Chomsky's, Sainsbury's, or Burford, for one of those famous scones!

After a lunch spent catching up, reading the Witney Gazette and — inevitably — sorting out whatever technological issue had arisen that week,

Grampy would take me to the stables. Often, he'd stay, and was always happy to do odd jobs, as well as shower whichever pony I was favouring at the time — Ellie, Red, Harry — with love and carrots. He was my dedicated equestrian photographer and assistant, whether that be in the sunshine, the freezing cold or the pouring rain.

Grampy's dedication to my passion for horses even went as far as learning to ride himself, so that he could join me on holidays. I have great memories of 'accidentally' going a little too fast on horseback with him in Ireland, and splashing through the waves on beaches in the Isle of Wight. Once, in Waterford, we got so lost trying to find a stables that we ran out of petrol and had to coast all the way back to Dungarvan!

I will always be so, so grateful to Grampy for enabling and encouraging a lifetime love of horses which would not have been possible without him and his willingness to become a taxi driver for all three of his grandchildren.

Grampy, thank you so, so much. Those Wednesday afternoons will always be ours. Ride On.

Zoe continued:

Over the last ten years, Mick and Jean really enjoyed special trips on Irish Music and Dance Holidays. They had wonderful times and made so many friends. Liam said he would often wake on receiving a text message at 3am from Mick, telling him what a great time they were having.

Mick's family were his whole world. They loved to socialise together, enjoying live music on a Saturday night, the closeness of the family has been long admired by friends. Jean said they have had a truly wonderful life together for over sixty years.

Robert was the captain of the wonderful football team that Dad had managed. We had stood together at our teammates' funerals, and now he was standing for me, talking about my Dad. I was as proud of Rob as I was of Dad.

Mick loved his football so much that not long after he'd hung up his boots, he decided to enter the world of football management. Mick and Jean somehow, like a scene out of the 'A' team, put together a young squad of local lads to challenge the best.

Luckily, we were very successful from the off, winning cups, leagues and tournaments on a regular basis.

Looking back now, these were our wonder years, no work, no women and not a lot else to worry about except our football. And as recently as Mick's seventieth, we reminisced about the good old days, and to see Mick's eyes light up on that night was so rewarding.

Rob regaled us with stories from another age. Of one of the team casually swigging a pre-match can of light ale, aged ten. Of the time we were one short at the kick-off of a key game, only for Dad to realise one of the players was halfway up a conker tree.

And then finally and probably Mick's finest moment ... due to a congested fixture list, we were to play the same opponents for two weeks on the trot, firstly in the league and then in the County Cup final at Oxford City's White House ground.

Well in the league it didn't go well, we were two of our best players down. I was having trials at Liverpool and Liam was auditioning for the school play ... well something like that.

Anyway, the team took a real beating and lost the match 7-0 ... this didn't bode well for the final the following week ... however, with a rejuvenated full squad, we gave ourselves a fighting chance ... As I recall, we were under siege for most of the game, shots blocked, tackles made, and shots saved, keeping us in it ... until up pops Liam with an exquisite finish to win the game 1-0 and crown us county champions. Some people said Liam was only in the team because his Mum washed the kit, but on this occasion, he delivered the goods and his Dad was the happiest man in the county.

The encounter that followed, with Dad humbly celebrating the virtue of teamwork in a brief confrontation with the defeated manager, had stayed with Rob all this time. I couldn't be prouder of either.

Terry meanwhile, was an ebullient raconteur on top form. He recalled and regaled, bringing new life to old tales in his rich west Belfast brogue. He shared the story of Dad's intricately designed and tiled floor mosaic around the bar in the Elm Tree and woe betide any future landlord who dares replace it.

Terry fabulously brought to life a story Dad had shared of going to a family funeral during Lent in Ireland … and while many were abstaining from drinking, one or two were tucking in to the whiskey. They reasoned that as they were drinking Bushmills — perceived as a *Protestant* whiskey — it didn't 'count' towards lent. Whether their greater powers offered the same opinion is not recorded.

They were beautiful, warm, witty and genuine memories. I was bursting with pride with what Rob and Terry had stood up and delivered. Dad would have loved it.

We listened, we had to, to 'Ride On' by Christy Moore. Christy has been with Mum, Dad and me through everything, he had to be here somehow. We'd seen Christy together in the grand and the unusual, the bear pits and the hushed, sober auditoriums. He'd lullabied Dad to his final moments and here he was again.

When you ride into the night without a trace behind
Run your claw along my gut, one last time
I turn to face an empty space, where once you used to lie
And look for a spark that lights the dark
Through a teardrop in my eye

With love, we left him in peace, with respect, we bid him farewell.

Zoe's tender words brought us soon to a close, and there was only one way this gig was ending.

Dad's final song was 'The Parting Glass' by Liam Clancy. When he found this being sung by the funeral cortège at Clancy's own funeral in An Rinn, Waterford, on YouTube, it was as if the whole point of the internet suddenly became realised. He could find content previously unimaginably accessible, content of substance and depth and meaning and soul and life. And then he could share it. And keep playing it. And so it was with this version of this song.

So fill to me the parting glass
And drink a health whate'er befalls
Then gently rise and softly call
Good night and joy be to you all

This was the Liam that I was named after, and how could they have chosen better? I'd like to think he knew me well enough to trust me to do the right thing here.

We returned to the Elm Tree, to be greeted by cacophonous comfort, and chatter and overwhelming love once again. The scale, the noise was suffocating, connections being renewed, a life lived and loved being celebrated appropriately. Steve and Tom from Hullabelloo played, they had to. The bar tab ran out. Then it got extended. And again. The noise was relentless, Kate escaped for the quiet harbour of home. Jess and Alex played later, Dad loved them too, and here the night grew raucous and messy and about as perfect as it could be.

In the circumstances.

March

For six weeks, we'd lived at home in a sort of pre-lockdown lockdown. Well, save for hospitals, funerals and about a hundred trips to see Rich at PrintReady. I walked or ran under the cover of darkness. Our food, presumably, was delivered by angels. Slowly that changed. I remember my first trip to town in daylight. A solemn, determined walk, taking the route over the rivers and streams across to Cogges one bright afternoon. The air was heavy and the ground was damp. It would be dark in an hour or so.

I walked to the bridges and Langel and stared at the slow waters of the Windrush. There were familiar ducks in turn diving, swooping and arguing noisily. Trees were showing signs of life, tiny green buds, hesitant still. There were young children being encouraged and cajoled and that yes, they were nearly there yet. Yes, it would be warmer at home.

Despite the end to the afternoon atmosphere and the apparent onset of spring, this felt like the beginning of my longest, cruellest winter. But, simultaneously, I was so thrilled to be out. I pulled my hat down low, still fearing everyone was staring at me, and walked straight through the bustling Marriotts shopping centre. I was grateful to see no one I knew and returned home to collapse in pride, relief and mental exhaustion.

Besides running, since relinquishing voluntary football club and school governor chairman roles, I'd found great warmth in Witney's music community. I'd gone through an unconscious, but with hindsight fairly clear change, from doing things for others, to doing things more for myself. And this way I gained so much from both running, and being part of Witney's music festival team. The Sunday night, I walked through the door of the Hollybush, alone, self conscious and with no hat to pull down low, uncertain, I was hit with an overwhelming wall of warmth, and hugs. A lot of hugs.

The music festival was set up to remember Jo Foster, who'd died suddenly, aged just twenty-one. Her brother, my friend Stu, was the heart, soul and life of the team and local music scene. On Sunday evenings he hosted 'FolkUs' acoustic sessions, where our suitably talented musicians could wind down the weekend. Tonight though, after a damp, dreary weekend, the place was heaving and beating with a 'something special's going on' vibe. So many friends I'd met through music were there, some wanted to talk to me, ask how I was, some to simply say hi. Each hugged me. It was emotional, both terrifying and exciting at the same time.

The ridiculously talented Dave, aka Mosa and Cate, were on now, and the place was buzzing. Harmonies, melodies, gently strummed, a gorgeous background to the hubbub. I was standing with Stu, Sarah, Leena and Marli, leaning against an inner doorway, within stretching reach of the bar, observing other people's lives, lives without a care or thought for Monday morning. I was suddenly aware of Cate's voice, soaring, complementing Dave's key change, singing a song I didn't recognise. It was literally startling. The low ceilings were an acoustic challenge as they amplified every whisper, yet suddenly the pub fell quiet. It was a pure respect for the performers, a pause for intrigue and wonder.

What was this?

My sensitivities were already heightened; this was a spectacularly breathtaking, piercing moment.

"But you're everywhere, yes you are
In every melody and in every little scar
Yes you are, you are, love"

The song concluded, the moment passed, the pub grew lively again and later, raucous, and it felt like the sort of night that should never end, and certainly not with a Monday. Stu stood grinning, surveying the enchantment he had curated. Dave later told me that the captivating, pub silencing song was called 'Habibi', made famous by a Belgian musician I'd never heard of called Tamino, and that it was fabulous and I must check it out. I did check it out the next day and it was fabulous, but not a patch on the version they played that night, and not a patch on the version they posted on their Mosa social media pages. I may be responsible for approximately 40% of its plays, and each time I've heard her sing it since, Cate has kindly dedicated it to me. It belongs to that moment. Each time I'm taken back to that night, that song, those friends, and all those hugs.

Habibi, my loves.

Music had never meant more to me.

***

We knew we had to go to London. We wanted to go to London and we didn't want to go to London. But we knew we had to. We had to say thank you to our hospital support worker and we had to see the place Patrick died.

It was one of those reasonably bright, reasonably grey, reasonably nondescript days. Enough breeze and chill to make the wait on the platform of Oxford station somewhat uncomfortable. In the distance, I spotted my friend John, a Spurs fan as it happens, in striking dapper, tight mustard chinos. The train came and we rushed to find seats. Euan and I were close, Kate and Niamh further down the carriageway. We tuned in and out of the guy opposite's conversation, preposterous though it was. He was organising, for the benefit of all within earshot, an Oxford

University gathering to celebrate something or other. It was to
be extravagant, lavish and outlandish. He dressed in a different
world to us, spoke a different language, lived a different life.
Yet here he was, squashed in with us, chugging past Bicester Village
and on, on towards Haddenham and Thame and High Wycombe.
He was utterly oblivious to us and our purpose today, our life.

We arrived at Marylebone and Kate took a call to say that
our support worker couldn't see us. She's very sorry but she can't.
It's a stinging and resounding disappointment. It's late morning,
and we are stood, literally half a mile away, deflated and wondering
what now. We're also in denial — surely she could pop out for
five minutes. We're frustrated — we've come all this way to say
hello, and thank you.

It felt, in the moment, that we'd been rejected. Patrick had
died over a month ago, we were yesterday's news, yeah, probably
hundreds of other kids had randomly dropped dead since then and
here we were, forgotten.

John hurried by in his brazen trousers and, smiling, I sent him
a message:

Nice trousers x

I smiled again at the idea of him receiving it, wondering how and
where I had spotted him in London.

We went to the station shop, just standing again, lost, bereft,
our intent dulled, and eventually we bought bright red tulips.
They looked so hopeless, pointless. We'd lost a son and the railings
would gain some flowers. Splendid.

It felt an interminable wait for a green light to cross Marylebone
Road. It wouldn't be hard to find Gloucester Place on the other
side. I'd stared at that still, horror phone screen on Find My
Friends, willing Euan and Patrick to catch that train. Why wouldn't
they move, why wouldn't they just catch the train, come home?
Follow this road, literally straight down the original A40, and to
our front door, to the house Patrick was born in, and breezed out of
just a few weeks ago. Keep following the A40 and you'll end up in

Fishguard, waiting for the ferry to Ireland. This would have been the route my Dad took in the opposite direction, coming to Britain for the first time, wide-eyed, expectant, grinning, and scared too I'm sure. The road that's taken me east and west, thousands of times, for hundreds of reasons, and once I've crossed it, I'll soon be standing where Patrick collapsed and died.

There's Gloucester Place, parallel to Baker Street, and we walked down it, pace slowing, heat quickening, with tears welling. The flowers felt ever more ridiculous. It took forever to get there, along the grand, wide avenue, a highly desirable area of the world's greatest city. Well picked Patrick. Euan halted us at a smart residence with a black and white tiled floor leading to a vast, closed, black door. I wanted to bang on it, demanding why nobody had rushed out, saving Patrick, turning back time, saving us. Truth was, three passers-by that night did everything they could, administering CPR, alerting emergency services. Missing their own trains, their locations not moving, maybe their families and friends wondering too. We sent cards and thanked them as best we could.

We tied the flowers, our forlorn, pointless tulips, to the railings. We stuck a Sunshine On Leith sticker to the lamppost, shuffled, stood, cried, empty. We knew the additions wouldn't last the first blast of street cleaning, but what else were we supposed to do?

That's what it's like when you're standing on the spot your youngest child died.

There was a coffee shop around the corner, and a chance to pause for a drink, a cake, and an absolutely half-hearted *it's what he would have wanted*. We took the tube across town, feeling the chill now as we surfaced and read the inscriptions at Postman's Park. Here we raised further half-hearted smiles at the bravery in the stories of those who'd tragically died trying to save others.

George Blencowe, aged 16: When a friend bathing in the Lea cried for help, went to his rescue and was drowned

Sept 6 1880

It's 140 years later and we're thinking of George, his mum, Dad, brothers, sisters ... what became, who knows? How did they come to terms? What wretched lives did they then lead?

After the dour grey brutalism of the Barbican we ate in Leadenhall market, and waited for our allotted slot at the Sky Garden on Fenchurch Street, one of Patrick's favourite London places. Here we left a more surreptitious sticker, admiring the awesome views, hating the city that had ruined us. The sun was striving to shine. Everything was before us and below us, millions of people and millions of people before them, millions of people and lives and flowers and doors and trains to come. Despite everything, some of them would even choose to wear mustard chinos.

John eventually replied.

I was in London at 10:45. That's my usual work time, what's your excuse? X

John, living his normal life, just being, just wearing those brazen trousers.

***

There was more normal life to try to reconnect to. Like work.

I'd been due to attend a training course in Bath on 15th January. As customary, I'd ummed and ahhed all the travel options, and the resultant early start was why I was feeling a little grumpy about picking Euan and Patrick up post-midnight from Oxford. That night, that wait, those minutes will haunt me forever, desperate for them to just get on the train. In the morning, I sent this email:

Devastating news from me — our youngest son Patrick collapsed and died last night. He was fifteen and suffered a suspected cardiac arrest — completely out of the blue — and we're all in pieces.

I was due at the C-me session in Bath today if you could inform them please. Obviously there are other impending work priorities too and I'll be in touch again when I can.

Regards, Liam

In the midst of everything that unfolded, I didn't hear anything back. Kate was overwhelmed by messages, flowers, and support from her workplace. I … I didn't hear a thing.

Two days later, I felt I had to send an 'I don't know if you received my message' … message.

Hi both — hope you received the below ok?

I've been signed off work for two weeks as part of the process. However at the moment I don't feel that I want to be out of the loop for that long and I'll be in touch, probably early next week, to discuss next steps.

Those were some of the most difficult and lonely words I've ever had to type. I found a reply from our HR director to that, and indeed to my first email in my junk folder. Of course, she had replied, sending thoughts soon after that first email, but not seeing that response made me feel terrible. In the weeks to come, communication remained somewhat sporadic in comparison to the support that Kate's workplace provided and it became an issue for me. The only way to deal with it was to return to work, probably earlier than ideal, before it ate away at me. So first I met my manager, then a week later, the managing director and the HR director, at the John Lewis café in Swindon. I drank tea, feeling uneasy talking through a sadly familiar précis of what happened, feeling more comfortable when the talk turned to work, normal stuff. The company message was a clear one: *take all the time you need.*

I knew I couldn't though. I knew I had to return, and pretty quickly before the isolation became irreparable. Someone actually asked if I had enough to do to fill my days without working.

It was clear that the support Kate was getting was literally exceptional: our workplaces are not prepared for or accustomed to dealing with such acute grief. It wasn't anybody's fault. They just weren't ready for Patrick to die suddenly either.

We agreed to a sensible phased return, and we'd take it from there. Of all the trauma I'd been through, I was actually terrified of the physical return to the office, and asked that I could be accompanied in. I met a colleague in yes, John Lewis, drank more tea, then slowly, nervously made tentative steps back, back through the car park, back up the stairs that felt like a mountain to climb, back towards my desk. I was prepared for some people being fine, some a touch awkward, some hiding — all that's perfectly natural. I wasn't prepared for some avoiding handshakes or hugs because of their Covid fears.

What was this?

Of course, I was increasingly aware that there was a rapidly developing Covid crisis but was oblivious to it already changing behaviours. That people would actually keep their distance or turn away, was incredibly tough. Hindsight suggests that they knew more than I did, however right then I felt absolutely bewildered.

Within a couple of weeks, there came enforced remote working, an organisational restructure, an announcement that the company was up for sale and even a new role. It was a thoroughly frantic, exhausting whirlwind of a time. The phased return was hastily abandoned, this was it. I threw myself at it with as much vigour as I could muster.

It was to be September before I drew breath, reflected, and thought, *I cannot go on working like this.*

***

March was always my favourite month. Winter turning swiftly towards spring, new life on old trees, lighter evenings after dark afternoons. St Patrick's Day. My birthday.

And at the heart of March, Cheltenham. The Festival.

All the weeks of waiting and expectation, willing the winter behind us and promise, possibility ahead.

It's the nascent coming of spring, the feeling of blood chasing through my veins as sensitivities re-awaken. The very predictability and permanence of the journey itself through the rousing Cotswolds — Burford, Stow-on-the-Wold, Ford, winding down, down and down Fish Hill is a life-affirming magic. We'll joke about catching the steam train, inching through the Winchcombe traffic jams, with a heart racing, *what if these jams last for hours*, holding our breath as cars squeeze through narrow streets. Everywhere is Cheltenham and everyone has the same feeling of longing, belonging, and being.

On past the golf course we go, up, up this time, catching sight of the first lambs and new buds of this spring as the fields and road undulate. Finally, finally a tight left turn and we're parking at the Rising Sun on Cleeve Hill. Sometimes it's packed, sometimes it's almost empty. There are people we recognise from year after year, there are strangers who aren't really strangers, not today. There's the first rush of Guinness, there are smiles, relief that we've made another year. The *Racing Post* is spread across the table, time holds its breath, we're smiling. Soon, we'll take a photo out on the terrace, to prove that we've made another year. The course, two miles below us, distant and waiting for us.

And in the corner, there's always the Man In The Red Trousers.

After an hour or so of bonhomie and a picture for posterity on the patio, we'd usually park off course, paying a fiver, then eventually a tenner for a field and a portaloo — and another habit — a picnic with pork pie and Pringles. We'd be quiet now, listening to Festival Radio, studying the *Racing Post*, intently, earnestly, keenly hoping for wisdom, inspiration, luck, insight. Staring at it, a most incredible work of opinion, and data and knowledge and sure things and contradictions. The answers are here somewhere. Or maybe they are in the notes from last Thursday's traditional preview evening in Eynsham, another glorious ritual as the festival loomed upon us.

It's too hard, find a colour: just pick the one in red and white or yellow and blue or what did you say your first pet's name was? And then, at last, the most glorious walk of the year, anticipated more and more keenly through those cold dark months of January, of February. The walk, to the course, haphazardly through the vast car park, smiling at the touts, blessing our good fortune and breathing, ever breathing.

We were here.

Dad introduced me live to Cheltenham or The Festival (not Cheltenham Festival, or The Greatest Festival of Jump Racing, or the World Series, just *Cheltenham* or *The Festival*) in 1992 and I did not miss one until 2020. I say 'live' because before then, I remember staring out of my primary school window, into the grey, howling March wind and wondering, imagining whatever world with galloping, jumping horses there could be beyond this one. This one with bits of sellotape stuck to my jumper and cruelly, another hour until home time. And as I stared and gazed at that empty green school field, I really had no idea what was to come.

Do I remember the first time? 1992? Everything.

Everything except the horses and the races. It was me, Mum, Dad and Kate. We'd stopped for a drink in a pub with a low ceiling at Winchcombe. I felt anxious that we were already behind the pace; everyone else was supping up and leaving, bustling towards their promise. Before long though we were parking in a farm and walking a mile to the course, walking, walking ever faster. Faster because I was excited to be here at last, and faster because I knew, I knew I had a sure-fire winner at a decent price in the first race. I can still hear Mum telling me to slow down. I just had to get the bet on. I can still feel the disappointment of missing the roar as the crowd welcomed the first race of the Festival going off, the disappointment of my horse winning, before we'd even got there.

I've not had many winners since. For years, we went to the Festival for just a day each year, usually watching from the raucous centre of the course, colloquially known as the 'cabbage patch' although more corporate names have followed. The vast hospitality tents would be full of lads, enjoying a smart annual day out, becoming more boisterous with the beer, their football tribalries eventually revealing themselves — West Brom, Wolves, Villa — this was a West Midlands day out, not the great Irish festival I'd read about, and yearned for. I was sure that that was happening somewhere else, yet this was fine enough, each year anticipated ever more eagerly.

Eventually sense and adventure got the better of us — transferring to Club or Tattersalls, enjoying the developments at the course. Here was a different crowd, older, more Irish, more tweed, more 'Cotswolds At Party Time'. Yet for all the differences, Cheltenham embodies a teeming, wholesome version of humanity and celebration. Finding the same people in the same places on the same days, year after year: the Man In The Red Trousers in the Rising Sun. Terry's mates from London in the Centaur.

One year, within five minutes, I went from being yards away from the Queen, to singing arm in arm, ankle deep in discarded plastic pint glasses with a bunch of lads from Middlesbrough in the Guinness Village.

So it is with some disdain that when casual observers ask only:

Did you have any winners?

I can say only:

Yes.

Being there, each March, is my winner. To go, be there, breathe.

With time came change. Long gone are the ramshackle stands and recurrent crushes as the crowds surged between races. Cheltenham racecourse quietly transformed into an exceptional twenty-first century sporting arena. Or as quiet a transformation as a precision operation for almost quarter of a million people over four days and quite a few horses can have. In doing so, it lost no charm, none of its beguiling spirit. If anything, its sense of occasion was amplified and enhanced with each innovation. Our anticipation grew and grew through each winter, each new March to welcome. Dad loved the freedom, and had an enchanting knack of finding his peace, his smile, among a crowd of sixty thousand.

He'd be watching horses on the parade ring, observing the grooms, looking for owners, trainers, signs, stories, mysteries, magic. Within the mayhem of bars fifteen people deep in the Guinness Village, of terraces densely packed and punters straining necks for sight or sound of their sure-fire horse, amid all that, the bonhomie, the *joie de vivre*, he'd have a quiet lookout for the jockey who'd never won here before, the trainer that had an impossible back story. He had an exceptional knowledge of these things — which is to say he knew, and understood about 2% of the real workings of the racing industry. One day he'd taken me to see one of uncle Maurice's horses working out at its stables. It was like entering Narnia or finding platform 9¾, a world within a world, beguiling, mesmerising, hardworking, humble and dizzily exciting. So one of the things that enchanted him with Cheltenham was the stories, the small things, the human things, the real things.

He was so pleased to share this purist equine love and respect with Niamh. Niamh, who would sit on the arms of the sofa at eighteen months old using handbag handles for reins. Niamh whose own love and natural draw to horses had no measure. Niamh, his precious granddaughter who he accompanied to a thousand days at the local stables, mending their fences and leading their ponies. It was as inevitable as it was beautiful that she inspired him to regain confidence to ride again, and their holiday hacking adventures exploring forests and galloping on beaches together became a regular joy unconfined. Niamh of course grew to love Cheltenham too.

For my part, I have a curious and particular skill — I am incredibly capable of remembering virtually nothing about the actual horses. Yes, I just about recall Best Mate's third Gold Cup victory and being convinced from my angle that he'd lost. Indeed, I cannot forget the shattering disappointment and almost spiritual dignity of the great Istabraq exiting the arena for the final time. Or the glories of Sprinter Sacre or Big Bucks, year after year. But I do remember horses that won for family and friends at fabulous odds, like the 40/1 Anzum, or Katie Walsh's winners or the descent down Fish Hill suffering the most savage 30th birthday hangover.

And I remember how Cheltenham makes me feel. Christmas for grown-ups indeed.

Dad loved these days. He longed for them and lived every second of them. He loved being at Cheltenham in March with a glorious ferocity. The view across to Cleeve Hill, the vast, ever-changing Cotswold sky. I couldn't avoid inheriting it if I tried. Which I didn't, as I felt exactly the same way. He wasn't a hefty gambler, although he'd pride himself on a couple of winners, he wasn't there for the drink, although he'd enjoy a couple of pints — it was too important for that. And when the racing was done, if there was one thing he loved more than being at Cheltenham in March, it was celebrating St Patrick's Day.

There'd be heady nights in the Court Inn, and later the New Inn, with old Irish songs brought to new life by Hullabelloo; meeting old acquaintances, the Murphys, O'Briens, Kellys and making new best friends. Nights that went on forever. Singing ourselves hoarse to 'Sally MacLennane' and Dad's favourite 'Weelya Weelya Walya'. The diaspora celebrating our Irishness with a rich, fierce spirit that the home-based Irish, never mind the English, would never understand.

And through it all, holding the purpose, identity and belonging of the whole damn evening would be the songs, the poetry of the Pogues:

> *Did the old songs taunt or cheer you?*
> *And did they still make you cry?*
> *Did you count the months and years*
> *Or did your teardrops quickly dry?*

It was always the best night of the year, of riotous, drunken, unpredictable cacophony and revelry, and when it eventually ended, when one day became another, it was my birthday.

***

2020 is different. Of course it is.

This year I dread Cheltenham. I both dread it and want to embrace it, look forward to its familiarity, for its nature and humility and sheer life to take me in and hug me and tell me everything will be OK. I've done it once before without Dad, but then, I knew he'd be back. I knew he'd come here until he died.

So, 2020 and, to quote Billy Bragg, as the world falls apart, some things stay in place. Despite everything, or maybe because of everything, I resolved to go. Sticks and stones may break my bones, but I will not miss Cheltenham. Rather more controversially than usual, played out with an emerging Covid backdrop, The Festival came and it went.

On the day I have a ticket to go, I wake with a fierce, raging temperature. I can't make it to the bathroom, never mind to Prestbury Park.

Give it an hour Liam.

I want to cry in desperation. An hour later, I negotiated a shower.

I'm going!

I'm going!

Stop me if you can.

I got dressed but was physically unable to get down the stairs. I withdrew to bed, sending Niamh and Euan with my friends Peter and Graham. I was proud of them, and I knew there were parts of them doing this for me. I was asleep within minutes.

Soon I'll be dreaming, but will those dreams be able to match what Dad was able to share with his brothers those last few years? With their father being a groom for country estates it was maybe inevitable that the two older brothers, Maurice and Jack, would initially pursue careers as apprentice jockeys while Dad and his younger siblings Bernie and Jasper followed different courses. Their racing interests had ebbed and flowed over the decades, but Maurice owning a modest succession of racehorses brought them close together in those later years. Dad would fervently relay updates on Missing the Craic or Sweet Louise or Fenno's Storm, loving the days out at Newbury, Warwick, Goodwood or wherever. The successes were celebrated proudly, the disappointments swiftly forgotten. Visiting a training yard was that personal, real-life invitation to pass through the wardrobe into Narnia, to await that train on platform 9¾. It's a captivating, hidden, magical world of dedication, devotion and desperation. Dad took so much from the experience and Maurice's horses each have a special place in our hearts.

Another Cheltenham. Like most years, I can't remember the horses. Unlike every year since 1992 and the farmyard and the late arrival and the missed winner, I wasn't there.

This year, there was no St Patrick's Day to celebrate either.

***

Days later, and this time, Mum beats Rob to the horrible news. I'm sitting at my desk working and she walks in, unannounced and interrupting my concentration and self-importance. I feel momentarily bristled and annoyed.

All she can say is:

Murph.

And immediately I know that Chris Murphy, another of my old teammates, the fourth of Dad's cherished football team, has died.

It's impossible.

I close my eyes, I close my laptop, grab a jacket and walk.

April

With April came lockdown, and with lockdown came ... nothing. The country stopped and the world stopped. We collectively reverted into introspection and contemplation, looking back in order to give us a chance to look forward. Lists of this, pictures of that, a national spring cleaning of memories. It was impossible to think that it was just a year since Patrick had been on Henry Box's Sports Tour to Lisbon in Portugal, an adventure he absolutely adored. Having suffered a knee injury a couple of years previously, he had endured continual recurrences, which were painful both emotionally and physically. He didn't complain, he just characteristically got on with it. Sometimes he would be more diligent with the never ending physiotherapy, sometimes his motivation suffered, each new diagnosis with a new expert hurting him a little deeper as initial hope of a swift recovery faded.

His football team at Freeland, led by Gary and Brad, were fantastic with him. They both gently encouraged and nurtured his rare playing opportunities, while ensuring he always felt part of the squad during his long lay-offs. It meant the world to him, and to us, that they'd provide him with a kit that there was little prospect of him wearing, and he knew there was a place there for him. Even so, if he had one aim for that 2018/19 season, it was to be fit for the school tour to Portugal. Through the winter he trained carefully with Freeland, building his strength and confidence week by week. I'd attend and watch from a distance, partly to let him find his own space, and partly because I was terrified that his knee would give way and desert him once more. March came, and his fitness had improved to such an extent that he was fit to resume playing again. However, with the tour imminent, we thought it prudent not to push it and not to take any undue risks. He was ready.

On 30th March, Patrick and I went for a Saturday afternoon kickabout at a typically wet and blustery West Witney sports field. It was just the two of us, and a football, as it had been on a million other occasions. We were minutes away from calling it a day, returning to the car to check on Swindon's progress and to get home and recover with a hot drink.

Patrick turned to strike a ball back to me, his boot catching the turf as he mistimed his action by a nanosecond. It was innocuous, but he crumpled to the ground in agony. With both of us in tears, I carried him from one end of the field to the other and bundled him into the car.

Once home and alone, I let out a tremendous release of anguish; it was two years of agony that Patrick had suffered pouring out of me in the purest, most primaeval manner. His flight to Portugal was less than a week away.

Swindon won 3-1 at Bury.

Somehow, Patrick recovered sufficiently to play a part in the tour matches. He loved playing football again with his mates, loved the socialising and we loved what he'd achieved. The pictures told of a close-knit group having the time of their lives, with stories and laughs to last forever. He was in his element.

A few weeks later, as Brad had recalled at the memorial service, he was surprised and delighted when asked to be part of Freeland's cup final squad. He told me quite bashfully, and I could recognise how chuffed he was. As far as I was concerned, it was a wonderful gesture from Gary and Brad to involve him, to have him there on the side with his kit on, while the boys who'd fought the season out battled away. Come the day, it was a tight, competitive game, against familiar yet friendly foes. With the score at 1-1, and the afternoon delicately poised, I took a deep breath of surprise and pride when I saw Patrick being ready to enter the action early in the second half. It wasn't purely an inclusive gesture, they wanted him out there to try to win the cup for Freeland.

After just five minutes, a clever touch here, a rusty pass there as he adjusted to the pace of the game, a crunching 50/50 tackle ten yards from the touchline brought the now too familiar sight of Patrick falling to the ground. Watching from the far side, I felt physically sick, helpless and not a little guilty that I'd thought he was fit to take part — both for his sake and the rest of the team too. I watched, helpless, as he was carried from the pitch.

This time it was Brad, bless him, in tears, doing the carrying. At least I had someone to share that burden with.

It was Patrick's last football game. After that, it was back to the hospital, more x-rays and MRI scans and second opinions and at last, at last, after almost three years, the recognition that an operation was required.

And to think we were concerned that the surgery planned for April 2020 would be right before his GCSEs.

So come this April, there was no knee operation for Patrick and no imperious march towards promotion for Swindon Town. The season had been stalled by Covid. Days out planned, tickets bought, train journeys worked out. All were now on hold.

**

The 18th of April has come and gone. I'd written an article; the passion and the words of anger and love and memory gushed out. I remember, indelibly, the moment I was compelled to write, the moment gripped me as I grasped the steering wheel,

a roundabout on the A40 on the way to Burford. Write I did: and
when 18th April did come, there we were on the front page of the
Swindon Advertiser.

You've gone and made everyone cry again, said Mum.

A few days later, there was a follow-up piece, with the heartfelt
reaction of the manager Richie Wellens, and our players, our
heroes. The messages and reaction were extraordinary, soon
the piece would be in *When Saturday Comes*, a monthly staple and
nourishment for me for thirty-plus years — and was then picked
up by the *Guardian*. 18th April was supposed to be Swindon
Town's last home game of the season. It was supposed to be a day
of glory when Swindon were crowned League Two champions
after a magnificent season. It was also supposed to be a day we
pause to remember, as just before the kick-off the names of those
supporters who've passed away during the year are read out.
It's a poignant touchpoint, a moment to reflect, to recognise
and to appreciate those lives and then to roar and to get on with
the game.

Each year is different, and each year is the same: it might be a
meaningless mid-table meander, or maybe more significant: either
way, within ten minutes, I'm moaning about a throw-in here, or
applauding a deft pass there. I've moved on from thanking my
lucky stars that while I may know some of those names, none of
them have carried my surname.

Football generally, and Swindon Town specifically, have
shaped and guided our family existence through generations.
Shared experiences, some glory glory moments, ill-fated Wembley
bobbles, all central to growing and living together. And now,
through tears and grief and mourning, we go on. We go on, every
day feeling like the four-year-old me terrified on those rickety steps.
Every step is a success, and every step is a step nearer to the top,
and to the next game.

Until Covid and there were no more 'next games' either.
This year, there is Covid and no last game of the season, no 18th
April and no chance to pause, to reflect or to argue about the referee.

And now of course, this most memorable, ghastly season limps towards a farcical mess of an end; quite absolutely in contrast to the vibrancy of hope, passion and expectation we had, and ultimately, of that life being ripped away, finitely, forever.

The photo of Dad, Patrick and I that was on the front page of the *Advertiser* said so much about us and, quite ironically and unintentionally, nothing about Swindon Town. Months later, I wrote about the picture during a 'Writing Memoir to Heal' webinar workshop hosted by Nikesh Shukla. I was engaged and interested, but not feeling remotely creative. Within minutes, as my memories of a picture painted a thousand words, those words tumbled onto the page, and I wept uncontrollably as I wrote. Somewhat incongruously, as it accompanied a heartfelt article about our love of Swindon, and football, we were wearing novelty Gloucestershire cricket hats, with Dad wearing a Waterford GAA shirt, in a town we loved for its horse racing.

This time, we were in Cheltenham for cricket. Rain had stopped play, and the crowd took shelter wherever. For us, in a vast marquee near the bar and the line of portaloos in front of the college. There is so much life in that picture; I can almost smell the air, fresh with the warm feel of July rain.

It reminds me of the first time I took Dad to Lord's. A test match where the Pakistan greats Wasim Akram and Waqar Younis tore into England with relentless ferocity and hostility. Sat deep in the Mound Stand, tasting the fear of the batsmen, Dad was spellbound by the pace, the life around us, the history wrapping us and freezing us in this moment, father and son. After decades of listening to Test Match Special, its secrets and senses were gently unpeeling, becoming life around us. He was entirely captivated. We went to Lord's plenty of times after that, whether for a day at the test, a Twenty20, or to see our friends playing for Shipton under Wychwood in the National Village Knockout Final. Each visit was unique, memorable in its own right, its own purpose, and with increasing familiarity, each visit was comforting and enriching.

As the rain in Cheltenham continued, the marquee became crowded. There was bemusement, ruefulness, excited chatter. We've had no rain in this glorious, scorching summer, and here it is, now it comes, all at once. We've looked forward to it for so long, just a simple evening out at the cricket — me, Dad and Patrick. Groups continue drinking, almost unaware of the rain — they'd come for the social anyway, a Friday night release with the weekend ahead. And in a sense, isn't that what we're all here for? A catch up, a release. Does it really matter if Gloucestershire beat Essex tonight? Is it even Essex? Maybe that proves my point. We're all here for so much more than the sport.

I can remember so many times I've been to this annual event in the cricketing calendar, the sights and sounds and temporary stands abutting the stunning college setting. But can I recall the games, the outcomes, the fifties and five-wicket hauls? Barely. There are books and lists and internets for checking that stuff. Or a friend like Peter will tell me. All the other times, as a teenager with Dad or feeling that moment of relaxing into a four-day game reading a paragraph in the paper literally between each delivery, of keeping up with the test match in the Montpelier tent, or the horse racing at the bookies, or even missing a sensational Phil Tufnell bowling spell because we had to get the bus home. Kids playing, learning and leaping, in the nets behind the open stand. All those moments, they're mine. And now, we stand, speculating on how long the rain will last. We take photos, preserving rain stopping play forever. Preserving us forever. In novelty hats.

I'll play the optimistic card, of hope laced with science: I check the weather forecast. It's a passing shower.

It isn't.

After an hour or so of this most stubborn rain, the match is abandoned. The crowd, soggy and more downbeat now, empty the few spots of shelter and we drift towards our weekends and lives beyond. Most memorably, vividly, we passed a lady, she simply had to be over eighty, and she was head to toe in a Gloucestershire replica kit. A garish look, navy and yellow, sponsor-laden polyester.

A John Terry for the octogenarians. When we talk about the evening — how unlucky we were with the weather — in the weeks and months to come, this is the image to which we return. A woman, dressed up for her passion on a Friday night, who made us smile.

We never went to cricket together again.

***

For Kate, work remained very much on hold — out of sight, if not out of mind. It was out there somewhere, but simply not a realistic prospect. Whereas I'd felt almost compelled to quickly return to work, for Kate, the opposite was true. Working in a school, where staff knew Patrick and all pupils knew our story, would simply be too much for now.

And so while my course of grieving became a more public one — going to running groups, returning to work, seeking music and a drink or two in our social town — Kate's was a more reflective one. Of asking questions, understanding similar stories, examining the evidence before us. Thankfully the two paths could coexist and complement. From morning one, our ground zero, she liaised with medical professionals and schools, found supportive charities and made contacts. She wrote, passionately and openly and beautifully.

The hospital had kindly called our older children's universities and our son's school to inform them. His school called to discuss how to tell the other pupils and which pupils to tell first. Myself and Liam needed to contact our workplaces to explain our absence. Cards, flowers, messages and visitors began to arrive. I tried various support avenues including the GP, but nothing would be available until a Child Death Review meeting was held. I didn't know what a Child Death Review meeting was (why would I?). I made another phone call to find out. Our family would be talked about, but we were not invited to attend. I cried.

The following days were a blur of phone calls, messages and visitors. I had a notebook to write everything in as I was terrified I would forget an important detail. A post-mortem was arranged and the subsequent conversation with the coroner was one of the worst of my life with Patrick being reduced to a collection of organs and tissue samples. The post-mortem was inconclusive, meaning further tests had to be arranged and this would take weeks, if not months. We were given an interim death certificate and gently nudged towards the funeral directors to make the arrangements. The funeral director waived all costs as there is a fund that pays for child funerals. Who knew? I cried.

I googled and googled trying to find other parents who had suffered a similar death. I found a charity (SUDC UK) and through them found information, support and a network of parents who had experienced similar deaths of their children. We went to a meeting in Birmingham just before lockdown to meet with the charity and to learn more about research into sudden deaths. We were able to talk about our experiences and learnt about the importance of those tissue samples to research and how easily we could have made the wrong decision when the coroner asked if we wanted them to be disposed of or kept for research. I cried.

At the meeting in Birmingham I spoke to parents who had received the post-mortem report in the post with no warning. I obviously did not want this. SUDC UK helped me to email the pathologist and family liaison sister in London to ensure that we would be called when the report was available and then invited to the hospital in London to go through the report. I was reassured, it was one less thing to worry about. I cried.

The Child Death Review meeting was eventually held, and we were allocated a bereavement support worker to take over from the support we had been receiving from London. She visited us at home and we began to meet for coffee. I cried.

Then, lockdown happened. Our support network dissolved overnight. My parents could not visit, I could not meet my friends or our bereavement support worker. Yoga and running groups were cancelled. Wrapped up in their own lockdowns the texts and messages from friends quietened. We got ourselves a new routine starting with a daily walk (ten thousand steps by lunchtime). The daily walks gave us the chance to pause and talk. We sewed, we baked, did online quizzes, looked after seventeen horses at a local yard and tried to fill our time. We cried.

As the weeks passed by I started to tackle the paperwork. Because we only had an interim death certificate, we were not able to use the government 'Tell Us Once' service. I went to the Child Benefit website to inform them. There is no tick box for 'my child has died' so I was forced to write it in the 'Any other comments' box. Two days later Patrick's National Insurance Number arrived in the post, a moment of celebration and coming of age for his older two siblings but not now. I was devastated and added it to a fast growing box of cards and paperwork. I cried.

A few weeks after this I received a letter from the government child trust fund carrying the headline 'I'm sure you can't quite believe it, but your child will soon be an adult'. I cried. I emailed to inform them and was sent a form that referred to my child as 'late' and 'deceased'. I duly photocopied all the documents, got them verified and returned them. I still haven't tackled his bank accounts; lockdown makes this difficult and they will have to wait. Luckily my work was more than happy for me to use their printer for printing and photocopying, I don't know how I would have tackled the paperwork during lockdown without their support.

Weeks passed into months — Liam had returned to work. Lockdown meant working from home, which was a relief to us all to still be together. The get-together we had been planning to celebrate our son's sixteenth Birthday had to be cancelled and we planned a quieter day together as a family. We would eat Patrick's favourite food, give gifts to his friends and climb the big hill we had gone to on the day of his cremation.

Among the flowers and cards was a letter with the stamp of the coroner's office on it.

Despite everything I had put in place, Patrick's post-mortem report arrived on his sixteenth birthday.

I cried and then I got mad.

The following weeks were spent finding out how to complain to the coroner's office. How to ensure that the tissue samples are kept for future reference. How to see a copy of the medical notes. How to register a death when you cannot visit the registry office. Thank goodness for the support of SUDC UK who helped me with all of this. They are a small charity started by three women whose children all died suddenly, without explanation. We were so grateful for the welcome from the founder, Nikki, that day in Birmingham, and the support from all. Thank goodness for the SUDC Foundation in America who provide support in looking at post-mortem reports and whose social worker asked me more questions than any other professional has to date.

The post-mortem report declared Patrick's cause of death as Sudden Arrhythmogenic Death, which means his heart stopped, but they don't know why. The Coroner recommended the family be referred to the Inherited Heart Condition Clinic. I called the GP to check he had got a copy of the report and was able to make the referral, but he did not. I checked with the Coroner who told me that copies are not automatically sent to GPs — they have to request them. So how would the GP know to refer us? I asked, 'good point' he said. Yet again I was photocopying and dropping the report to the GP so that he could make the referral. I cried.

Slowly, I am able to meet friends again and go on walks with my bereavement support worker. I hope to be able to return to work successfully. But I worry, I worry for all the families having to face this catalogue of obstacles, mistakes, paperwork and delays without the support that we have had, and who do not have the knowledge and confidence to find support. Surely there are things that could be done to improve this for other parents.

It is just months since Patrick died and we are only just beginning the lifetime journey of grief for him. I have read books on grief, found support groups online and connected with other bereaved parents. We are determined that he will not be forgotten and that we will go on and find happiness in life and take him with us. We cry often, on our own and together.

Thank goodness for the work of charities such as the SUDC Foundation, SUDC UK, Helen & Douglas House and SeeSaw. I know that for me, I want, eventually, to be able to support other parents through this maze of decisions, paperwork, emails and phone calls and work to make it easier for parents so that they can concentrate on the hard work of grieving for their dead child.

May

Regan, one of Patrick's friends, has arranged to visit with his Mum, Lindsay. While it's emotional and obviously difficult, he's also self-assured and suddenly seems mature beyond his years. He presents us with a red Swindon shirt with WALSH 7 on the back, and it's been signed by all the players. In keeping with the way our club has been managed, Regan has paid for the shirt and organised the signatures directly through Anthony Grant, one of the players, as the club has been indifferent to his requests. Another friend, Finley, had said they didn't even reply to his. On one hand, it's remarkably difficult to not be perplexed by a professional football club so indifferent to the death of a dedicated fifteen-year-old season ticket holder. On the other, I'm humbled and beyond proud at what Regan and his friends have done. As May winds inexorably towards Patrick's sixteenth birthday, Regan shared tenderly-written daily posts of his memories of Patrick on social media.

Another friend, Hannah, organises a magnificent quiz. It lifts us through the humdrum routines of lockdown, grounds us with our grieving friends and community, and most memorably introduces us to Swear or Chair ... quite possibly the most entertaining quiz round testing our knowledge of Swedish soft furnishings and profanities that I've ever come across. At the end, as I attempted to mutter some acknowledgements and thanks, I was overcome at the gallery view, and the sheer number and faces of all those who'd taken part.

A lot of people will never visit IKEA in quite the same way as before.

***

Meanwhile, I resolved to share some more stories before Patrick's birthday. What began as simple intent to share became a daily outpouring of emotion, bittersweet memories and tangled feelings. I somewhat startled myself with how raw it made me feel, increasingly uncomfortable writing so openly and painfully.

I this, *I* that … is that really me?

The feedback was humbling. Alan said he'd stay up late waiting for the daily instalment to be posted and the kind words kept coming, so I kept chugging along. A plan gently formed, and by day ten, Patrick's birthday, I allowed myself some quiet satisfaction.

This is what I posted, one day at a time.

***

1/10 (991)

In the days until what should be Patrick's 16th birthday, I'm going to share a story.

It's not about Patrick, well not for a few days; perhaps it's a little about each of us. Don't say I didn't warn you …

So, you find yourself drawn into reading a piece about hurling — and no, it's not Ireland's version of curling — but the fastest field sport in the world. By way of a gentle introduction, its roots originate in ancient times — by which I mean the Celts of two thousand years ago rather than anything that happened just before the Premier League was invented. It's fierce, as you might expect if imagining overhead hockey, and the pace utterly unrelenting. Its players are all amateur, genuine and often humble representatives of their communities. Were it not for ongoing debates about TV coverage (Sky v terrestrial) and governance (the GAA can make the FA look innovative and inclusive), you might get sucked into thinking this is a model of honest, sporting utopia …

And then, then, your county, your team, your identity gets on a roll, and primeval sporting passion takes over: there were 83,200 tickets available for the Croke Park final in September, and I just needed a couple … Could George Clooney help with finding me tickets for the All-Ireland hurling final?

It's August, and I suppose, all things considered, that few of the words written, the dreams dreamt and the hopes realised, of Waterford's semi-final victory will have come from the sumptuous shores of Italy's Lake Como, where Mr Clooney and I were both holidaying, albeit, not together.

Fewer still, from a second generation follower never having lived in Ireland, never mind the county, yet accustomed to finding ever more creative ways to watch, to believe and to feel, but maybe that's what hurling does to you.

And hands up, when that holiday was booked months ago, I barely paid attention to the date (we of the Déise have a somewhat troubled history of semi-final Sundays in August) or the location and its attraction to film stars.

Anyway, let me take you back to Italy, to semi-final throw-in time and I'm sitting with a pint of Guinness. My new friend and foe, Joe from Cork, informs me that this is the only bar for hours around that will be showing the match, so I should thank my lucky (film) stars that we're staying a couple of decent puckouts away. We only spotted the bar in the first place as tempers beat earlier: there was nowhere to park the car for miles around, no hint of a shop serving even basic provisions. Yet there was a sign on a hand-written whiteboard, promising, teasing (is this some absurd Italian idea of a joke?) Cork v Waterford later. This could have been Tramore rather than Tremezzo.

But really, I know that this is providence. I know that it's providence because it's easy to be clever after the event, but mainly, as I sat and plotted Waterford's path through the hazardous qualifiers to September after that drubbing from the Rebels in June, I knew that this would be like no other year.

Without wishing to make this all about me, or to deny our manager, Derek McGrath, and maybe some of the players due credit, my role shouldn't be overlooked. It would be harsh, maybe petulant of you to point out that I've done nothing, never stepped on a pitch in my life, barely understand my full forwards from my half forwards. I'm a football fan, no, worse, a soccer fan, I'd even be a little disappointed if you didn't mock me so, but like I said, this is what hurling can do to you.

It's another story but my introduction to live hurling came in the 1990 final between Cork and Galway at Croke Park in Dublin. It came, extraordinarily, because me, Mum and Dad sneaked in, via the huge, unguarded and slightly open gates to the Hill 16 terrace. No one wanted a fiver for their trouble, nobody was mindful in the wake of the Hillsborough disaster, to the horrific dangers at an overwhelmed stadium.

Really though, hurling came alive for me with Waterford's semi-final defeat (hey, get used to it) to Clare in 2002. Watchful of our progress and resurgence from afar, my Dad and I took our first day trip from West Oxfordshire to Croker. Little did I know that that taste of being so near yet so far, of being so proud of what these players give for that jersey, so hopeful that next time, next time we'll get it right, would become so much a part of me and my identity.

The near misses came and went alright, the day trips turned into weekends, into family holidays. The first time Patrick flew, and shouted *again, again* as we landed in Dublin. The days of listening from afar, of the vivid Mícheál Ó Muircheartaigh commentaries, of endless expectation and ultimate disappointment. The coming of the internet, of live streams and cursing connections and cables. Of celebrating the contributions of fine players and grand men whose races were now run, to watching the coming of a new generation. Of feeling I have the only English accent in Pairc

Ui Chaoimh or wherever, of feeling so familiar yet so much an outsider. Always though with that hope eternal in spring, and always too, always the fragility or the heartbreak or the hard luck of the summer to come.

The Déise found endless ways to lose semi-finals, to carry that yearning on for another year. We were usually there — against Clare, Cork, Kilkenny, Tipperary, whoever, whatever. Always. So near, yet so far. And then that astonishing weekend in 2008 that Ronnie Drew, legend of The Dubliners died. For once not drowning Guinness-flavoured sorrows, we headed for O'Donoghues, the spiritual home of the guardian angel of Irish musical culture. Waterford had beaten Tipperary, a first semi-final win since 1963; cause enough for concentrated celebration of sport, of life. All around us were half recognised faces and familiar voices cheek by jowl, as a mighty traditional music session took hold in honour of the great man. We raised our parting glasses to Ronnie for the last time and left, twinkling, burning with the soul of what we'd privileged. The next day, the national press reported the evening, filling hazy gaps and lending names to faces and voices.

For sure, we don't get *The Times* or the *Guardian* eavesdropping on our nights at home in the Elm Tree, we chortled, as we skipped along Grafton Street.

You know, it's easier for me at home or wherever the internet connection has taken me: no week-long media inquests, deliberations over pints or ribbing from work colleagues. Waterford have lost, I can turn off, and pretend, pretend that it didn't happen or doesn't matter; after all, I have a new season of supporting Swindon to struggle through yet. Even so, I'd be deluding myself to suggest that the hurt doesn't add up, that Waterford's last All-Ireland victory in 1959 isn't an invisible weight to carry with me through each long winter.

Nineteen. Fifty. Nine.

Back to me and the credit thing, and come to think of it, it's a bit tenuous. However, in the aftermath of last season's semi-final heartbreak at the hands of Kilkenny, with Derek McGrath emotionally and publicly considering his future, I *nearly* wrote to him. I so *nearly* told him to keep the faith, to keep believing, to keep innovating. His day, our day would come. My eloquent and persuasive tome would have warmed his autumn evenings and helped his deliberations. It would offer support, insight and inspiration in generous measures. It would be welcome and detached perspective from the other side of the sea. One true hurling heart to another. Ultimately he would thank me at the final in September — and I would say no Derek, thank you.

So, we fast forward and back to that bar in Lake Como. After watching an epic Waterford victory against Cork on the big screen, Joe offered his hand in congratulations, and without wishing to offend his Galway friends back home, hoped that the Déise would win the final. I hoped so too, how I hoped so too. Tickets? *Que sera sera.* George Clooney might be interested — will it help if I bring him along? Joe said, *phone your Dad, he'll be a happy man.*

My Dad has beaten seventy-five of those winters, and there's more than a chance that, if the wait goes on another fifty-eight years, neither of us will be around to finally enjoy it.

Maybe that's why, when fate and the semi-final draw apparently conspired against me (plans were in place, bookings made should we have faced Galway), I had instead already arranged to be in Waterford in the lead up to, and then Dublin itself for the final weekend.

Providence? Or just hope? It's funny what hurling does to you.

***

2/10 (992)

It was shortly after midnight on 1st September 2017. I'd had a pint or two and I needed a lie down.

It had been a glorious day, one of the best ever. We were in Stradbally, in county Waterford, living a dream of seeing the hurling team, our team, win their first All-Ireland since 1959. Nineteen. Fifty. Nine. You already know that. The county was entirely captivated, a community enthralled, united and excited beyond humble comprehension. All we needed were tickets to the final in Dublin on Sunday. Problem was, so did everyone else. I'd tried and begged and cajoled, then phoned and wished some more, but every trail was cold.

Still, this was a magic, special, surreal time: if national radio broadcasting live from the local GAA club three minutes stroll away in the morning doesn't convince you, maybe the local pub having Ireland's newly crowned national champion at singing with a bucket on his head in it will.

Feel free to re-read that last sentence.

Buoyed by the drink, heady with hurling anticipation, I left the hubbub in Whelan's Bar, Stradbally, behind and took the hill towards Ballyvooney Cove with Mum, Dad, Maurice and Margo.

Grinning. Yet something bugged me.

Embracing the sudden calm and sweetly breathing the chill sea breeze, lightly giddy with Guinness and catch up chatter, I checked my phone.

I'd done 9,117 steps during the day just gone. That last pint had taken me into a new day. It was the first day since March that I hadn't done 10,000 steps.

Being me, just the fair side of obsessive, of course it bugged me a little. But after that day, and that evening, honestly, honestly, I wasn't too bothered.

***

3/10 (993)

The next day, we left Cappoquin, Dad's birthplace and another proud town held together by flags and bunting. Charmed by the inspiring, incredible displays of good luck and sheer hope, we headed for the hills. We were on a mission. Dad was looking to find his mother's McGrath family home for the first time in more than thirty years. The omens weren't good: between us, we'd tried before, we'd failed. And here we were again, a single track road, always searching, another mile, more flags, more bunting, ever more remote, up and up, now less hopeful. Looking in the wrong places although we knew we were on the right road. Another mile. Trust me, there's a certain despair when the optimism and excitement slowly gives way to quiet, to tension, to fading hope, to stinging frustration.

And ultimately, a resigned acceptance that maybe it wasn't going to be our day. There weren't any more miles.

We were virtually in county Tipperary.

Eventually, mournfully, fatefully, we turned the cars around and headed slowly, quietly, ruefully back downhill. I felt crushed. My head was spinning with regret, we wouldn't get this chance together again, tears were forming behind my eyes and my breathing tightened.

A lone horse, its head poking over a gate, soon compelled us to stop. It allowed us space to halt, to gather our feelings, share our disappointment. We took in the air, several degrees cooler up here than the seaside we could see fifteen miles away in the distance.

As Niamh patted and indulged the grateful horse, we smiled, it was comforting and calming for all. We were joined by a farmer. Arms dripping with blood and gently enquiring as to how our day was — or perhaps he meant: Who the hell are these strangers come halfway up the mountain to prod my precious horse?

So we explained, and he explained. He was in the middle of calving, this was no ordinary horse, it was a racehorse, his daughter was a Shakespearean actress in Stratford, he knew Oxford right enough. He spoke faster than we could Google to verify his wonderful stories. It was utterly captivating. There was more explaining. He explained that his family had bought the land from ours in the 1960s, and sure, McGrath's cottage was still standing. We were but a few hundred yards away and he would take us there right now.

And of course he did.

The structure was still sound, it was made of hardy mountain stone and had withstood over a hundred winters. These were moments of astonishing coincidence, unforgettable significance, with deeply emotional resonance. The McGrath house was now his pig sty. Moments that I instantly knew that I would remember and cherish forever.

We'd only stopped to pat the horse.

My gran had two siblings who had not survived their toddler years; they had literally starved to death in this harsh environment. Kate braved the brambly track for a closer inspection and pictures.

Our host's name, the farmer, was Donal Fennessy and he had brought magic to our lives.

I glanced at my phone and saw a missed call from Paul, back home in Bampton. I took several deep breaths, started the car and dared to dream.

***

4/10 (994)

We took the single track road back down the hill to Lismore and its familiar castle. I could have skipped those miles. The sky was a breezy mix of foreboding low cloud, yet with enough blue sky to make a Dutchman a pair of trousers. Reflecting that summer afternoon, I already knew that we'd just had an extraordinary encounter.

As the rest of the family entered the stunning castle grounds, I made my excuses, hung back and listened to Paul's message. The castle has always been special for us, as my Gran was in service there and we've long loved roaming the gardens. Always pausing to giggle at a Gormley statue here and to take staged pictures there by the same trees as the children grew older. They resisted and then endured it with characteristic equal measure. It's an evocative place of peace and serenity, scent, beauty and memories and bloom and a hidden tennis court. Our pictures that day captured a relaxed, playful family.

Paul's message said: *I might have good news for you.*

I didn't know Paul especially well and he didn't owe me anything. Some years earlier, my friend Ossie had said we should meet, that we'd get on famously, then we talked some more about football shirts, and nothing happened. It was seasons later before we did meet, agreeing a deal to supply kit for Tower Hill FC. And fair play to him, I thought, heading up uhlsport in the UK, alongside his own developing gloveglu sporting business and an inquisitive, insightful blog. Brave and sharp enough to make a decent and fulfilling living in a way the rest of us would love to. I might not say it often, but Ossie was right.

Now here Paul was, leaving me a message that caused my heart to leap, jump, stop, leap some more … I daren't tell anyone else … he'd only said might, he might have tickets. Tickets! Tickets for Sunday in Dublin! Might wasn't enough right now. I wandered the lush avenues, posed for customary pictures, imagined my gran joyously picking flowers, and said nothing.

It felt like hundreds of days, and thousands of missed calls before we eventually spoke, all of twenty minutes later. And he had, of course he had found a couple of tickets. I was giddy with waves of relief; joy unconfined. I knew how much this would mean to Dad when I could tell him. How could I tell him? What words were there to share perfect moments like this? I waited for a quiet spot, breathed, gulped, hesitated and then blurted out the fabulous news. And wow, it did mean everything.

I knew, because he said nothing.

I'd blagged through Father's Day a couple of months earlier, saying I'd get tickets for something or other, maybe some cricket. We'd have a day out, I promised. I must confess, come early September I'd missed most of the cricket season and I really didn't have the Déise's second final in over fifty years in mind when I'd said that. Almost immediately, that delight turned to stark realisation, a blast of tension. Neither our ticket saint, nor anybody he knew, would be going to Dublin. So we were on the south coast of

Ireland, and the tickets were apparently stuck, in Belfast, about five hours' drive away. I would have driven to the end of the world and back for those tickets, but Paul conjured a solution. I trusted him. I'd merely have to find the only man in the whole of Ireland with two spare tickets on Sunday morning in the capital.

So yeah, how I needed that pint.

I knew that I'd have to find a way to repay Paul some day. I knew him well enough to know that he understood and felt sport the way I did. That he knew how much the phone calls he made to sort tickets meant to me, and to Dad.

***

5/10 (995)

Come Sunday morning, we hugged our farewells to Maurice, Margo, Ismay, Georgina and family and took to the road. Thousands of other Waterford fans were doing the same, the flags hung from every house, every conceivable point and every car, limp in the relentless, gentle, Munster rain.

It was the last Patrick would ever see of the Comeragh mountains, no more would he sweep through the Vee admiring the dramatic vistas of Clonea strand or Dungarvan bay. Over the sumptuous Greenway, his ancestors had toiled to build and work as a railway line. Maybe the mists that morn foretold us; hiding and wrapping the simple natural beauty, the Mahon falls, a forlorn tree now bereft at Lismore Castle.

I met a tall goalkeeper from the distant north in the doorway of a Travelodge in the Dublin drizzle. He handed me an envelope containing the golden tickets, and wouldn't take a bean for his troubles. At risk of offending him, I then offered humble thanks once more, and cartwheeled through a slowly waking Temple Bar.

As ever, we walked and walked: O'Connell Street, Parnell Square, Mountjoy Square, over the canal to Drumcondra. There we met cousin Paurick and Jack, and smiled and chatted and stood, and walked some more, and smiled again and drank in the occasion. We'd been to Croke Park many times, but there was a rarefied tension today; neither Waterford nor Galway had won the ultimate prize in many, many years, and the desperation felt almost frantic. It's what hurling does to you. Hundreds of fans begged for tickets on cardboard signs, no one was selling. Resigned, beaten faces. 83,000 golden tickets and nobody could contemplate selling, not now. I have never been to another major sporting event where there is neither sight nor sound of a tout; we had hit lucky alright.

Waterford lost, of course, but it wasn't about that. I thought back to Joe from Cork who I'd most improbably watched that semi-final with in a bar on the twinkling shores of Lake Como. I thought back to all those times listening to Mícheál Ó Muircheartaigh so vividly describing a game I barely understood. I didn't need to. I thought of the first time we flew out and back to a semi-final on a day trip. I thought of having the only English accent in Pairc ui Chaoimh, and a conflicting sense of absolute belonging, yet feeling so completely an outsider.

We didn't need to say much, there wasn't time for talking. It was a rare, raw, poignant privilege to share with Dad. Retracing the steps his mother made to the high temple of Irish sport for that last triumph in 1959, perhaps accepting that we might not get too many more shots at fulfilling this passion, this odyssey together.

As I said at his funeral, he was there in Genoa for David O'Leary's winning penalty for Ireland in Italia '90, he was there in Cardiff for Munster winning the European Cup. He was here, there and everywhere supporting Swindon, passing on his passion, whether we'd asked for it or not. He was there at Cheltenham, welcoming spring every year. And here he was, at last, in Croke Park, watching Waterford on All-Ireland Senior Hurling final day.

He was there.

So I knew I'd have to try to thank Paul some day.

***

6/10 (996)

It's late February 2020, the week after Dad's funeral, and I read on social media that Paul is embarking on a charitable challenge. I remind myself that I owe him one. I've started running myself in the last couple of years and am intrigued by his aim: to run 5k for fifty consecutive days leading up to his fiftieth birthday, to raise £5k for the We Love Football Academy in Cape Town, South Africa.

Why didn't I think of something like that? Some days I read his blog, and marvel that he finds something different, something natural and motivating to write each day. Sometimes, I push the boat out and give him a like, or kudos or a thumbs up. I resolved to join him for one of his runs and to stick a few quid in his pot. It was high time we caught up.

I read a bit about his chosen charity, and something strikes a chord. Then, Covid hits, and there are no more chords to strike. Fifty flippin' days and I never did get to join one of those runs, and rued that maybe circumstance meant he didn't get the support or recognition he deserved. Paul modestly, successfully completed his fifty-day challenge in April, glowing, no doubt fitter … and still a little short of his charity target.

Today, please read some of Paul's words:

Done. Finished. Completed.

Running 5km a day for fifty days to raise £5k and to finish on my fiftieth birthday.

I just wanted to do something to celebrate my half-century, to try and make a difference in other people's lives and to, perhaps, learn a little about myself.

I'm not sure what I entirely thought this challenge would be like. I did know that there would be days when I would think — 'there is nothing worse that I could think of doing than go for a run when it's cold, wet, rainy and I've had a crap day at work'. And, of course, those days came.

But here's the lesson I learnt. I learnt that when you really don't want to do something, just do it. Push yourself. Take yourself outside of your comfort zone. Those days were the most satisfying. It was those days where I came in after my run feeling energised and feeling so satisfied that I'd bothered to make the effort.

And I think this is a lesson that I will take into life (even though it's taken me fifty years to learn it!). Push the boundaries and just do it.

I've read about headspace and people finding time to think and de-stress, and how running can be a fantastic outlet for this. I've read about it, but never really got it. I've heard people talk about it, but never really listened!

But now I get it. I had times when I'd had such a rubbish day, or couldn't get my head around an issue or a problem and running was a huge help.

On a deeper level, this challenge was about improving people's lives. Helping those families in the We Love Football Academy in Cape Town, and trying to help fund improvements for them.

We set off at pace and raised funds quickly in the early days, but then things changed.

And so that takes us to the end. Fifty days have passed. Fifty days of running every single day. I have loved it.

I remembered that I wanted to help him and had an idea.

It's four days until Patrick's sixteenth birthday and I need you to hold my hand through this.

***

7/10 (997)

Patrick loved his football shirts didn't he? As a toddler he recognised Ronaldinho in Brazil's yellow and Christian Roberts in Swindon's red. I don't know which is more improbable. While like so many he always wanted the newest kit, he was equally happy in Euan's oversized hand-me-downs, or maybe a holiday knock off, or a more obscure shirt. He didn't really need, or care for other clothes. I remember being exasperated at the mess in his bedroom — and finding nearly fifty football shirts of various shapes and sizes, fabric and fashion, clubs and countries. And the smell.

I was proud when he actively supported Niamh's 'Shirts for Lesotho' campaign. Not only did he (not entirely willingly) part with kit from his own collection, he encouraged Tower Hill teammates and schoolmates to do likewise. Before we knew it, we had almost too many to send out and had raised some money for charity too. When the pictures eventually came back from Niamh in southern Africa, it really was one of those take the breath away, never forget moments. I sat, staring at my phone at work, tears in my eyes, in a Coventry office. A gorgeous example of the power, the universality, the global community of football — and a wonderful reminder that a smile is a smile is a smile, whatever the country or culture.

Looking back at those pictures now is so evocative and still makes me feel emotional — I can see Finley wearing Arsenal, Casey in Real Madrid, Connor the green of Ireland, Patrick wearing Swindon. I can smell the early autumn cut grass at West Witney and see more smiles and hear excitable chatter. What I'd give to be in those moments again. Meanwhile in Africa, alongside those shirts there's a new team parading their uhlsport Tower Hill kits, not only supplied by Paul but painstakingly, agonisingly, bespoked with head office in Germany. And there they are, half a world away.

Here we are, ourselves now a world away.

And if I get a wish today, it is that those grateful faces in Lesotho are lucky enough to get even half the meaning, fun and friendship, life from football that we have. Patrick would want that.

So thank you again, Paul, for reminding me through your project in South Africa of our own modest efforts, and that moment in time. The We Love Football Academy in Cape Town is a shining example of pushing personal boundaries, it's a 'now' moment.

It's fascinated me these last few months, reconnecting with people through circumstance, how little we know and make of all the connections that bind us and our community and circles of friendship together. And what we could achieve if maybe we all pushed our boundaries a bit further, and talked to each other a bit more. I look at the incredible cushions that Kate has made out of Patrick's football shirts, and my mind wanders.

I wonder at the connections between Hibernian and Freeland, Swindon and Barcelona, Henry Box and Valencia. Or right now, Lesotho or Cape Town and Witney.

And there's a little of us in those answers, and a lot of us in our possibilities.

***

8/10 (998)

Three more to go, and to be honest, I'm uncomfortable writing all this. It's getting tougher. I started off with a simple idea: I didn't expect it to turn into such a soul-searching, emotional wringer. So yes, I feel awkward writing about myself, it feels indulgent and earnest writing 'I this' and 'I that'. And today, I'm meandering off plot and, more me this and me that. Which is where, literally, so many of you come in.

It's getting on for three years since those heady days, leaving Whelan's bar and Stradbally and the man singing with a bucket on his head. It really was a mini Sommermärchen, that unforgettable, unsurpassable unity in Waterford and a damp, wonderful day of destiny in Dublin. Clearly much has changed. Blimey, so much so these last few months. But what I'd never have guessed, downing post-match pints in O'Donoghue's, another Waterford melodrama at an end was how quickly the winds of change would blow.

Just over a week later, I was made redundant, went home, and went straight out to meet and be inspired by Dan and Tamsyn Wymer for the first time. Wearing my Tower Hill FC hat, I was curious but sceptical about whether a parkrun at West Witney could ever be more than a pipe dream. Within an hour of their passion, not only was I determined that it must happen, but that I would be doing it too ... and if I was doing it, I'd be doing it the best I could. Fast forward towards spring and I'd enjoyed my first parkrun, settled into a long-term working contract in Birmingham and joined the Witney Music Festival team.

One simple sentence with extraordinary life within it. Tomorrow, hey look forward to this one, you'll get some stats, interesting analysis to brighten your day. Today, it's about you. Of course, I treasure all you family and long-standing friends, forty-plus years for some of you, and I hope for forty more.

Today particularly, it's an enormous virtual hug to all the new people, new friends I've met along the road. Whether through early running mornings or late music nights — and occasionally a blurring of the two — or from someplace else, most sincerely, thank you. It's just a simple thank you for the endless variety of energy, fun, inspiration, motivation, friendship and smiles you've brought. Here's to be able to celebrate all those joys together again, sometime soon.

Reflecting, contemplating; it strikes me not how much I've lost, but how much I've gained.

I should get back to the story, and remind you of Paul's charity in Cape Town, but I'll save those for tomorrow. Are you ready for 999?

***

9/10 (999)

Sorry, was distracted there yesterday. Promised you some numbers. I meant to say that after that late night Stradbally pub blip, I soon jumped back on my ten thousand steps a day bike, so to speak. So much so that all this time later, I'm still on it. I've had plenty of wobbles, but have never fallen off.

I've done ten thousand steps every bloody day since.

Does that mean anything? No, and yes.

No: it's just a number, so what, who cares, etc, etc. On what planet would anyone be living to actually bother, not let it go? Life is for living, not counting, not knowing the price of everything and the value of nothing.

Yes: the end justifies the means. Every day I have to plan my exercise and consequently, I'm lighter, fitter, quicker, generally happier. Some days it's easy, some, a dismal begrudged struggle. I'll do it, whatever. Illnesses, injury, indifference have come and gone. Three winters. There's a hint of OCD and a fair dashing of madness. It's become part of me.

It's offered me new perspectives. Working in Birmingham was a challenge: fancy a 4-5 mile walk or run on a cold winter's night after a long working day? No, me neither. So I built a walk into lunchtime whenever I could. Walking along the A45, come rain or shine, ridicule and bemusement. Learning to first notice, then see the trees changing through the seasons, blocking out the relentless city dual carriageway. Or discovering squirrels scurrying alongside a stream in a nearby park, while marvelling at the plants and flowers thriving at the end of the runway as planes thundered in.

Speaking of which, I'm distracted again. Have you spent your life gazing into the blue sky, wondering where those jets a million miles up have come from, where they're headed? Or of the stories they contain, the ambition, new beginnings, perhaps fear, anticipation, sad endings, hope, within? And however quickly our lives unfold, however, we gaze and wonder, technology does it quicker, cleaner. This morning, I watched the plane and its vapour trail in the vast expanse of blue sky, for probably twenty minutes as it caught, then kept my attention. An app on my phone focuses my gazing, and tells me it's a Boeing 747 travelling from Chicago. In less than an hour it'll land, with its beginnings and endings, in Frankfurt.

East it flies, over Abingdon, Marlow, Heathrow, central London and remarkably it's over Kent before I lose sight of the picture it's painting in the sky. I'm reminded then, less of the dreams on board, and more of the connections I wrote of yesterday. The silhouetted skyline of Chicago that came up in Hannah's fantastic quiz for Patrick's Place in aid of SUDC the other night. I remember my one school exchange visit to Frankfurt airport, to the soundtrack of Nena's one-hit wonder, '99 Red Balloons'. More pertinently, Niamh's changeover there as that precious cargo of football shirts was headed for Johannesburg (another Hannah quiz skyline!) and on to Lesotho.

It's a huge, tiny world. Connections, connections ...

As the walks turned into runs, and the runs turned into parkrun, into Dan's Tuesday Group — slippery slopes these — to

Witney Roadrunners, I realised that running could be social too. It is as possible to chatter, to ease into a run as it is to stretch, to push personal boundaries, to achieve. There's still so much for me to learn and to enjoy, but this I do know … it helps get the steps up sharpish.

Why the obsessive focus on ten thousand steps? Every day? Why does that matter? I don't know. Maybe I'm fearful of what will happen if I fall short or stop, like the ravens leaving the Tower. I'm met with equal ridicule and support from those closest, and that feels about right. But on and on I've gone, walking on through the wind and the rain, through many a storm, dreams indeed tossed and blown.

It doesn't feel like an actual achievement, like Paul's 5 for 50 for 5. This just is, it's just who I've become. His was planned; a considered, intense, short-term burst of effort. Mine, a long-term meandering accidental adventure. Which just so happens to have changed my priorities, every single day.

Walking on, hope in my heart, always. As he completed his 50 runs in April, something else nagged at me, my fingers and thumbs couldn't quite do the adding up, so I had to check, and I did.

I'd like to talk to him about it.

***

10/10 (1000)

Today it's Patrick's birthday and there simply aren't the words to describe how sad I am that he's not here for it. I set out ten days ago to help raise awareness of, and fingers crossed, a few quid for the We Love Football Academy in Cape Town for Paul, knowing that he was so kind to me when I needed it. Clearly it's become something more deeply personal, possibly cathartic, hopefully part of our ongoing healing process.

There aren't the words either to describe how much your support throughout means to me, and the family. I will keep the kindness and love safe in my heart, til they're needed on a rainy day.

To end where this ten-day journey started, I'm driving up a single track road again, a little anxious and feeling emotional. However, I sense a tingle of excitement, not knowing what I'm going to find beyond this impossibly glorious countryside.

I can see for miles.

This time, there's no horse, no magic farmer fresh from the calves, no mountain, no Waterford flags adorning every proud property. Instead, eventually, there's an implausibly pretty village, there's a Union Jack, presumably hung for the recent VE celebrations — although this place has changed so little, it could pass as an original from 1945. There's a haphazard straggle of entirely perfect, honeysuckle Cotswold cottages. There's a village pub, closed of course, and sat waiting on a bench, there's Paul.

It's an astonishing country idyll, the sun is shining, entire counties have less beauty than what surrounds us. Quite clearly, as Mum has said, it's a good year for the roses. We run together, we swap stories and barely even notice another stunning village as we chatter through it. Some of the things we either talk about, or perhaps should have, include:

The hurling tickets, Dad and Dublin

We Love Football Academy in Cape Town

Sending football shirts to Lesotho

Friendship

My ten thousand steps obsession

Patrick's last evening

The deep-rooted role of sport in community

Running, cycling and the challenges and the hopes that drive us

Work blah, blah, blah

These gorgeous hidden Cotswold villages

How difficult and unpredictable fundraising can be

Getting injuries

That some things never change, and some things do

The 5k run flies by in a way that's not always the case, and then we wander around the village; more sumptuous stone, more roses. It's a calm, special time and we ponder the binds that tie people together, through friendship, through connections, across years.

Before we say farewell, Paul asks what the numbers at the top of my posts mean.

With a slightly awkwardly inappropriate grin, I say that I love it when a plan comes together.

Because today it is Patrick's birthday and also the milestone day I will hit one thousand consecutive days of doing ten thousand steps. Because it's exactly a thousand days since leaving the Irish pub, embracing the calm and catching the sea breeze, a touch giddy with Guinness when I cursed myself at seeing my 9,117 mishap.

***

Kate, Niamh, Euan, Mum and I walked up White Horse Hill together, as we had on the saddest, sunniest day after Patrick's crematorium service in February. While we cannot see what's ahead of us, we can see for miles and miles. We try to argue about which woods are in which direction on the horizon, but our hearts aren't in it.

Alone I walk to the sports field at West Witney, and crumple and cry and remember: some of my earliest memories are here, and some of my happiest. This evening though, it feels impossible to drag myself up off the ground I know every blade and bump of. Eventually I wander, picking up white feathers, leaving a Sunshine On Leith sticker on the lock-up. I turn away from the wide open spaces and familiar tree avenues, and head for home, to complete my milestone of ten thousand steps on each of those thousand days.

***

It's 14,745,370 steps on from that Guinness, and now I understand that some steps mean more than others. In a minute I'll type a full stop and then, then I'll take some more, gentle, steps, hope in my heart. I remember we sang 'You'll Never Walk Alone' at Patrick's memorial and 'The Parting Glass' at Dad's funeral and recall the We Love Football Academy quoting Nelson Mandela:

May your choices reflect your hopes, not your fears.

As I see another plane piercing the blue sky, I remember Frankfurt, and it's 1983 again. Sorry Nelson, but I need a deep, insightful and resonant ending here. With half a smile, I settle on Nena's denouement in '99 Red Balloons'.

I think of you and let it go.

***

The night before Patrick's sixteenth birthday, there was a super flower moon. It was wondrous, an extraordinary sight to behold. I stared and stared in wonder, wondering of all the life and love that is doing the same as me right now, right across the planet, of all the humanity that has gazed and wondered at this moon before, and the future generations who will wonder at this moon again and again and again.

I quietly sing 'What Shall We Do With The Drunken Sailor' to myself, just as I sang it to Patrick the first night we welcomed him to the world and I cradled him to sleep in my arms, just as we sang it at his memorial service a few months ago.

The moon may be wondrous and extraordinary and everlasting, but life can be very, very cruel.

June

Patrick's room remains a place of sometime solace and occasional despair. A bed, a desk, a wardrobe, a map of the football world. Teenage kicks.

It carries an air of permanence, of him, his presence, of time stopped still. His clothes and scattered belongings are still being sorted: gently, sensitively and absolutely painfully. Barely used weights, a green Adidas jacket hanging on the back of the door. It also feels that this cannot be permanent: how do we deal with the bedroom of our child who has died? What will become of this room, this space? What can become of this space? The door is always open, it always will be open. One day maybe he'll spring through it, or jump out from behind the door, having played the biggest, cruellest trick of all time.

What I'd give for that impossible cruelty to become the tiniest possibility.

There's a stack of *Beano* annuals. A Christmas present every year yet untouched and unread.

My eyes ache from emotion, this unrelenting pain. The ever-present grief. The weight of a hundred pipers marching in my head. The sense of loss is so visceral that for a nanosecond I think it feels a privilege to endure this depth of being. It is as close to an out-of-body experience as I can imagine. In what form does whatever is left of me exist, I ponder.

On Patrick's desk, the PlayStation slowly enters into rest mode, the blue light, faint now, fading before me. Eventually red, eventually yellow and then nothing.

Nothing.

And tomorrow we're going to meet the doctor, the serious lady who told us that Patrick had died.

***

We don't quite believe it until they're here, but our hospital support worker and the doctor who told us Patrick has died have indeed come to visit us from St Mary's Hospital in Paddington. In the real world, we greet them warmly by name, but we suspect that officially they shouldn't be here. That they've chosen to come and explain the post-mortem report in person, to support us out of their own generous conscience, possibly in their own time, because of the dreadful mess and upset caused.

Most notably because we received Patrick's post-mortem on his 16th birthday.

Nobody mentions it, so we suspect that's probably the case. Our appreciation for them coming to see us knows no bounds.

Kate and I steer them towards our slightly rickety wooden table, covered today with a crisp, patterned tablecloth. We sit around it, making small talk and discovering their connections to Witney and Oxford. The world can be small and charming sometimes. It's late morning now, a perfect blue summer's sky with the sun up past the yardarm, so at least one of us has to make a start on the homemade cookies. Coffee is served and further pleasantries exchanged, a robin lands nearby suggesting vague interest, and the dog wanders hesitantly out to investigate. Not sure whether she's more perturbed by the heat or the visitors, she settles in the shade, observing at a safe distance.

Eventually, we have to do this, the doctor produces the post-mortem report and we have to understand it.

With the sun shining brightly and the birds singing, we review Patrick's post-mortem line by line, word by word. It's painstaking and painful. It's difficult not knowing what Sudden Arrhythmogenic Death Syndrome actually means, and even more difficult knowing that understanding it wouldn't make a jot of difference anyway.

We're looking for a needle in a haystack, but we know it isn't there.

As if Kate's going to spot something hidden in the data, written in the words, ask a magical question and the medical professionals who live and breathe this stuff say:

You know what, you might be onto something

The brutal reality is that there's no reason Patrick died.

He just did.

And if there was a reason? Then what? What does that change?

For us though, and this is important, it's about genetics, that's why we need to know. What if I'm a ticking bomb? Or Kate? What if one of us carries a gene — still undetected — that killed Patrick?

And if that gene is here, now, in the garden, waiting for its next chance, lurking deep inside one of us.

Or Niamh?

Or Euan?

Or love of life willing, some future progeny?

That's why we need to know.

But in the here and now, sat in the gorgeous summer sunshine, the fresh green leaves contrasting with the vivid blue of the sky, wondering how well those trees will bear fruit this season, here, now, the brutal reality is that we don't know, can't know, and there's no reason Patrick died. He just did.

***

Forty-odd years ago, Dad came home from work one evening, excited by a package he'd recovered from the skip at a house he was renovating in Abingdon. And impressive it was too: a haul of letters sent by a soldier stationed in the World War One trenches. Some personal mementos. Newspaper cuttings. It was extraordinary;

history in our hands, almost the smell of the front line. Then the grim inevitable too. The letter on New Years Day 1916 from the regiment Chaplain, informing the family that everyone thought so highly of George, and had laid him to rest that morning.

I did a sweet school project on it and then forgot all about it.

Last week, sorting through stuff, Mum found that precious bundle, still in incredible condition. Dad had kept it safe and cared for in his bedside cabinet all that time, waiting for a time that never came for him. It was remarkable, my senses tingled. We read some of the letters, held the Tommy's tag and wondered at a time that was absolutely horrific and world changing.

So we wondered too, if the marvels of the modern internet could help us now.

Quirks of fate and all that, but we had some prior family experience of the role of the internet in understanding family history during World War One.

***

It was 2014, and we'd known for a few years we'd be doing this. We'd spent a summer holiday on the Normandy coast, enjoying the steam running through the garden of the gite, walking the pebbly beaches, eating baguettes, feeding horses. We paid due respects at the beaches of the World War Two landings and ventured inland to the Somme and World War One. We'd planned this meticulously as we were on a mission to find the grave of Kate's great uncle. And in 2012, we did find private Tom Foulds, buried in a quiet, dignified, entirely French village; the blood and stench and senselessness of ninety-something years ago utterly unimaginable. I felt a sense of guilt that I'd not even bothered to look my own family up. I'd managed to ensure we had WiFi to watch Swindon's first round League Cup match, but I hadn't thought about the sacrifice the English half of my family had made in the Great War. Within thirty seconds of getting home, cranking the PC into life, I'd located one of my Gran's brothers, Reginald Greenfield. He was buried just outside Thiepval, barely a couple of miles from Tom Foulds in Mesnil-Martinsart. The guilt morphed into a degree of shame and then resolve.

So I knew we'd be back.

I didn't know this though.

As we arrived at the car park at the vast monument at Thiepval, a guy poked his head in the car window. He was from French TV and inquired gently if we were casual visitors or had a particular purpose, maybe a relative to search for. Did he not know us? Of course, we had a purpose!

Ahhh bien, he was interested in filming us, joining our story. It was October 2014, and we were just a couple of weeks from the centenary of the most horrible war starting. I glanced in the back of the car for affirmation, and was met by three steely, reluctant stares. Stares that said with solidarity and certainty, no way Dad, we didn't need additional intrusion. Just let us be.

Of course, I said.

Parlez-vous Francais?

Un peut.

And so began an extraordinary couple of hours. Or rather, it began just before the monument as we passed through Albert, the central town for Somme battlefield visitors. We passed a florist, perfectly situated for visitors such as us, to pay respects, to remember, and to simply dignify the sacrifice of our forebears. I drove by, as I was now on a mission, our mere presence would be memorial enough. We didn't need flowers.

Our amiable host, whose *peut* English was marginally better than my long withered *Francais*, nudged and encouraged us this way and that, with the TV crew maintaining a largely discrete distance. We lingered at the memorial, a grand solemn stone arch at the top of the hill that will stand forever, visible from miles around, carved with the names of thousands of the dead. The dead without even the respect of a grave. The lives that ended, suddenly or tortuously, maimed, dismembered, stinking and dead. I could stand here each day for the rest of days, stinging with the bitterness and inhumanity of their dreadful waste. Back inside the museum building we were filmed pretending to research on the public PCs, in a pathos-rich *Who Do You Think You Are* moment.

I didn't stop for those flowers though, did I, how's that going to play out on prime-time French telly?

With or without the accompaniment of cameras being thrust in our faces, this was a preciously emotional experience. As we parked the car, and started to walk through the mist up the hill towards the small, symmetrical cemetery at Mill Road, there was a peace, a crunch of gravel underfoot. It was us, reflecting, absorbing the contrast of the violent futility of a hundred years ago with the quiet stillness of a cool October morning.

Or so I thought.

We were called back by the TV crew to do this walk again, a little slower *s'il vous plait*, a touch more thoughtfully please. The boys were giggling now, they'd remembered Joey Barton's interview in a French accent, and worse still, Steve McClaren speaking double dutch. They were imploring me to not go there, whilst simultaneously daring me to.

Go On Dad, do it

Just be yourself Dad, don't make yourself any more of an idiot.

If there was any sense of emotional punch-packing, prime-TV-award-winning theatre, it was gone now. At the point of finding the grave of my great great uncle, who'd died, ridiculously young, in the name of his country and for the sake of temporarily capturing a few yards of mud and a nice hill, I was worrying about sounding like Joey Barton or having a giggling turn. We found Reg, I had three seconds to pause, gather myself before I was asked how I felt.

I should have brought some flowers

That's what I felt then, and what I feel now. Maybe, one day. I deflected the next question in my worst franglais to Euan, and melted away. I was rightfully and mercilessly ridiculed for my clumsily accented answer.

A few days later, our two hours were distilled into a ninety-second clip on TF1. I wondered if there'd be a Christmas special instead.

They didn't get back to me.

Tom was thirty, Reginald nineteen. They died a month apart, leaving mums, dads, brothers, sisters, friends, and their communities bereft. I think about my lovingly remembered gran, Ethel, and how on earth she was told that her precious brother had been killed in the Somme. How on earth did she, her siblings and her parents cope?

***

While I drifted off remembering our short-lived 2014 fame, Niamh was in the 2020 real world of an internet search engine, and she had a mission.

Minutes. If that. An identity tag, a name, and in moments George isn't a number, but a full life. A young lad, of course, but now he's a son, a brother, a chorister, a solicitor's clerk, a picture, an Oxford boy. It was mind-blowing to discover, so quickly too, that George, one of 886,000 British military personnel to have died in the First World War, was one of just a few to have been so preciously remembered. His story, lovingly researched, preserved forever on a local history website.

Ahhh, how much we wanted to be able to return this golden discovery to his family.

Just another couple minutes later Niamh said — do you recognise this name from your twenty-plus years working at Unipart? I said:

Yeah, of course I do, Geoff's worked there even longer than that, and now you're telling me he did the research about George?

Could that be too simplistic to be true? Sure, it's more than plausible that someone else has the same name, that this journey will take a different course. But Google only offers the one hint and it's a guy I've known since 1997.

And it felt right.

Literally fifteen minutes later — maybe a full, glorious, grinning half an hour since the research actually started — I was walking across the meadow on a breezy summer's eve and with a spring in my step and a smile in my heart at the magic of the story, when my phone pinged.

Yes! The identity was swiftly confirmed. It didn't just feel right, now, it was right … George's great nephew, a friendly, long-standing work acquaintance was right there, on my phone and wondering what on earth I was so excited about … *long time no speak and all that hey Geoff*.

(Euan said my eyes sparkled, *it had been a while, Dad*, he said).

***

Just a few days later, I sat in the garden with Geoff, chattering vaguely about work while we both stared at the box I was about to hand over. We talked of family history, of research, of the chorister, the clerk, the son, and our own trips of discovery to the Somme; that my own great uncle was buried just a few miles from George. That his own father had even written of the bundle in his diaries, and that they were presumed long disappeared. Lost in a skip perhaps.

It's no exaggeration to say that handing that box of treasure over to Geoff was one of the most joyful acts imaginable. We'd both lost our fathers recently, and my, how much they'd have wished to be right here, living this miracle. Still, the sun came out, how proud they'd have been, how utterly perfect this moment was.

The discovery was for his family now, and finishing his coffee and needing to dwell no more, Geoff took George with him, back home.

***

There had been weeks of speculation as to how the 2019/20 football season should be concluded. Abandon it — frozen in time? Wait, wait, wait until this Covid thing blows over and carry on

— readjusting the next season if necessary? Or, as slowly became apparent, apply a points per game formula, draw a deep line and get ready to go again. All were flawed, all were pored over, all who ventured an opinion did so primarily out of self-interest. On 9th June, Swindon Town's points per game promotion as champions was confirmed. This was different from those other league-winning seasons. The record breakers of 1986 culminated in a crazy night against Chester and a wild day in Mansfield. Or 1996's class, with a promotional party in the Tower Ballroom at Blackpool. And fast forward to Di Canio's expensively-assembled ensemble in 2013, a champagne performance to seal it against Port Vale, and a somewhat unique Party On The Pitch to celebrate together. Patrick bought the fetching, brand new Tipperary/Boca Juniors blue and yellow away shirt. Paolo sang 'Dancing In The Moonlight' with the actual Toploader. Come on 2020, how to trump those?

Well, this time we had a special asterisk to remind us for posterity that we won it on the cheap.

League Two Champions 2019/20 — Swindon Town*

It was an emotional day, and I appreciated supportive messages from friends far and wide. It felt some kind of vindication for the torrid season it'd been — from that initial togetherness and collective will of the fans, to the feeling it would be Dad's last season, to Patrick. For them, as the *Swindon Advertiser* had emblazoned it, we were:

CHAMPIONS FOR ETERNITY

That sense of destiny felt in the Autumn had come to pass, just not in the way anyone could have predicted, or wished for. It was a valedictory moment for a world that had now changed.

I'd lost my Dad and a son, but hey, we'd gained an entirely unexpected asterisk.

Even by then though, serious, serious questions were being asked about the ownership and direction of the club. The owner, Lee Power, has made gradually fewer but increasingly inconsistent public comments. Was the club for sale or not? Who were the mysterious third parties being alluded to? Court cases suggested extraordinarily complex shenanigans and manoeuvrings. A message I received from a diligent investigator in Waterford, whose football club Power also owned, was as enlightening as it was scurrilous and terrifying.

For all the rampant speculation and worry, one thing became clear: Lee Power, who had for five years divided opinion, but for many was better the devil we knew, and thus been given the benefit of many supporters' doubts, had now dug himself a very large hole.

It rather seemed that an asterisk over the promotion was the least of Swindon Town's concerns.

July

Jack Charlton has died. In this year, of all years, I can't be too sad that an old man, cruelly suffering with dementia has found his peace. And maybe I'm not sad. But I'm nostalgic, proud, sentimental and fiercely emotional. It's thirty years since Genoa, Italia '90, 'Nessun Dorma'. The arc of Jack's life is clear enough: the Geordie living his playing career in the shadow of his sublimely gifted younger brother Bobby, winning the World Cup together, then managing a succession of clubs before taking Ireland on an incredible decade-long joyride. In many ways his steadfast, traditional, stubborn, forthright ways made him an easy caricature. The reality is more complex. Jack was enigmatic, a gifted moment seizer and the stories he spun etched into our being, deeply personal and transformational. And so it was for Dad and I.

Given the individual talents of Liam Brady, Johnny Giles, Mark Lawrenson, David O'Leary, Frank Stapleton and others, as a child I was entitled to say:

Dad, why are Ireland always rubbish?

He'd pin another green and white rosette on me and say:

Liam, our day will come.

Boy, how it did. One autumn evening, Gary Mackay scored for Scotland in Bulgaria, sending Jack's Ireland to the 1988 European Championships, and with one shot, realising millions of dreams.

We didn't go to Germany for the tournament, we didn't see Ray Houghton stick the ball in the English net but we could celebrate Joxer going to Stuttgart in song, we could celebrate the release of the barren years. Jack Charlton, an English honorary Irishman, with a pragmatic, unifying, liberal use of the playing diaspora at his disposal, made it ok to be Irish with an English accent. Sure he didn't mean it, bless, he'd rather have been fishing, but the success of his teams gave the dreamers, the sociologists and thinkers, the writers the material. The pied piper of Ashington was single handedly creating the Celtic Tiger before our eyes, was he not?

Not content with that, he was fuelling mine and Dad's relationship, moulding my identity, laying out our adventures before us. These were ancient times. There was not wall-to-wall football on telly, Sky Sports barely existed. It was nigh-on impossible to watch an Irish football match in England. The entry for Setanta Sports is still in Mum and Dad's prehistoric contacts organiser. We'd have to phone Marie in London on the day of the game, and she'd tell us the nearest pub or bar that might be showing it. Although she couldn't promise. Ah no, I can't be sure.

Devoid of options, throughout that incredible glorious period, we'd be on the march with Jackie's Army, searching for a game we might or might not see on the telly. We'd drive to the Tap and Barrel in Swindon, or to Gloucester or Cheltenham or Oxford. Once we spent forty-five minutes finding a pub in the middle of rural south Oxfordshire, who, it transpired, had no intention or interest in showing the match. Two other gutted lads had made a similar journey in hope, in their green shirts, their rosettes, with their dreams.

More often though we'd travel all the way to London, to the GAA club at Ruislip or a vast old cinema in Ealing. The atmosphere electric, the release of now, now at last, of being Irish and in the right place at the right time. Expecting to win away in Spanish citadels.

Jack gave us that.

Jack gave us the World Cup adventure of Italia '90.

I finished my finals in Swansea, skipped along the Mumbles Road and down the Kingsway, and cartwheeled all the way to Heathrow. Dad and I took off on our most special journey.

Landing in Milan was more than landing in another world, it was landing in the world, our world. We stood, open-mouthed, silent, in the grand station watching fans of every nation greet, cheer, rush here, pause there. It was a mesmerising celebration of people and peoples, the astonishing and unifying power of football.

And we were here.

Eventually, we took the late train to Genoa, not arriving until the early hours, no plan, no hotel, no tickets. Tomorrow though, Ireland were playing Romania, for a place in the quarter final of the World Cup. We were in the right city. And so, it became clear very swiftly, were thousands of other Irish supporters. It became equally clear, almost as swiftly, that they had no beds and no tickets either. We were going to need those sleeping bags.

We hung out in a small hotel, or possibly someone's front room, as long as we could and at 5am retired to the concrete comfort of the station floor for some sleep. Hundreds of others were merrily doing the same.

The next day, the greatest day, began a couple of hours later when I took a wake up kick in the back from a gentleman officer of the *carabinieri*. Within an hour, we'd bought a coffee, croissants and, and, and not ridiculously overpriced match tickets off a Belgian guy on the station concourse.

Blurry, aimless, tired, we left the station to explore. Even in the early morning, the heat was rising as the city stretched gently into life, pockets of football fans searching out cafés and coffee shops. On and on we walked, entirely without purpose or direction. A busy dual carriageway, the industrial grey sights and shouts and smells of the working docks. This was not the world with representatives of every nation at Milan station, this was not the Genoa of the early hours with 'Fields of Athenry' ringing around the late-night bars. This was me and Dad, arriving at another noisy ring road junction, suddenly listless as tiredness, heat and dehydration hit and starting to wonder what on earth we were up to.

We were lost.

It was late morning now, and walking still, at last we found a small bar to regroup and refresh, and a welcome coffee. We'd left the docks behind and found signs that there might be a World Cup on. There was a World Cup on, and there were still Scotland fans — humiliated here by Costa Rica, perhaps the shame was too much to face going home, perhaps the craic was too mighty or perhaps, perhaps, this was the World Cup and perhaps this was as good as it got.

The next few hours in that bar were as good as it got. It's hard to relay sometimes the joy and celebration of fans mixing in major tournaments, the being alive rejoicing of the moment. Here, a far cry from television images of fuelled-up jingoistic nationalists hurling plastic chairs across majestic city squares. Here, here set the pattern for future travels and adventures with Dad, Ireland's presence or not, how we loved the big occasion. Today, those pockets of Scottish fans, hordes of Irish and a scattering of willing extras, beguiled and bewitched by Jack's Party. Together, we shared the moment. We sang each other's songs: the Irish singing 'The Sash', the Scots reciprocating with Irish rebels songs they wouldn't naturally be comfortable with. We took a young French student under our wing as the heat and the alcoholic haze intensified. Dizzy with the enchantment of it all, he staggered off the bus still miles from the ground. I smile in wonder at what became of him, and my daring removal of a *carabinieri* helmet as Dad tried to take a picture. I smiled at my first glimpse of those magnificently striking red corners of the Stadio Comunale Luigi Ferraris, one of the enduring images of Italia '90. Most of all, I smile when, still nearly an hour before kick-off, I look down from my upper tier seat with a vertigo bar, at the rectangle of green beneath me. I look down and as the players are walking the pitch, taking in the breathtaking

number of tricolours already in place all around the ground.
I smile as I look down and the first player I see is Alan McLoughlin.

It's 25th June, 1990, and Alan McLoughlin is my hero.

***

Macca had joined Swindon Town from Manchester United, his
pedigree clear but his lightweight, flighty, ball-playing nature
not immediately beneficial to an heroically direct Lou Macari
team. At Manchester City, in his hometown, we sat distant in the
away end at Maine Road, thrilled at McLoughlin's raw potential.
His eyes, body and two City players went one way in the centre
circle, his hips swivelled the other, shifting the ball with them,
opening up acres of green to his left, another counter attack.
How Dad rejoiced, recalling this single vision of footballing dash
and élan for years to come. After four years of remarkable success,
on one hand, Swindon were close to the hallowed land of mixing
with the big boys for the first time in the club's history. On the other,
the approach had grown stale, formulaic, and could be hideously
dull to watch. Swindon's success-saturated public had grown
restless and increasingly bored, crowds were poor, increasingly
apathetic. Swindon lost a play-off to Crystal Palace and soon after
we'd drifted desolately out of Selhurst Park, where we'd had an
unimaginably glorious play-off evening against Gillingham just a
couple of years earlier. Macari departed, few lamented. A couple
of weeks later, we were on holiday when I picked up an English
newspaper in Galway:

Dad, Dad, our new manager is Ossie Ardiles!

This promised to be different, and possibly fun.

It was all that and rather more. The first game I saw was a
pre-season friendly away at Hereford. We won 5-4, and that set
the tone. Instead of scanning the sky for the ball, wondering where
it would eventually land and who was chasing after it, the same
players, Lou's up-and-at-em runners, were now treating the ball
with affection, caring for it, gliding around the pitch in exotic

patterns, looking like they were enjoying it. At the fulcrum, at the tip of a new-fangled midfield diamond was Alan McLoughlin. The skinny, bit-part player of a couple of months ago now epitomised and led our transformation, weaving this way and that, dazzling us, confusing us. Yeah, we let four in, but hey, we scored five.

And that was the pattern of the most remarkable season. Set against the backdrop of financial scandal and looming punishment, the team, Ossie's team now, danced their way towards the playoffs once more. McLoughlin was the heartbeat of this astonishing reinvention. On New Year's Day, he scored twice at Watford in one of the most wonderful performances in a Swindon shirt and of a Swindon team I can recall. Dad, with Mum a willing passenger, drove us around the country watching our team, our team now. This joy was ours to behold. At Wolves, Dad had a standoff with one of West Midlands constabulary's finest, and they stood in Molineux's vast crumbling South Bank, deep within each other's personal space, too proud to take a step backwards. At West Ham, we crept up on friends in an East End wide-boy bar and Dad startled Rob with a broad West Country 'where did you park your tractor' in his ear. We parked our tractor near and far following Swindon that season, meeting my student housemate Bunny in the Gardeners Retreat at Stoke on a glorious fancy dress last League match. Dad tried to pay at the turnstiles with a £50 note. That didn't go well. At Blackburn, at the Fox & Hounds they were serving Lancashire hot pot and that did go well. We grinned at Darwen Road as coach after coach of Swindon fans crept past in the play-off traffic, spilling out of the skylights, noise and readiness filling the air. We were nearly there. Watford, West Brom, wherever — we'd be there.

Wembley awaited.

On 28th May, 1990, McLoughlin scored the play-off final winner at Wembley, as we obliterated Sunderland in surely the most one-sided 1-0 victory in a hundred years. At last, Swindon had reached the promised land: milk, honey and all. Except that wasn't quite the case. Ten days later, as I distractedly completed my finals at Swansea, Swindon were demoted two divisions (reduced to one later on appeal) for illegal payments to players. It was absolutely heartbreaking. The sage DJ John Peel opened his evening BBC Radio 1 show with a state of the nation address:

My heart goes out to my friend George and all the Swindon fans. This is a monstrous decision.

Jimmy Greaves wore a 'Swindon fans are innocent' t-shirt.

Dad said:

Let's go to the pub.

We went to The Plough, the quietest place we could find, and quietly reflected. We quietly fumed and planned and plotted and set the world to rights. And this is what we did for another thirty years. Issues and debates, family or global were taken to the pub to be considered, debated, argued and agreed. Calmly, lovingly, *quietly*. Together, it's how we did it.

In the meantime, Alan McLoughlin received a fortuitous and certainly controversial, very late, call-up to the Irish World Cup squad. Jack was taking our Macca, our hero, to Italy. He made a couple of substitute appearances, helping recover a draw against England, and today, there he was, in Genoa, in green rather than red, living his dream and ours, as he surveyed the pre-match scene around him. In sunglasses, short shorts and strolling casually, at home among Jack's heroes, the picture will stay with me forever.

Three and a half years later, we'd driven to the GAA club in Ruislip to watch Ireland's decisive World Cup qualifier with Northern Ireland in Belfast. The Republic needed a point to secure a place in USA '94, and the build up was relentlessly rancid and bitter, amid a background of sectarian killings. It was the most acrimonious football match. Jack, who'd remained steadfastly and consistently oblivious to the context of the troubles in the north, had one card left to play. The hosts were leading 1-0 through a goal by Jimmy Quinn, another of Macari's old Swindon trailblazers.

Jack's ace was Macca, now a Portsmouth hero, still appreciative of Quinn's welcome when he joined the Town. Alan McLoughlin, always the substitute, so often the bridesmaid for Ireland, crashed home an equaliser. Ruislip erupted, *que sera sera*.

We're going to U-S-A ...

Dad and I floated home along the M40.

***

Back to the greatest day in Genoa, one of the world's finest players, Gheorghe Hagi, the Maradona of the Carpathians, tip-toed this way and that for Romania, gliding with a grace and verve that Ireland's workhorses couldn't match. But the boys in green, roared on by thousand upon thousand, kept the opponents out, dragging a cagey, uneventful game goalless through half-time, full-time, extra-time. All the way to penalties. Boy I needed some water now, and wondered what had happened to the French lad. My ears were sore, my head ached, my throat was dry and Ireland were a penalty shoot out away from a World Cup quarter-final against hosts Italy, in Rome.

Packie Bonner made the crucial save, David O'Leary calmly dispatched the winning penalty. The words, the pictures, the memories have become national folklore. The noise, delirium, joy, songs, emotion, thrill of being there was life itself. Our hero though, as at Wembley just a month earlier, was Alan McLoughlin.

That he was an unused substitute didn't matter.

As we poured out of the stadium, wide-eyed fans roared: *We're going to see the Pope*, surely the unlikeliest of all football chants ever? Rome awaited the team and the journey. For us, to Milan and a simple bed.

It was, the greatest of days.

***

The next season started with the club re-energised by the injustice of the summer, intent on making good. McLoughlin began in sublime form. Still early in the season, Macca led the Middlesbrough team a merry dance as they hacked and pulled and tried to drag him down. Eventually they succeeded, kicking him off the park. The team fell apart, Boro soon equalised, an old teammate of mine from boys football, Robbie Mustoe, cruelly scored the winner. Dad was wistful. Robbie was genuinely one of our own, playing occasionally in Dad's team too, coming on tour with us to Holland, going on to have a fabulous professional career. Alan Mac was patched up and soon back, but it was never the same again. As a tremendous asset he was dressed up and sold, clearly reluctantly and ultimately pointlessly, to a Southampton who had no idea how to utilise the talent they'd bought.

The team fell apart.

The club fell apart.

With Ossie's dream over, he was replaced by Glenn Hoddle who prevented relegation and brought us fresh hope. Eventually, it was slowly and painstakingly renewed.

Alan McLoughlin went on to play over three hundred games for a rightfully appreciative Portsmouth, followed by spells at Wigan Athletic, Rochdale and Forest Green Rovers, but he was always ours.

Always ours, capped forty-two times, too many of them substitute appearances. He played in two World Cups despite playing most of his career at Championship level. He was always there for Jack, for us. He was one of Jack's. Jack knew.

Jack didn't create the Celtic Tiger, Jack didn't deliver the Good Friday Agreement, Jack didn't wave a magic wand and spirit up an exuberant, globally confident nation. But by heck he gave us a football team and played his part alright. We put 'em under pressure. We marched with Jackie's Army. We lived through and roared on the boys in green. There were dreams and songs to sing. He gave me, and Dad, and a million others, magic, and sometimes, that's more than enough.

***

It's 14th July, six months since the night Patrick collapsed and died.

We've kept it low-key, and are feeling low-key. Two friends — Christina and Marli — remembered and sent us messages. We know we can't expect or hope or wish that everyone marks everything, tiptoes around our sensitivities, always saying or doing the right thing, when we don't know what that means itself. I know that my biggest fear is that people forget Patrick. We cry and take time to remember him, to feel proud of him — how happy he was, how loving he was, how sparky, how tactile, how gorgeously argumentative he could be too. Euan reminds us that he was far from perfect. I'm grumpy to Mum and she texts about seeing Patrick in her dreams.

Sometimes he feels even closer than a dream, so close as if he's part of a conversation we're having — I find myself waiting for him to comment with a little laugh, a little sarcasm watching lockdown football on telly, *the usual quiet crowd at Arsenal* or, or …

But he doesn't, and he's not going to.

August

So many people have said since Patrick's memorial that they didn't know 'Sunshine On Leith', the centrepiece song of that starkly solemn, beautiful, miserable, and somehow uplifting February day. A couple of years ago, Euan, Patrick and I had crept over the border to Gretna Green before watching Swindon win so memorably at Carlisle. It was to be Patrick's only venture into Scotland despite the fondness he'd developed for it.

Today, we're staying in Edinburgh. Today, we're going to Leith. And seeing as not everyone knows this heart-wrenchingly magnificent, sweeping Proclaimers song, not everyone will know that Leith is the port on Edinburgh's shoreline on the Firth of Forth, and that Hibernian Football Club, one of Scotland's finest, are based at Easter Road, in Leith.

Kate, Niamh, Euan and I walk, taking the scenic route from Edinburgh city centre via the Water of Leith. We're already wet from the constant summer rain. At Dean Village we're met with roaring water, a perfect urban idyll of trees tumbling into the river, rocks breaking the flow, picturesque cottages competing for postcard-pretty potential. It's a breathtaking surprise hiding beneath the city streets. We walk on towards our purpose, the Forth. As we settle into our stride the waters become becalmed by Canonmills. The rain here is soft, and it doesn't deter the

Scottish national cricket squad training in the park alongside us. Their determined cheeriness contrasts with our cussed demeanour. Our purpose carries us on.

Quieter and quieter the walk becomes. The tourists don't come here. Still, when we might least expect it, there's a Gormley statue in the water. We're quiet, respecting each other's needs for reflection and space within the family. The sheer surprise of the stark, graceful Gormley in the river is an emotional whack.

I start to cry.

I cry thinking of our last trip to Port Vale and those moments and how fresh they still are, of meeting Bunny in the pub in Burslem, and that bloody awful picture Patrick took of us. Nobody sees me crying, nobody knows I'm crying.

We trudge on and just as Leith is within a couple of miles, the path is closed. Closed for repair, although most of the plastic diversion signs have blown over anyway. They could have chosen anytime to repair, but no, they've chosen to schedule it for our visit. There's an improbable diversion, reluctantly signposted, confusing us. It feels a little too deliberate, that they're poking personal fun at us. Just let us walk the path!

That we're now walking across the lushest, greenest grass that these islands have surely ever seen in August is of scant consolation. Leith does not feel it's within a couple of miles any more. We need a drink, a break, oh please we need a break. On and on. The walk, initially springy and driven, is now a recalcitrant and weary plod. Our precious silence is now less respectful, more curmudgeonly.

In time, the landscape changes. Eventually, we're back at the river. The water is a murky industrial brown, the sky is a bleak, heavy grey. The traffic-lashed grand old works buildings, long forgotten, purpose distant, are an uncertain mix of the two.

We make it to Leith. There's no sunshine today.

Given the unremitting closeness and damp of the day, the few people about are huddled in cafés, while the Trainspotting-famed Banana Flats contrast with a soon-to-be development and the vista opens up to Arthur's Seat's magnificence. It's a startlingly glorious juxtaposition. Where else? Where else is it like this? I feel this demand rising through my senses. The sensory overload of Edinburgh is an epic sensation. It is an awesome, magnificent city. Each angle, each view, is unique, almost provocative in its challenge to confound and inspire.

And meanwhile, there are our own contrasts: on the outside, we're just more damp visitors to a stunning, beguiling city; on the inside, we're pained, aching and miserable.

Still, we persevere. We can't agree where to stop and eat, refuel and reflect. When we can agree, they're sorry, they're full, so we disagree some more. Our legs ache and our bellies are empty. Leith, Edinburgh, world: you need to feed us.

Perseverance: what does it mean? Today, it's a street name. It's another Proclaimers song, and it's a sign in a second-hand shop we pass. It's walking as far as we can, reaching as far as we can, and sticking a Sunshine On Leith sticker on the cold, bleak wet steel of the bridge across the Leith. This bridge is here to stay for many thousand more days like this. We'll be back Patrick, we promise to each other. Maybe we'll see the sun, and maybe it doesn't matter.

In time, we were heartily nourished, and we marched on, almost revitalised, towards Easter Road and Hibernian FC. My senses are still in overdrive. Easter? Redemption? Rebirth? Renewal? I grimace, providence feels in short supply today perhaps, but those very words feel loaded with questions and meaning, encouraging life. I appreciate the moment, the calm of pausing to think, feel and be. I appreciate again the city we're in and enjoy the way it makes me feel like this. Alive, present, in the moment.

The stadium peers at us through the streets. We're here. It's an odd, unlikely and very private pilgrimage. We're here because Patrick developed his Hibs connection through his last months. From Irish rebel songs, to Celtic anthems, a green and white hop to the Hibees. To his retro shirt, the stickers we bought him for Christmas, the 'Sunshine On Leith' lyrics print. We're here because of him, for him, and nobody knows, and therefore nobody cares. It seems peculiar, like there should be a welcome committee, sympathising with our loss, loving our story, our voyage, hugging their forevers, taking us as Hibees for life.

But nobody knows, and therefore nobody cares.

We spend too long in the club shop, almost browsing beyond decency, waiting for something to happen, for magic, for connection.

It doesn't. Nobody knows, and nobody cares. I bought a T-shirt, it was simply a transaction.

Outside again, we leave some stickers on a turnstile. Being here, then leaving here is so bittersweet.

Later I'll take the tale to Twitter

... so, loving football shirts he bought a retro shirt (yeah the sponsor fell off) ...

... found some stickers to leave in random places ...

... or maybe at Easter Road some day ...

.... and loved his Christmas present ...

... just a month later we were singing 'Sunshine On Leith' at his memorial celebration ...

... we've continued to leave stickers in random places on our very occasional travels ...

... and today, at last, we found Leith, if not the sunshine.

Despite a few touching, delightful responses, the Hibs community aren't really listening. I'm searching, reaching out for a Celtic cousin connection, something magical to tie this peculiar diversion together. Others might seek spiritual solace, answers in medics or see magic orbs in photographs: I expect magic or to bump into a random Donal Fennessy, our Irish mountain farmer, in a club shop. It doesn't happen. It's raining again.

We're caught again in our own reflections as we turn away from the ground. We walk together, yet very much alone. You'll Never Walk Alone? Of course, somehow there's enough hope in our hearts to get us up the next hill. It's so different to the hubbub and buzz of a match day, every detail visible without the crowd. The battened up pubs on corners, huge waste bins, touching graffiti on a bridge for one of their own resting in peace.

It's not Patrick's place, or peace.

The streets around a rectangle of green are waiting to come back to life, to weave new stories on Saturday week. We get to the top and pause for family photos at the Easter Road signs. I feel a belonging, and even more, wanting to belong, and a longing to be wanted.

It might be dreich, fret or oorlich, smirr or stoating, goselet or yillen. Whichever, it's raining.

Whatever.

Patrick's Hibs, our Hibernian, the Hibees, are top of the league. It won't last.

***

It's GCSE results day, and this year is unique in that students couldn't complete courses or take their exams. There's a predictable hoohaa about gradings, and rightly so. For us though, we're determined that Patrick can be part of the day, and that we get to congratulate his friends and yearmates and wish them well in their ongoing journeys.

With Rich's help as ever, we design a simple postcard and badge using our Patrick's Place heart logo and deliver them to school to be handed out as each student collects their results. It's an extraordinarily bittersweet day, our crumpling pain assuaged by the joy, relief and smiles of celebrating 16-year olds, and their gratitude to us too. We collected Patrick's results, it's sweet and appreciated that he'd been remembered, his schooldays formally acknowledged. I resist the temptation to stare too mournfully at them, lamenting the futility, or to rage against the August sun.

To escape the intensity, we drive into the country, walk briskly up Broadway Hill, and stumble back down to a tea shop with welcome cheese crumpets and jam and cream scones. I'm not sure an afternoon out in a twee picture-postcard Cotswolds village would have been Patrick's preferred results day treat, but it helps us through.

September

I'm at work. Or rather, I'm working, from home. As is the rest of the world, months into this interminable pandemic. We all live in a desperate cycle of arguing about global data and trends we don't understand, chorusing 'you're on mute', willing a vaccine, an end, and to be able to begin again.

We know that we will never begin again.

Still, it's another Teams call and the same four walls. Half-baked ideas scrawled on post-it notes, aches in my shoulders and a garden that's tantalisingly just yards away. It's hot, and I feel the temptation of stretching out to welcome the September sunshine, and closing my eyes. The sharp spring hues and excited growth have given way to the onset of autumn brown, and there are the first signs of curls on leaves as nature begins its seasonal shrink. The garden now is peaceful. How I miss the vibrant energy of children at play in fantasy worlds, watching Niamh create her version of the Badminton horse trials out of upended benches and flower pots, a washing basket for a water jump and alas, just a wooden hobby horse. Or Euan or Patrick living out imaginary football dreams. That's not a rickety wooden strip of fence held up by sturdy stakes to protect the carrots and tomato plants, that's the Town End goal at the County Ground and it's Charlie Austin scoring in it. Or Lionel Messi completing the perfect hat-trick in front of the adoring Camp Nou.

Sorry about the flowers though Dad.

Dad, Dad, come and play, imploring and persuading.

Of course I do. I'll throw, kick, catch. I'll encourage, challenge, inspire. I'll smile, laugh, joke.

I can live in a dream too.

Maybe sometimes I do those things. Maybe sometimes I'll whinge, bark and frown instead. Either way, we repeat, repeat, repeat. Either way, when we do play, rain or shine, there's one rule: finish on a good one. Whatever the task or game, no matter how long it takes, repeat, repeat, repeat, it'll end on a high.

I sigh, and turning away from the memories and screen, catch a picture of Patrick. It's there everyday, he's watching me, his then early teenage innocence smiling goofily over the room. I wonder what he was thinking about at that precise moment, what he had done that day, what came next.

I burst into tears.

I'm hit by waves of intense and throttling grief. I'm literally overcome, and gulp, struggling for breath with the realisation that I won't hear his laugh or touch his skin or see his smile ever again. Within a heartbeat, I'm a million miles from work, where no one asks or mentions or knows. The feelings in those minutes that follow are unbearable. I can't do this, my head is faint and I'm nauseous. The pain is never ending and always will be. There is surface respite, there is acting and there is temporary relief, but this numbing sense of loss is always there. I lie on the bed and cry and cry and cry.

All of ten minutes later, I have restirred and composed myself. Still, I resent having to walk back down the stairs, sit in the study and pretend. I talk to someone about work stuff that is seemingly important in the here and now of other people's lives, but does it matter? Really? Does it matter whether we get Nigel or Hamza or Tish to do the work this week?

***

I'd wanted to run the Oxford Half, or Swindon Half Marathon in aid of SeeSaw, and either would have been fantastic, so it was pretty demoralising when both were cancelled due to the ongoing pandemic.

But really, I thought, maybe a 'solo' effort starting and finishing at West Witney Sports & Social Club and joined and supported by some of my favourite people was meant to be.

Once I'd decided and started organising, honestly, I couldn't wait.

It was a special place for me as a small child: I watched Dad play football here by day, and looked forward to seeing Gannon's Guitars, my first favourite live band, play at night. I'd fall asleep under the tables in the bar. I swear I even spotted the real Father Christmas flying through the sky one starry Christmas Eve. I played football and cricket here until I was nearly grown up, and more occasionally when I was kind of grown up.

It was such a vast, free, special place for Patrick. He simply loved playing football for Tower Hill Football Club here, just being here. He treasured every moment and remembered every match, every friendship he made here. Every goal he scored and every laugh he had. And to treasure it and remember it and laugh at it some more, he would endlessly watch the end of season highlights DVDs. They're dusty now, abandoned on a hidden shelf, waiting for a moment I am not ready to contemplate.

More recently for me, it's become a special place again through Witney parkrun. The thrill of improving, the satisfaction of meeting new friends, the perfect start to the weekend. A year ago this week, Dad had just been diagnosed with mesothelioma, I ran my fiftieth parkrun, and I ran a personal best. The sun shone magnificently and stoically. It was his only visit to parkrun and his last to West Witney, where he was one of the first committee members, most of a lifetime ago.

Come the day, it's sunny again, conditions are perfect. All week, I'd felt under the weather, with a niggling, nagging calf injury. Real? Or are you feeling the pressure, the tension Liam? Maybe it's a week too far. Feeling ready, I'd run the distance, in target time the week before. Peaked too soon? I procrastinated, hesitated, and time drifted on. I knew I had to do it — the fundraising, goodwill was just overwhelming, there was no choice … and the weather forecast next week was rubbish. It was now or never.

I wasn't late, that was a start. There were a few photos, a small, self-conscious socially distanced gathering, and I was off. I'd chosen Graham, as one of my oldest, dearest friends of course, to kick off with. He'd been there to take those cherished pictures of Patrick's shirts and mementos in those horrible in between days bookended by Patrick and Dad dying. He was there for me then, as we'd been there or thereabouts for each other since primary school. A thousand pints, a hundred gigs, nights at the dogs, dogs of the nights and the greatest of friendships. And today, our first run. Today I was wearing a Patrick's Place football shirt, with the heart badge containing the pictures that Graham had taken. Today there wasn't much space for such sentiment, we had a mile to run in eight minutes and that was it. I slowed Graham down, he was keen, enthusiastically eager but I had another twelve of these to do. It felt too quick, as we zipped along Downs Road.

Waiting for us at the golf club entrance was Paul. Paul was smiling, as he had been when I met him in that postcard Cotswolds village the day before Patrick's sixteenth birthday, the day I could finally thank him for those Croke Park tickets. Graham continued with us, and already I felt something rather special building. We were calm, relaxed. I was to enjoy this. Paul and I had spoken of the importance of connections, of friendship and here we were, putting those words into action. It turned out that Graham and Paul had met through work twenty-plus years ago, now, now this.

Now, we were running through Curbridge and here was Rupert. Another greeting, another smile. Rupert had been incredibly supportive through the year, from turning up on the doorstep with a huge lasagne the day after Patrick died, to organising raucous nights out with Ossie, Leggy, Alan and Lee in the windows between lockdowns, to messaging, checking and being there. In the midst of having the toughest of personal years himself, it was incredibly appreciated. That's why I gave him an uphill leg into the wind.

Graham and Paul had dropped back a few yards as I caught up with Rupert. I didn't need to, I'd seen him a few days before, yet here we were nattering away like long losties. All this chattering was going to do no good for my time. Everyone who greeted me with a cheery grin from here on in would follow it with a *how's it going?* I'd respond — I'm struggling, I feel rubbish — because in a running sense, I was, I did. None of my training had prepared me for such wonderful company. I wish I could have run thirteen miles with each of them. Instead, I was running at a decent pace, and having glorious conversation at the same time. This made me smile, while simultaneously wonder how long I could sustain the sheer effort, not to mention the pleasantries and platitudes for.

I was in the zone now, in a running rhythm at the planned pace, and right on time, it's 9:54am and Sally is waiting for me at Deer Park Road. As Run Directors at parkrun, Sally and husband Fraser had been inspirations to me throughout my running journey. Fraser would be ahead of me, sometimes way in the distance. Each time I record a run on Strava, Sally or Fraser have done an extra one or gone an extra mile or a little bit quicker. It's inspiration by increments. It's been like this every week since I started parkrun. With their daughters too they're fabulously, consistently, yes, inspirationally active. I'm still relatively fresh into today's run, and as we run on the path, the cycle path developed 60 years ago to take workers like my Mum and Dad to Smiths Industries, the familiar mound is to the left and slowly developing trees and bushes to our right, Sally is asking the right questions, keeping me at the right pace. In a couple of minutes she'll slow down, handover, and she'll see Rupert, who she doesn't know and say *didn't I come to view your house the other day?* It's a small thing in a small enough town perhaps, Rupert's house was for sale, Sally and Fraser were house hunting — yet hey, still a gentle quirk of fate that reaffirms ... connections, connections.

Next up are Lindsay and Regan. Regan had written those incredibly open memories of Patrick each day in the lead up to his birthday. He'd delivered the signed Swindon 'WALSH 7' shirt that he'd organised and sorted. He'd been Patrick's best friend at primary school, a foot taller, his blond curly hair clashing with Patrick's red, making them an unlikely pair. He'd been brave, he'd been to our house and rung the doorbell. We have such admiration for everyone who's walked down our steps, wondered who or what was going to greet them, had second thoughts, wished they were somewhere else, and then reached for the bell. Regan, and his Mum Lindsay, had that bravery in spades. Regan's writing, open and tender and evocative, was rewarded with a fantastic social media reaction. Their heartfelt friendship has been a huge source of strength for us, now we were running together. As we headed along Downs Road and left onto Range Road, Regan darted ahead. I wasn't having any of that, I was more than content to keep my pace, chatter to Lindsay, drawing more strength. On the corner, was an extraordinary sight.

Protesters? I could see placards. About what?

They were shouting something too.

Surely not!

These weren't protesters! No, closer now, it was mum, my auntie Sonia and cousin Valerie. Oh bless them! It was gorgeous. And through the run they popped up time and time again, appearing in random corners to provide cheers and strength and love. There they were, wearing decorated, customised shirts as well, like a glorious scene from Father Ted. Here they were again, I could pick out the wording this time ... Keep Going Liam, You're Doing Great, You'll Never Run Alone and Run On, Run On With Love in Your Heart.

I did.

It was an amazing and delightful surprise.

Now we were joined by Ben and Billy, two more of Patrick's precious friends. I'd coached Regan and Ben for years, taking Regan to Wembley to watch Swindon, after meeting the Wealdstone Raider. I'd put my arm round Ben's shoulder as he was nervous at the prospect of playing a six-a-side on the hallowed County Ground turf. That rectangle of green, divided into four smaller rectangles of green, with dozens of young players living out their own dreams. That day Patrick scored at the Town End and that day he lived out his dream. Billy had his own yellow and blue reasons for our dearth of Swindon connections. The three boys were running together, each wearing a different Patrick's Place football shirt — Regan in Henry Box red, Ben in Coventry City sky blue, and Billy in the yellow and blue of Oxford United. Tracking just behind them, each with their own WALSH 7 on their back, it was an emotional moment. I know how much Patrick loved them, because he spent so long shouting at them on the PlayStation or chanting with them in the garden. I know Dad loved them too, because he knew how much Patrick loved them. I was glad that after five miles at last I could run without conversation: it gave me a break and more fundamentally, watching those lads, seeing them smile, being with them … I know I wasn't capable of talking.

10:18am and here was Chris, smiling, ready, concerned as to my wellbeing. I told him it was awful and that I was struggling terribly etc etc, then we banged out another spot-on mile. I did have a concern meeting Chris back out on the road to Curbridge, as he seemed to be waiting well before the expected mile marker. It seemed that my Fitbit and the original plan were all out of sync and I hadn't run as far as I'd thought. Our running journeys had been similar, both taking such joy from our weekly parkruns, occasionally volunteering, then dashing around our course, enjoying a catch up afterwards. Chris was ideal for this halfway leg, he'd always see the big picture, understand the value, not the effort. His encouragement was calm and energising.

Eric was next, and possibly the only friend I thought was going to greet me with a momentum-breaking bear hug. I dodged that and despaired that my Fitbit tracker was now so far behind — I'd be running a nearly fourteen-mile half marathon at this rate! No wonder I felt compelled to tell all and sundry how awful this all was. Eric had drawn the same short straw as Rupert, into the stiffening breeze and mildly uphill. Listening to him though, we were battling up the steepest Cotswold hill, fighting the unforgiving storm, daring to achieve. That's how it felt after seven miles, a mild September breeze can play havoc with the emotions. I'd known Eric through football, but more lately he'd carried out an heroic job in developing Witney Music Festival. As chairman, he'd reinvigorated it, grown it, passionately championing opportunities for all. I'd had a fantastic time with a beautiful team making it happen these last couple of years, Eric made that happen. One night we'd joyously discovered trance together at Fat Lils at 3am, and five hours later I was blearily watching Morris dancing at Bampton. We'd drunk Montana's finest whiskey all night, listening to Fleetwood Mac. We'd celebrated being 'All Together Now' on stage with The Farm in front of five thousand people. Now he just had a few more hard yards of this mountain and hurricane, and this was a baton he could hand over. Fingers crossed he'll be keeping hold of the music festival one for a long while yet.

For Patrick's memorial service I'd asked the parkrun community to help, and of course they stepped up to be there for us. Gill was there on the early shift, helping set up, put chairs out, asking what more she could do. She had become a friend through parkrun, although it had taken some time. Before we'd met, I'd recognised her husband (another) Paul's name on the weekly results, always just a few places ahead or behind, yet I didn't know who he was. He'd been a neighbour until he was about eight, so it was probably 40 years since we'd played street football together, and now, I didn't recognise him. In the back slapping and bonhomie that followed each week we'd find ourselves in different circles. His wife Gill was a regular volunteer and runner too, but I didn't know who she was either. The building of our parkrun foundations right there. So many possibilities of new friends, so many connections to be fulfilled. It must have been a year until we were mutually introduced, with a welcome smile from them too, as they'd similarly wondered who I was.

Come that memorial service, I still didn't know Gill too well, and was deeply touched that she cared enough to volunteer and be there for us. Gill also sent the most beautiful message, which I didn't even see for about six months as it lay hidden in the depths of an unread inbox. One night at the running club, I was running alone, doing ok, yet lonely among the crowd. Gill ran with me, talked to me, asked me how I was, listened to me, told me her stories. It was such a brave thing to do, to reach out, to make friends and to be a friend, at completely the moment I needed it. So months later, I really wanted Gill to run with me, being a friend. It was fabulous to run with her now, and the mile flew by.

And by now, I knew who her husband Paul was too.

Gill handed over to a guy I recognised first from his awful scruffy blue drill top. It looked like a relic from about thirty years ago, and was frankly a ridiculous choice of clothing to run in on this warm early autumn morning. I didn't tell Shaun that, I was too busy telling him that I felt rubbish and wasn't enjoying this. It was fabulous to see Shaun, and even better to be running alongside each other. We'd spent the better part of thirty years turning up together on FA Cup final weekend for reunions of our old Leicester Uni football team. Most of those years Shaun would turn up in far better shape, fitness and fresh-faced style than the rest of us, only to pull a hamstring after five minutes and spend the rest of the time drowning sorrows and resolving to be fit for the next year. Now, he'd travelled up from Wycombe, to run one incredibly special mile here. I was running with him, thinking — what if I pull a hamstring now? How much stick would he give me for that? We had about eight years' worth of catch-up in eight minutes and neither of us pulled a muscle.

Shaun still had that heavy, faded blue top on when we caught up later. I hadn't clocked it earlier: it was our old football club training top from student days. Like us, it was indeed a relic from thirty years ago. Where on earth he'd dug it out from who knows, but if I hadn't been caught in the glow of just completing the run, if I hadn't been facing a different emotional direction, I think he'd have got a cry out of me, just for wearing that.

It hits me, deep in retrospect, how different these friends are, and how different our stories are. Marli was next, leaping out of the trees, bringing another different story. When we first met, Marli was running her own half marathon challenge, and hers was the first time I targeted: if she could do it, so could I. More recently she'd brought a fresh, different perspective to grief. She would say the things others hadn't thought, ask the things other friends didn't dare. And all these miles in, today I needed Marli to be different. And she was. I was greeted with a honey-based energy concoction, and blaring from her phone a song, her song, 'Fight Song', which I know had given her strength as her Mum died. We ran a precious, higgledy piggledy haphazard, honey-fuelled mile and finished along the shaded avenues through the trees at West Witney. We ran a different way back to base point, catching all by surprise.

Next was Dan, as it had to be. Before I met Dan and Tamsyn, I had a quite different perception of running. After my football playing years, I would have an annual constitutional run, as if it was my physical MOT. I would run, as sharply as my legs would carry me for about three miles, collapse in a mixture of relief, triumph and blissful ignorance. I would ache in all the wrong places, proclaim that those who did this for fun were idiots, and mainly sit down for another year. I was happy in my confident certainty that I knew best.

I met Dan and Tamsyn one evening in the Windrush pub because I had to. I was chairman at Tower Hill Football Club, and I had to listen to their optimistic dreams about bringing parkrun to the site. I'd planned to then go home, reflect for a while, and tell them that unfortunately it was impossible for a multitude of clear reasons.

Sorry guys, I'd say.

That afternoon I was made redundant, and that evening I resolved to help bring parkrun to Witney. In the time it took to drink a small glass of sparkling water, I was convinced, sold hook, line and sinker. Their passion, determination and meticulous planning with options and maps and logic and everything was simply compelling. It was going to happen. And if Witney parkrun was going to happen, I was going to do it, and if I was going to do it, I was going to do it as well as I could.

I figured I had around six months of planning time to change my annual service-based approach to running, to give it a go properly.

There was still a significant car parking obstacle for parkrun to overcome. Each weekend the West Witney site was overcome with cars. Cars carrying kids to play football, to learn tennis, there were cars on verges, double parked, barely parked, just cars. It was a long-standing issue; there just wasn't enough space to accommodate everyone. Adjacent to the site, in the industrial park, there was a large, empty at the weekend, car park, owned by Blenheim Estates. They would begrudgingly allow us to use it for just one weekend a year, for our annual six-a-side competition. And they charged most handsomely for the privilege too.

Kate's brother Jim was over from Brisbane, and he arranged to meet an old friend, Steve, from Sheffield, who coincidentally now lived in Witney. Coincidentally, Steve had a senior job working for Blenheim Estates. Coincidentally, Blenheim Estates had a new, community-minded CEO. Coincidentally, Steve was about as close as it gets to local running royalty, although was now ravaged by injury. Of course, he'd be supportive of the parkrun ethos and would love to support it coming to Witney. Coincidentally, Steve was a long-term friend and former housemate of Dan ... the path forward was clear. A mutually beneficial car parking solution was soon found. I like to think that in the course of about a pint and a half of Hobgoblin one night in the Elm Tree, Witney parkrun went from an aspiration to a reality.

A few weeks later, Punam led the nascent organising committee and local stakeholders, including supportive and influential local councillors, around the proposed course. It was an inspiring, heart-warming and genuinely thrilling morning. I now had about five months, and I knew that I'd be ready too.

Dan was waiting in the shirt Swindon wore in the club's one dismal, unforgettable Premier League season. It was the Loki-designed, bright red one with white swirly bits on it. Unfortunately, while worn in some style by the likes of Jan Åge Fjørtoft and John Moncur, it was also synonymous with conceding a hundred goals in a single league season, as well as two consecutive relegations. Anyway, good morning Dan. I'd passed him earlier as he warmed up and now he was going to accompany me on my toughest mile. This was the one I found tough, I didn't just say how bad I was, I meant it. Dan encouraged me, kept talking to me, kept me on the right pace and didn't get much in return.

I had a mile left, and as we arrived back at West Witney to greet Euan, I felt relieved, almost euphoric, and ready to finish this.

Euan was smiling, looking pretty splendid in his matching Patrick's Place shirt, I just had to rein him in in case he tried to accelerate away. He did up the ante, and I gave what I had to rise to the challenge, along Burford Road back to the roundabout at the top of Tower Hill, I knew every step. I knew every yard and felt every breath. As we turned and headed back along the cycle path, half a mile to go, quicker, still quicker, we quietened. Lost in the process, the concentration, the simple act of one foot in front of the other, breathing, reaching for a little more.

To our right, fields, slowly turning golden, gentle slopes down to the river, criss-crossed with footpaths and trails. This Windrush valley, freshly discovered and rediscovered and explored during this cruel lockdown year of all years. The wooden bridge over the river, the ancient boundary, Wessex to Mercia, to the old mill and simpler times. A simpler time when the fields were farmed rather than built upon, and the River Windrush still glistened as it meandered on towards the Thames.

To our left, houses. As a child I'd looked left here, to fields and more fields. All these fields until we could get to West Witney, and kick a ball around its wide open acres.

Now though, houses.

Houses which I'd helped tile with Dad some thirty years before. I was fortunate to work with Dad through my student holidays: floor tiling, wall tiling, and a lot of grouting. We were a happy pair, enjoying Pogues cassettes in the van, the only *Guardian* readers on any building site at lunch time, working hard. His was the only unmarked van in town, renowned quality and trusted reputation were the only advertisements he required.

After each summer at home, Mum would say how much Dad missed me when I returned to student life at Swansea or Leicester, and I knew that he didn't mean so much at home or in the pub or at football, he meant at work. In the van, in a tight bathroom, in the working company. We had a tight bond and a precious, private world.

Other friends would summer in forlorn factories, or pack, pack, pack until their senses were numb, or maybe stay on a kibbutz or coach kids tennis or just laze. I had my Dad.

So those houses to our left. Many of them were built by a major national house building chain, the 'all fur coat no knickers' type. Dad had taken the tiling contract, and as needs sometimes must, at a low price, cut-throat rate favoured by this margin-slashing construction giant. I was concerned that we'd be effectively halving our wages on this job — and it was a lot of houses.

No son, we'll be spending half as long working in each house.

It was a valuable life lesson in practical economics.

So, apologies to any who bought a dream Deer Park house only to be disappointed by shoddy tiling or clumsy grouting. It may have been me. I was reminded of this very recently when Kate asked our building friend Fred about his old groundworker.

I've still got his spade, said Fred, *well, one of them*. He had a half-sized spade for day rate work, and a full spade for priced jobs. Fred referenced Nietzsche and Jung in the same conversation, but neither trumped his digging colleague.

At last, Euan and I entered the huge field in the top corner, running through the tree avenues, past the Tower Hill lockup, past a fading Sunshine On Leith sticker. I felt the emotion in the pit of my stomach, my eyes welling, Euan was beside me still. Quarter of a mile, the last minute. I knew where the ground dropped away slightly, where the roots protruded. I'd known this ground since I could walk, a million memories and a lifetime of feeling flashed through me. I remembered lying on the floor in despair on Patrick's birthday in May.

We swept through the last trees, the bowling green hidden and forbidden beyond the neatly trimmed hedge to our left, and there was a small welcoming party ahead.

Socially distanced camera phones clicked, the race was run. There was some applause, some well dones, a few hugs, a homemade 'Patrick medal' from Kate, and eventually some water. The protesters/cheerleaders were there. One cousin, Michael, took more photos and another, Andrea, refreshed the cheerleaders. I thanked every lucky star imaginable and, beyond chuffed with beating my target time too, walked back to the car and drove home.

It was a special time, in a special place with special people.

Showered and feeling fresh and super-special, we wandered into town to grab some lunch and enjoy the sun on Church Green. Henry at Sandwich de Witney made me feel like an Olympic superstar, demanding that I bypass the rest of his queuing customers, making a song and dance about the run and serving and treating us, on the house. It was typical of Henry, and wonderful. Later in the evening, still glowing, there were drinks, a pub garden, and many more drinks. The stories, the achievement, and the incredible pace were all gently and lovingly embellished.

It was a glorious, floating end to the best of days.

***

The next day, and the day after, and some of the day after that too, are terrible. The run pales utterly into insignificance. I'd done this for Dad and for Patrick, and they're not here for it, and never will be. What's the point of going to all this effort, training, chasing sponsors, a dedicated shirt, every last detail, when I don't get to hug Patrick after it? He doesn't get to make a little fun of my earnestness, Dad doesn't get to take a gulp of beer, a breath and tell me he's proud. Nothing. It's just a horrible emptiness. The total raised ticks over £4.5k, and I'm monstrously grateful for every single pound. I thank as many of the hundred-plus sponsors as I can, but still not enough. My energy and purpose has deserted me. It's an almighty shock to be thumped with such a low. It was a waste of time after all. A self-indulgent mistake that I won't make again. All that effort and not even a day more of Patrick to show for it.

***

And all the things we won't do.

This is the reality of our September. It strikes me how much this time of year is a real new year: new football season, new school term, new beginnings, new hopes. For us though my friend, not so much. The opposite effect sinks in. This is our truth, our precious not normality. There is no peace and this is how it is.

Every photograph seems so vivid and so alive and so in the moment. I stare deep into a picture of Patrick sitting in a vast colourful stone chair taken at the ski centre in Oslo — it was two years ago, yet feels like yesterday. I can feel the strop he spent almost the entire visit in, rush through me. I'm aware that I'm missing Patrick more and more. There's an empty space at the table, a quiet in the car, a huge gap where our Friday night music choices and sharing should be. If I stare hard enough can I preserve that feeling forever? Turning the past into the present and a future? Can that be a hope? That the photo never fades and the moment always lingers? Can I live my life by stringing together such moments? Given the burning intensity and such strength of feeling, such will for it to be real and such hope, surely he can become real again? I stare and stare until the gentle tears that form make my eyes sore, until the quiet rage that knows I can't turn the past into the present or the future, until that peaks and sadly, gently fades. I walk and pace around the empty house as words form in my mind, and stand in Patrick's Place. His room, his presence and let those words tumble out with the tears before me. I've overspent my lunchtime, and have to find a way to put a different face on, to take a deep breath, and act my way through another afternoon at work.

This time, I put my hand up at work and say:

We need to talk. My superpower veneer is wearing off. I need a respray. I might look ok, but I'm not.

***

Swindon have had an indifferent and inconsistent start to the season. There has been a huge turnover of players since last season, the guts of our champions for eternity team ripped out. Even our unique champions asterisk feels grubby and awkward. Richie Wellens, our previously effervescent and almost provocatively confident manager, seems increasingly withdrawn and distant. It doesn't even feel a surprise when Michael Doughty, our one player of genuine class, becomes surely the first professional footballer to retire in his prime to launch a brand of sustainable and eco-friendly trainers. It is abundantly clear that we have a weaker team in a higher division. This spectacle is being played out without fans in stadiums, adding to the feel of futility and disconnection. So our matchday habits have changed too. No drive, no optimistic walk down Shrivenham Road, no peeking for the cat or cheery nods to friends and familiar faces. This is a season to be followed, or endured, online. In an attempt to breathe life into the matchday experience, Euan and I try different pre-match pubs in Witney. But whether we try the Wychwood Brewery tap room, the Eagle Tavern (home made sausage rolls and Hooky on tap!), or The Plough, it makes little difference. We haven't got a decent goalkeeper and the brief, sweet glory days of Ginger Pele must have been a dream. It's going to be a tough season.

How tough becomes too clear, too soon. Wellens has seen the whole of the moon and leaves abruptly, and tartly. Lee Power replaces him with John Sheridan, ushered into his tenth managerial role in five years, and his third in five months having been spectacularly unsuccessful at Wigan Athletic. It is an astonishingly bizarre and grim appointment.

Oh well, I say, bewildered, *at least he won't be here long.*

October

Due to a twist or two of fate, and shared connections, I'm talking to Aodh. Aodh is a Breathnach, the Gaelic version of Walsh and we share our versions of Brecon/Breathnach and Welsh/Walsh heritage, and how one version is rather more specific than the other. Our flavour of post-agricultural age West Waterford Walshes helped create the railway. It's now the magnificent tourist-pulling Greenway, testimony to what a little creativity, ambition and social responsibility can deliver. Nestling to the north are the dark greens, the rocky crags, the bogs and the loughs of the Comeragh mountains. Situated to the south is the Copper Coast and the Celtic Sea, the sweeping views of Clonea Strand.

Views, nature, hues, beauty, all unchanged for generation after generation.

Our family history is entwined with that railway line: I imagine my forefathers building the spectacular viaduct at Durrow, the tunnel at Ballyvoile and for sure, working the signal box at Kilmacthomas. Sitting proud on the old platform, it's been left in some disrepair almost as a monument to the efforts and lives of those generations. Here, here is where my great grandfather worked. And which his father built. How much I would give for an inkling of their thoughts, an insight to their lives and ambitions.

Did my great grandfather Maurice stand in his signal box, in the shadow of the mountains and with the coast ahead, and wonder at the miracle of the railway and where it might take future generations of Walshes?

And now, by way of the railway and the sea, a hundred-odd years later in England, we have a Kerry Walsh talking to a Waterford Walsh about the precocious essence of life.

Fate and twists and connections and whatever. I'm only talking to Aodh because Patrick's died.

Aodh is working for Storyvault Films on a documentary for the BBC about sudden death, following the story of a young man (coincidentally) named Patrick as he tries to understand the unexpected death of his young sister Lauren. Aodh has spoken to Niamh and Euan, and Euan has agreed to take part in a group counselling session in London as part of the film. With time short, both Aodh and his team and we as a family move heaven and earth, call in favours and compromise other arrangements to make good the organisation. At last, I'm ready to take Euan to London.

The evening before, Euan phones to say his whole flat must self-isolate after a Covid outbreak.

After all that, there's nothing anyone can do. A day out in London is very much off the agenda. Perhaps we can catch up with Aodh again sometime. I've never met a Breathnach before.

***

Breaks, holidays, treats — how on earth do we manage these in a post-life still pandemic world? We're craving sunshine and peace somewhere far away, but opt for fresh air and new views along the rather more local River Thames.

Over a couple of days, Kate and I walk from Hampton Court to Westminster, taking in about twenty-seven miles through south-west London including a couple of diversions.

It's amazing. How serene and graceful and beautiful and green London by the river is.

It's an incredible city, I can think of no other remotely like it. I love this city, this vast, contradictory, beguiling old girl, but I will never forgive it.

I hate this city.

I trusted her, let her welcome Patrick and she took him.

***

I'd long heard Dad's stories about nights out at his cousin Maurice 'Louie' Power's pub in Tooting, south of the river in London. I always took them in, enjoyed them, and gently questioned him in return. But as with so many things, that was it — a surface appreciation perhaps. I barely wondered how a boy from rural county Waterford came to be running a pub in the heart of London, how horribly little I knew of that journey. Now, as Euan joins Kate and I, weary after those twenty-seven miles of walking, reflection and contemplation settling within me, how I wish I'd dug deeper, how I wish I'd felt a walk in his shoes.

It's too late.

I imagine Dad at twenty-six springs young, buoyant and delirious surely, on 15th March, 1969, skipping up the tube steps at Tooting Broadway station with his friends, after Swindon had won the League Cup across London at Wembley. I'd heard the summary, but suddenly, now, right now, I craved the minutiae. Which route did they take to get here? How did they arrange how they would get back? And what about Mum, at home, readying herself for my birth in three days time? All those times I've heard the sketchy outlines: always Don Rogers this, Don Rogers waltzing around Bob Wilson that, walking the ball into the net. That the Horse of the Year show rendered the Wembley pitch virtually unplayable but we'd have beaten the Arsenal anyway, about Princess Anne and her skinny pins.

But really, I rolled my eyes the same way my boys switched off when I'd bang on about Glenn Hoddle, Ossie Ardiles, Lou Macari, the good old days, *hey, please indulge and smile with me …*

I realise it's too late. It's acutely painful, just when I need the details. Even as I nagged Dad to recall that Wembley winning team, desperate in his last days to keep him alert as his body was ravaged by the vicious mesothelioma, I wanted names, numbers. Facts. Right now, I wanted context, shades, stories, humanity, memories, feelings.

I wanted my Dad.

I emerge from the underground into the bright lights of Tooting and its city sounds of evening rush hour, without bearings. It takes thirty seconds to steady myself, and to work out which direction The Castle is. It's just a long throw-in away.

The pub is enormous and shiny and it's very definitely 2020. Even so, within seconds I feel I'm a million miles and years and dreams away. I can sip Guinness and imagine my imaginings, feeling the feelings of 1969 and Dad's other trips here. I'm lost in myself. Kate and Euan are chattering and I'm fifty years distant.

I look for tell-tale signs, pictures on the wall, any remnants of connections — but fifty years have passed, this place has changed. I'm supposed to be sitting down concentrating on not catching the virus, but when I do wander, I find that John Wayne visited before filming locally and that I'm the king of the castle, you're the dirty rascal. Cursory research later records the Faces and Mott The Hoople as playing here.

It was clearly quite the place.

It's a massive venue yet I see no evidence of a plaque saying Mick and his country bumpkin Swindon mates stood here, laughing and celebrating the night away on 15th March, 1969. No evidence of Louie, a legendary Irish landlord. Today though, today it's about what I see when I close my eyes, not when I open them. And in my mind's eye, I'm with Dad and Patrick and about a hundred thousand other Swindon fans who've come and gone since, and we're having the time of our lives.

I'd longed to know more about that distant day, to know how the wide-eyed country boys had fared amid the bright lights.

When John, Dad's friend of many decades recently died, I knew another jigsaw piece was lost forever. At John's funeral, when I was faced with the chilling familiarity of the same location, same funeral director, same celebrant as we'd used, I was somehow taken by surprise. I was shaken up by the overwhelming emotion of my situation rather than the here and now for John, his family and over a hundred mourners gathered here. I collected myself, swept along by the warmth and memories in the room. John may not have seen Swindon play in many years, yet here, now, at his reckoning this was how he was being defined: how proud he'd been to see Swindon lift the League Cup in 1969.

I loved how that definition of John had endured. That being a supporter can be so much more than those actively attending years, its habits literally part of life's arc. John left the County Ground, but the County Ground never left John. And I loved still more how Dad had held tight and dear to those matchday habits. The rituals, frustrations and occasional highs as life's ebbs and flows played out with a rectangle of green before him. For him, for Patrick, literally their and there forever.

Later, with my questions still gently forming, and before I could even ask, John's brother Graeme told me, eyes glistening, voice brimming with emotion, all about 15th March, 1969. About who drove the minibus, about who marvelled at Princess Anne's skinny legs, about the joy, about life. And about The Castle in Tooting. About the disco, *there was a disco Liam!*, about the marvellous revelry, about Dad's landlord cousin Louie having a truncheon in his jacket.

Bampton and Ducklington landlords didn't carry truncheons.

More than anything, Graeme told me about my Dad.

This was all I needed to hear. Somewhere else, Nick Hornby was ingraining defeat to the country bumpkins into his psyche.

I became aware of all the Swindon fans sitting around us, with their awful West Country accents, their absurd innocent glee, their delirious disbelief. I hadn't ever come across opposing fans before, and I loathed them in a way I had never before loathed strangers.

Here, the bumpkins were kings of the castle.

Before long, we were out into the newly dark, bustling early evening hubbub of Tooting Broadway and looking for the way back to Kew.

Euan says he wished he was able to drink more with his Grampy, to see him happy and buzzing. There was nothing more fitting or evocative to say.

***

We're in The Farm, a pub deep in Bristol that can only be found with the benefit of satnav and a careful eye. There's me and Euan, Aodh and Lindsay. There's Paddy Mead and his son Patrick. Patrick's sister Lauren died suddenly, like our Patrick, and the Storyvault team are completing their programme about the number of young people who sadly die each year, undiagnosed, misdiagnosed: effectively forgotten by the system while their families crumble. Aodh and Lindsay are gentle and sensitive, expert directors of the situation. I'm sat in the corner, warmed by the fresh October fire as the intermittent showers lash the forlorn beer garden I'm staring into. I'm just out of earshot of these two young men, sharing their fragile souls in the hope that awareness saves other families from this. There's a noisy coffee machine. Strangers an hour ago, now they're talking about how they coped the night their siblings died. They have to pause if anyone goes to the loo and uses the hand dryer. The pub gets busier and filming gets harder as locals, inquisitive at seeing a TV crew filming in their local on a weekday afternoon, arrive from their day's work, then tuck wholeheartedly into their own reasons for being here. Euan has another pint. At the end of it, the pub air thick with sweet Bristol vibes, I'm proud of Euan. I'm proud of this Patrick, new to us, too, and of everyone involved in creating this programme: it deserves every success when it airs in the spring. A few pints in, Euan is warm and keen to renew acquaintances with friends on his old Gloucester Road student patch.

I drive back home alone. I think of journeys up the M5, and through the Cotswolds with my Patrick. I miss him enormously and desperately, but trust the moment to pass before it overwhelms me. Gloucester, Birdlip, Seven Springs, past Kilkenny and North Leach and Burford. Frank Turner sings about 'Redemption', Solange about 'Missing You' and Lorde about loss and moving on, as shuffle works some kind of magic and carries me through the dark, the autumn leaves, and home.

November

I catch myself reflecting, looking into myself, still unsure what the mirror is telling me. I'm thinking about what I've found out (learning would be an exaggeration, I know that much) about grief and, in a sense, it's a relief, my good fortune, that I'd been broadly insulated for so long.

So long, innocence.

But there's something becoming clearer about perspective. How to appreciate rather than mourn those who've lived, weaving rich tapestries into their late seventies, eighties and beyond. How to come to terms with aunts and uncles taken in their sixties yet much too young — Pete, Bernie and Janet and what each of these gave me, and their wonderful families, over decades — and still had years to rightfully give. And then, the stark, dramatic loss of my football teammates in their forties and early fifties — Marcus, Lea, Kevin, Fish and now Murph — the impact on their still young families, and a reminder of my own ageing and greying and mortality. Then there are those in their twenties and thirties — like Nick and my cousin Kelly — how brutally unfair and cruel and random life can be, when it's barely even started adulthood.

How on earth are we supposed to grieve and survive these?

And then, then there are the shattering losses of lives barely begun. Like Liberty, a daughter of good friends tragically killed while walking to school. Like the children of all the bereaved parents we've now met. And, of course, like Patrick.

***

Covid has necessitated a condensed All-Ireland hurling championship season and reversion to a format which is as incredible as it is incomprehensible, and all power to it for that. And Waterford, having not won a single championship match since I shared that Guinness with Joe from Cork on the shores of Lake Como three years ago, will slowly rouse and come to life. So it is that we beat Cork, handily enough, in the Munster semifinal to consign them to the national bear pit of the playoffs, but then lose to Limerick in the final, enabling us to lie in wait for playoff winners in the All-Ireland quarter-final. Normally this would entail a period of waiting in the long grass while the playoff contenders tear themselves to bits. This year, the waiting in the grass bit is a week, rather than a month. Barely long enough for the players to return to their day jobs, revel in some glory and then let the excitement build again. It's a savage programme for amateurs. It's played out in obviously pandemic-empty GAA stadiums, the vast open spaces of the playing field and the towering terraces somehow amplified now.

The coaching teams are animated and demonstrative, wholly consumed in their endeavour. The pundits are sage, canny, wrapped up from the howling wind and sweeping rain that accompanies each new weekend, wherever the venue.

And next to me, there's a space.

I've never watched hurling alone before. I've never sat in silence, watching the season unfold before me. I've never not had anyone to share the successes with, to agonise over unfair defeats with, to be with. So it is that they're hurling in November rather than June, and that I miss my Dad impossibly.

***

Meanwhile, it's nearly Kate's birthday. We've all dealt with our grief in different, often quite separate ways. Reaching for support, for energy and for sustenance, hope maybe, in those different ways can bring its own challenges, but as long as there's a central place of love, of family, of shared experience and shared coping with the present and grasping for a future, to return to, then there has to be a way. So for every time I've pushed lockdown rules to the limits, met friends to drink with, found music to stay out late for, Kate hasn't. She's found inspiration and been inspirational in different ways. And then we return to that central place. Kate then, has read every book on grief, joined every support group, learned about all the miserable, grizzly medical stuff, and reached out to every charity. All the things I haven't done, and don't have the energy to even contemplate.

Sometimes, given our hectic and frantic work schedules too, it feels we're navigating a cruel world in the only direction each of us can manage. Sometimes we manage to dock in the same harbour, and it's that which keeps us afloat.

Kate doesn't want a birthday and she doesn't want anything for her birthday, save for some socks from Patrick, which has fast become a tradition in our central place. What she has heard about, is an initiative called Grief Café and immediately, this feels a potential source of new energy. She runs a proposed Facebook post through me, proposing kicking off the Grief Café concept in Witney. She has already lined up Fat Lils to host it. Our town has lost too many, too young, too early and she wants friends and family alike to have somewhere to go, to talk, to be safe, to grieve, to remember, to celebrate and to be. As we hoped, it took Paul at Fat Lils all of about five minutes to jump at the opportunity to host and support it.

Before we can even picture a scene where grief is talked about, openly and painfully, the post has had a tremendous response, with friends pledging books from all over the country. Once more, the support is immediate and humbling, our re-energising reality. Over the next couple of weeks, the Amazon delivery guy practically has to join our Covid bubble, as over forty books arrive. Each will have its own inscription, its own purpose and life. Life to remember and to live on in a stack of books at the Grief Café.

It's a moment to reflect and be proud of the way Kate is positively leading her own grief journey. So for each occasion she struggles with the music in the house, or I struggle with the silence in the house, or she goes to bed and I go out, we have a dozen more where we have our central place, and safe harbour to dock in.

Kate writes a beautiful article for the Good Grief Trust to share for National Grief Awareness week. She articulates what I can't, about how she's coped and how we've painstakingly built our resilience. How we've talked as a family — some of it lockdown-enforced as we've walked every field and found every footpath, every secret forest and an awful lot of puddles. Kate has developed a trusting and caring support network, in person, online and through reading. She describes her Bereavement Support Worker from a local charity, Helen & Douglas House, as her 'Switzerland' — for she is completely neutral and can give a fresh perspective on anything that's thrown at her.

Initially Kate, previously a voracious reader, could only read self-help books and took inspiration from the likes of *It's OK that You're Not OK* by Megan Devine. That permission that it is ok not to be ok was really important, helped her find solace within her grief and allowed her to let the waves hit and roll through. She managed to progress to biographies and enjoyed *Lady in Waiting* by Lady Glenconner, who wrote about the trauma of losing two sons.

Kate took these insights and reading of the sad experiences of others to develop her own strategy around self care and finding people. Self care for Kate started with consistent basics: getting out of bed every morning to walk the dog, showering, washing her hair and getting dressed. The mundanity of these tasks masks how profoundly difficult they actually were.

Kate did each of them every day.

From there she started to run — cautiously on the treadmill, then more confidently outdoors, and returned to yoga classes as lockdown allowed. She focused on cooking nutritious meals for herself as the lone vegetarian, and the rest of a sometimes fussy family. She gave herself permission to enjoy buying and wearing desirable clothes and beauty products. Kate found meaning in fragrant and calming candles to light each evening at the dinner table, another day survived.

And as much as anything, she needed to find the right people to connect to. She needed to find other parents who had experienced the loss of a child, and hence by definition, survived. She found some local mums to talk to. She had found SUDC UK, a charity dedicated to funding research into the sudden unexplained death of children. Through them she began to understand the importance of research and the retention of tissue samples. They supported us when we needed to complain about our treatment by the Coroner's Office. She found CRY and SAD, who support families when a child dies of a heart condition. She joined bereavement groups online where parents find a safe place to vent their frustration and anger.

Kate drew strength from each of these ways of supporting herself and the love of the family harbour, but she really felt the lack of obvious community-based local support. She discovered the Good Grief Trust and, more importantly, the pop-up cafés. The café support concept made complete sense and it didn't take long before she was desperate to open one herself. She found beautiful and inspirational friends in Claire and Faye, and they were off, a veritable tour de force. The café meets once a month at Fat Lils and provides an opportunity for anyone who is experiencing grief to meet with others to share problems, thoughts, ideas of things that help. It has quickly become a safe and welcome home to share grief, and I am so proud of her for it. The garish orange sweatshirt is less fetching though.

We don't sing happy birthday. The birthday quietly comes and goes, it's not a happy birthday, although a hundred social media wellwishers implore it to be so.

Happy? Do you really think so?

Next it'll be happy Christmas and then it's January.

***

I'm getting ready to fly to Dubai for a week of work in Sharjah and I have aches in my arms, in the same places in each arm. Previously it was on my shoulders and stopped me doing Pilates. I'd wince when extending them. Years ago, I would struggle to take throw-ins properly, as they would twinge. Now, they hurt. It's the worst in the mornings and I can barely reach my arms up, when I instinctively reach out to grab something, I shock myself, the pain sears into me. Yes, I know I should get them looked at.

I'm lying in bed, unable to sleep as I need to be up at 4:30am to get to Heathrow, to get the plane. And while I'm lying in bed, unable to sleep because I have to get up to get to the airport, the demons of the middle of the night take over. I have an arm disease that is surely different to anything anyone else has ever had. And this surely incurable disease is spreading through my body, spreading through the silence and the dark of the early hours. It becomes obvious that I'm dying of, of, of … *something*. I wonder if I will actually die of this unique arm disease, and in the moment, I genuinely need this to be swift.

For one, I have an urge and need to be with Patrick, with Dad, and for two, I can't be faffed with the hullabaloo that's going to come with being the only patient in the world associated with such a special, night-time creeping, haunting, debilitating painful disease. The alarm breaks me out of panic, and I make it to Heathrow in good time.

Maybe some clever scientist will discover and diagnose this unique arm debilitation some other time.

December

The flight leaves the bright summer's heat of Dubai and I fall asleep. When I wake up, it's already dark and winter. Dubai denies definition. It is, simply Dubai. What to say about this crazy, bewitching, billion miles an hour place? It's a brash, garish, melting pot of every culture on earth; innovative, friendly, creative, mesmerising. Almost every downtime minute in the city that I share with my wonderful colleagues Robert and Nicola is spent laughing, marching, teasing, drinking or laughing some more. Occasionally we break from the merriment to work in Sharjah, splendidly hosted by our working partner and guide. He goes the extra mile for us, then another one, gently teaching us about the local ways, sharing its majestic story of development. Our clients over the creek in Sharjah are unfailingly warm, eager to keep us happy and keen to learn. Nicola's endless enthusiasm endears herself to the chairman, and one day we find Robert sharing lunch in the security hut. At times, I'm guilty: when everyone else is home in the cold, suffering the endless reality, we've enjoyed so much, and here I am, *laughing*.

It's a trip I was due to make last January, before ... before everything intervened just as I was about to check in. I've brought with me one of the last Sunshine On Leith stickers. Not fancying the potential ramifications of sticking it on a lamppost, I decided to give it to the team at our client. It's such a personal thing to me, so much to try to explain — Patrick, the Hibs connection, the song, oh the song, the stickers and how we use them — that I'm nervous and hesitant about doing it. It's just a little green and white sticker. I try my best to explain it to their team and they are visibly appreciative, supportive and touched. They discuss quickly where to put it, and decide to stick it on a framed photo of their own visit to Scotland. It's a beautiful and emotional moment. There's a pause for calm and I need to leave; listening to the sound of my heels on the marble floor as I go, distracting myself from tears.

And now I know that when I come back to Sharjah, there'll be a place where Patrick is waiting for me.

The signs say *Smile, You're In Sharjah* and *Dubai: Nothing Is Impossible.*

How true.

In the space of five glorious hours last Saturday, Swindon scored two late scrappy goals to win at Oxford, and Waterford delivered an astonishing comeback to beat Kilkenny in the All-Ireland Senior Hurling Championship semi-final.

I'd watched the pulsating hurling alone, nursing a Guinness in a local Irish bar, and as the game unfurled I knew that win or lose this was a glorious, heartfelt, do-or-die, life-affirming performance. It was such a thrilling, captivating, raw-intensity two fingers to 2020, such a privilege to behold. Gasping in the still, warm night air, I skipped across the countless lanes of zooming traffic, and returned to my hotel to hear the celebrations on WLR: a local radio station living the Déise's glory and sharing it with listeners at home. Sharing it with singers with buckets on their heads, with the diaspora around the globe, with Liam in Dubai and with the living and dead. My Dad would be a happy man and I thought of Joe from Cork and the last victorious semi-final and the vibrant greens and glistening blues of Lake Como. Except this time I couldn't phone Dad to just be. I couldn't phone him to say nothing, knowing that nothing was all I needed to say. I thought of Patrick and what Swindon's win in the derby would have meant to him. I messaged Euan knowing what Swindon's win did mean to him; I read some congratulations.

I wept and closed my eyes and drifted off to sleep again, as the plane cruised on towards the English winter.

Dubai hey, it was good to be back.

***

On arriving home, there was another return to negotiate. At last there was to be a limited and short-lived return of crowds to sports events. We were months and months into this never-ending, cursed pandemic, and as a society we still didn't know what to do for the best. But when Swindon announced they'd be able to welcome crowds of two thousand to the County Ground, despite the unmitigated mess they were making of the season, despite the ongoing Covid risks, despite the emotions we knew would be set to unravel, our names were first in the hat for the ticket lottery.

Our wish was granted, and our lucky golden tickets arrived for Swindon Town v Fleetwood Town — we were on our way back. I picked Euan up in Oxford, as if somehow taking a different route, the A420 past Faringdon, Shrivenham and the White Horse roundabout, would miraculously mask the reality that there were only two of us making the journey.

It didn't. We made small, meaningless, distracting conversation instead.

Did we stop at that McDonald's once on the way back from somewhere?
Yeah, I think you're right.
I'm sure we did, where had we been?
No idea, think it was a day out somewhere.

Utterly inconsequential in the grand scheme of things, absolutely consequential in the moment. We were so consciously and actively saying nothing that we forgot to put BBC Wiltshire Radio on for the team news.

Announcing the team was Patrick's job.

Everything was odd, eerie and peculiar. In the miserable mid-December afternoon, it felt dark before it had even become light. With the crowd maybe a quarter of what it would have been, there was precious little traffic, no buzz, no away fans were allowed. We'd parked in our usual place out of habit rather than necessity and took sharp intakes of breath walking along Shrivenham Road. The loneliness and despair was palpable, yet so too, the sense of achievement and even a whiff of excitement.

We were back.

We didn't see the ginger cat.

We walked silently around the ground. We'd missed this place so much. It was horrible. Temporary steel fencing ringed the stadium. There were as many hi vis stewards as fans. There were checks and stern looks and barcodes and clouds. This was not football as we knew it.

Once inside, there was no lingering in the concourse. We had to sit in our allocated seats, appropriately socially distanced, equally spaced in a discerningly regimented fashion. It was a sharp jolt into the reality of 2020. Still, this was our fun, our leisure time, our weekend. Our choice. George Orwell, where are you?

Somewhere on the pitch, the players of Swindon and Fleetwood went through their carefully orchestrated warm up routines. I say somewhere, as this professional choreography was taking place with sixty-two people on the pitch. Sixty-two! It takes sixty-two people to get this show on the road. I wondered what Dad would make of it, accustomed to days of yonder when eleven v eleven would hurtle onto the pitch a couple of minutes before kick-off, kick a ball into the air, finish their cigarettes and fly into bloodthirsty action on ploughed up pitches barely fit for cattle.

I'd had the fanciful notion that the shower of a bunch we'd been watching remotely online week in, week out would transform into a vaguely coherent and discernibly organised, committed team when backed by the mighty roar of two thousand passionate ultras. That Fleetwood would tremble and disintegrate in this fervent atmosphere. I was woefully ambitious. Distracting myself from the pain of the action, I noticed the flicking lights of a plane on a flight path over the North Stand ahead of us. The sky was turning darker still, the air cold and in these locked down times it felt odd that there was a plane, high above us, escaping. From despair to where? I wondered of the lives within it and the hopes they were carrying to their destination. The linesman had his flag up again. *That was never offside.* The plane traced west towards Bristol, out of sight, out of mind and forgotten.

After an interminable forty-five minutes, the shrill half-time whistle came and at last, it was something to lift us out of our seats. Just as we were talking about whether Patrick would have tried to sneak a cheeky dirty burger and maybe some chips, I saw a slightly bigger version of him doing just the same. He was wearing the right clothes, had the same hair and a similar frame and gait. It felt as freakish as it did despairing.

I caught Euan thinking the same.

I know I did because we didn't say anything.

Fleetwood were tidy, compact and winning. In response, Swindon looked meek, lacked guile, and were abjectly leaderless. As the floodlights shined brighter, the early optimism waned further, and desperation set in. This was a relegation struggle, for real. I summoned my flagging energy, and seeking any form of helping the team, did what any sane and rational supporter would. I bellowed and howled and barked my frustration at the linesman in front of us. It was in vain, he gave us no assistance, no comfort. Now, more forlornly looking for signs of hope, inspiration, anything, I recalled that the seats we were in — Don Rogers enclosure, near the Stratton Bank end — were close to where we'd sat one night when Euan was tiny.

With about twelve minutes left that night, Swindon were two down to an impressive Sheffield Wednesday side, and lucky to still be within reach. A quarter of an hour later, we had astonishingly fluked a 3-2 win, and I remember, as if it were happening right now in front of me, Super Sammy Parkin knee-sliding in celebration right towards us. There was a madness and intensity in his eyes. He was in another world. I evoked and implored with all the might I could muster, but for the life of me could not see Brett Pitman repeating that.

He didn't. We lost 1-0.

It was just me and Euan that comeback evening, and it's just me and him now, with not even a cat for comfort.

Night-time had descended, and if 2020 didn't feel like the end of the world before, it did now.

***

Every night, I walk past Patrick's room on the way to bed. Every night, I look and check, but he's never in it.

Sometimes I expect, always I hope, that he'll jump out on me to surprise me, like we always did to each other. He was expert at waiting patiently for his moment, catching me unawares, then, *crash*, make me jump out of my skin. I hated it, the feeling of my heart almost bursting through my chest in shock, the feeling of pride dented. He'd got me, again.

He never does now. I walk past his empty room, and nobody ever jumps out.

This year, the build up to Christmas takes forever. The advent calendar must have a hundred windows. We have to hide through all of it. The nation is grim and there's an almost tangible necessity to pretend that festivities are normal and joyous, peace and good will to all and all that.

Merry Christmas!

Happy Christmas!

It abundantly isn't. And for us, it's horrific.

There are Christmas cards and messages that don't mention Patrick or our loss or a simple thinking of you, and they hurt. I think of all the times I have failed to understand or acknowledge others' losses before, and I feel both inadequate and sympathetic. I'm new to this. But right here and now, I just want this season to do one.

It's raining hard on the windows, and it's a world falling apart at the end of the worst year.

***

On Christmas Day, Euan and I run around Blenheim. The sharp frost and crystal clear day are in contrast to the sweeping rain and floods that have forced neighbours on Bridge Street out of their homes on Christmas Eve. Kate and Niamh feed horses and deliver food parcels in Oxford. I wander around town looking at the flood water on Langel, wearing a smart black overcoat of Dad's now tailored to fit me, thinking it wasn't supposed to be like this. Rueful, resigned, I wish the day away.

Christmas too, besides the holly, the lockdown, the short days throwing sharp cold light across the neglected garden, is a break from work. I'm freed from the relentless monotony of talking to people through the screens in the study, the impossible chase to complete work which surely, surely someone else could do? And so Christmas offers time and new space, a break for reflection, overdue catch-ups and belated thank-yous. A reset and readiness for January which, well, we have to plan for being tough.

But what Christmas brings, really, is suffocation. Patrick is everywhere and nowhere. There is literally no escape from the crushing loss, maybe it's not the grief of the loss, it's the actual physical loss. I miss him and basically, his contribution to and enrichment of my day, so much. He's not here to mimic a distant cousin I've just heard from, he's not lying on the sofa demanding that I scratch his leg, he's not pulling a face because we've run out of Cheerios, he's not lazily wiping the oven half clean, he's not designing new football kits, he's not chanting with his mates on PlayStation, he's not only done some of the recycling, he's not still in bed, he's not endlessly flicking through old photos on someone's phone, he's just not. He's not making me smile, anxious, frustrated, caring, sigh, or loving. He's not making me parent him and I miss that need so much, it suffocates me.

So with all the time in the world, I don't have time to get dressed or to do the rubbish. Instead, in default mode, I pick up my phone and idly waste all the time in the world checking Twitter and checking Strava and checking Facebook and then reading something about nothing. I'm distracted and all the time in the world has gone now and it's a dramatic rush to do something suddenly important but with no consequence whatsoever.

And I know Mum is doing all this too, in her way, because Dad isn't there either and I'm a little short of energy to be much use right now.

I have hidden my way through and denied this relentlessly awful Christmas so much that I don't even hear 'Fairytale Of New York' and I don't hear 'Last Christmas'.

However, there was one evening of relief. Patrick's friend Hannah organised another online quiz and as well as being rollicking good fun, it was again fabulous to feel the connection of so many, near and far, in our treasured community. Feeling a tiny bit more hopeful and positive I turned to 'When The Thames Froze' by Smith & Burrows — it is an entirely perfect winter song:

At the end of Christmas day
When there's nothin' left to say
The years go by so fast
Let's hope the next beats the last
So tell everyone that there's hope in your heart.

2021

January

Ah well, if Christmas was tough, and New Year's Eve was a desolate, empty one to hide deep inside the duvet well before midnight, now it's January and we have the anniversaries to cope with.

Despite the date, we keep telling ourselves that it's just another day, that it's just twenty-four more hours, but there are mantras and there is pretence. The one year-anniversary is indeed just a day, but its significance is unmistakable. There's nowhere to hide now. Patrick had collapsed late on the 14th, and was confirmed as dead just after midnight on the 15th. If there's solace, it's that we are able to share private family time late on the 14th, and remember more publicly on the 15th, the 'official date'.

At around 10:45pm on the evening of 14th January, the time Patrick collapsed, Kate, Niamh, Euan and I huddled around a small fire in the garden. We are warmed by our memories, our love and our resilience in getting this far. It is a heartbreaking, tender, proud moment. Kate lets off a single, spectacular firework and as it fizzles and crackles and bangs, in between our tears and sadness, we feel a shared sense of defiance.

We have worked on the premise, the hope, that the more we plan for the 15th, the more ok it will be. Unprepared, we'll get a huge shock. Christmas was planned to the minute, new year too, was, just, survivable.

This isn't, it's the worst day.

It's never-ending, it's cold, it's miserable, it's tense.

Some people, and it's a recurring theme that becomes starkly obvious on anniversaries and special occasions, don't know what to say, so they say nothing. Otherwise there are acts of beauty and kindness from friends and relations that are incredibly touching. Without them, who can possibly conceive how difficult this would be? We have asked people to make decorations to adorn Patrick's tree. The response is simply incredible. The time and love and attention and creativity that has gone into each one is humbling. There is huge justification in putting them in a box, and saving them for our miserable rainy day, when we can be reminded of the support we have. But no, these are to go with Patrick, his tree, and to weather and age and fade with nature, and to be. And each time we look into the garden in the days, weeks and months ahead, there they are.

***

Even after these touching displays of — very literally — remembrance, I'm still worried about Patrick being forgotten. How does that impact me? Motivate me? It was one of the first things I felt, when he died, *don't forget him!* and it still terrifies me. What if nobody came to his memorial service? What if people just forgot to come? It was a Friday after all, they'd be thinking about the weekend, be too busy. And I am here, a year later, still acutely aware that memories will start to fade, his friends will move on, become adults, they'll fade away. I think of Nick, and 1993 and Manchester, and never telling his family that yes, yes I remember, yes I care, yes I've valiantly traipsed up and down those cemetery paths, yes, I've fairly frequently visited his tree in Swansea.

And as I walk I feel that impossible sensation, that Patrick is absolutely with me, alongside me, while at exactly the same time I find myself clutching and striving and reaching to remember him better, to prevent him sliding away. Surely this is why I need to write about him, to tell stories, to share and to implore you, plead with you, not to forget him. Sliding away into photographs and witty anecdotes and cushions and as a bloody tree. No! I can't bear to believe he'll just become a fuzzy memory, a star that sparkled, and then ... didn't. I need Patrick to be a living, breathing, arguing, loving, laughing, debating, kicking, screaming part of me. I'm not sure what that means, but by now it's raining. I pull my hood up, fasten the zip higher, breathe the cold January air and march on towards today's ten thousand steps.

I get home and President Biden is being inaugurated. At the moment of his greatest achievement, he's a father remembering the two children he's lost.

Naomi Christina Biden.

Joseph Robinette Biden.

It's a minor detail in the magnitude of this immense Washington day, but here in small town Witney, it inspires. If he can do it, so can I. America's youth poet laureate Amanda Gorman then begins "*When day comes, we ask ourselves where can we find light in this never-ending shade?*" I'm together with Kate, Niamh and Euan, we stare in awe at the telly, desperate for light in our own never-ending shade.

We've been without Patrick for a year now. It's been torture. We've suffered enough.

***

Come the evening, come lockdown lower-league TV viewing. Swindon lose in quite pathetic fashion to a fluid, attractive and hungry Plymouth team. Withering and embarrassed, I stay tuned on local radio for a debilitating post-match interview with our manager John Sheridan. At one point he's asked:

What's gone wrong and what are you going to do to put it right?

Sheridan was a magician in his own playing days, a gifted member of the boys in green diaspora, a hero who could make the ball talk and sing. He was wonderful to watch. More recently and pertinently, sadly his parents both died over Christmas. However sympathetic that makes me feel, his football team, my football team, are useless. He responds:

So I can only I can only go by what's going on. I always think we'll score goals, I think attacking wise but we need to be switched on it's not about ... the second goal is a absolute ... from a this is, we've took a, whatever we've tried to put a ball in a box it should be a better cross breaks down ...

I feel energy seeping out of me as I try to make sense of what he's trying to say. I have another five minutes of the interview to listen to; our players have to listen to it each day, make sense of it, and then somehow weave it into a strategy, a compelling game plan, executed to mesmerising perfection.

We're second from bottom.

Sheridan has managed four clubs in a year and three of them for less than a dozen games. He is enduring shattering personal loss. Surely he should be on compassionate leave. It defies logic as to how he can be expected to organise, motivate and lead a professional football club when, from my perspective, he is manifestly unable to form coherent sentences.

Today, I have absolutely no idea why my son died and I have no idea why John Sheridan is manager of Swindon Town Football Club.

***

All year, there's been such an intense focus in our loss and grieving for Patrick that sometimes it feels like we've given Dad a raw deal. I feel horribly guilty that we've not mourned him. I'm aware too that this may come back to slap me around the face at some point. I was so close to Dad, he was fit and strong, and he went so quickly, quietly taking the back door. He wasn't there any more. We've missed his calm, presence, and humour. Our gardens have missed him.

Kate reminds me every time I attempt some DIY that Dad would have done it quicker, better, and unquestionably with rather more enthusiasm. Mum has coped increasingly admirably and independently, but their house is empty without him.

His ashes were stored in Patrick's room, among the cushions, part-sorted school books and football medals. We'd agreed a plan to scatter half of them and just needed the *worst* weather to help make it happen. The day came, or was sent to us, perfectly, on a Saturday the day before the anniversary of his passing. Kate, Mum and I wrapped up, drove to West Witney sports field and faced the eye of the storm. The sleet was horizontal, the wind howled, the ground was flooded, the 'feels like' temperature was minus four.

Fantastic. This is exactly what I wanted. This is how I'd pictured it. It was bitter and brutal.

There was a Dad playing football in a makeshift goal with a young boy. Was this parental cruelty or inspirational coaching? I saw myself in that moment, both as a demanding, desperate lad and a demanding Dad. This is the irresistible lure of the moving ball. We photograph the fading Sunshine On Leith sticker on the lockup, and pick our way through the puddles on the tree-lined avenue. It was a truly vicious day, and we struggled to peel open the first box, then we started to scatter, scatter, scatter. Into the deep pools of water, around trees, careful not to stand downwind. It was a relieving, almost exhilarating experience. It was freedom, and it was right. We scattered, we sprinkled. We continued through Deer Park woods, sprinkling here and there on the fresh wood chip of the parkrun route, tentatively negotiating the steep slope and miraculously all staying upright.

We trudged through the mud back into the West Witney field; it was a desolate scene of waterlogged pitches and as the sleet turned to snow, the clubhouse was barely visible through it all. The water crept through my boots, socks and found now defenceless and soon sharply stinging toes. We scattered some more, in each of the goalmouths, first Mum, then me. As I shook the box to empty, the ashes blew back and caught me sharply in my face. My eyes stung, as the last remnants of Dad accidentally got absorbed into me.

Maybe it was symbolic, meant to be, a sign of his humour and mischief. Also though, it hurt, and it was flipping cold. We shivered our relief into the car, and drove silently home.

Later, we attempted a bonfire in the garden, to pause again and think and remember and celebrate him some more. It was soaking wet, miserable and futile. The smoke choked and the few flames stalled. He'd have done a better job, got the fire crackling and leaping, and he'd have whooped his pleasure, cupping cold coarse hands together in rich satisfaction. But we couldn't make a magic fire, so we went back inside, and had a cup of tea and a piece of cake instead.

He'd have appreciated that too.

February

I'm sat at Patrick's desk, trying to write. The words are coming more slowly now. I torture myself trying to understand why. Is it my energy? My love? My memories? Where are they when I need them? It feels as if each word has to be wrestled onto the page, twisting, turning and contorting as it forms, finally settling into place, uneasily sitting next to the others.

The words are staring back at me with disdain, provoking neighbours and taunting me, their parent.

So what are you going to do about it?

I am being bullied and threatened by my own words.

Patrick's room has undergone gradual and sensitive change. After an impossibly long time, his duvet was removed and the bed dismantled. It's another heartbreaking full stop.

You can't come back now Patrick because you have no bed.

There are slats, a mattress, some screws. It's just constituent parts now. Taken apart, left on the landing at the top of the stairs, waiting for someone to collect it, reassemble it and bring it back to meaning.

That's how I feel. Bones, flesh, brain separated, waiting at the top of the stairs, wondering whether I'll be taken to the tip or with fresh life to come. Now the bed has been replaced by a low blue sofa. I look at it pitifully and can't imagine sitting on it, but what else do we do with the space? Kate has put it together herself, partly because putting a cheap self-assembly sofa together is useful, but mainly because it takes some time up in the never-ending emptiness of a lockdown half term. There are no dashes to family in the north, or a couple of days' break, no memories to make. The photo albums will feature nothing from February 2021 half term, another blank page.

The room is Patrick's Place now, a neon sign says so, so it must be.

The best we can do in there is to lose ourselves in memories and cry or do yoga or pilates or watch the football or bury ourselves in polyester covered cushions made out of Patrick's sports kits. A retro adidas tracksuit, the black and red of Henry Box school, an England training top, an old Swindon away shirt. They're sat there, individually reimagined, carefully stitched with Patrick tags. Lovingly handcrafted yet completely devoid of the life, the laughter and the body that once filled them. It's an ordinary place and an extraordinary place.

There's something about yearning, the need for Patrick to be remembered, Dad's life too of course, but it feels that when people die at roughly the expected age that there's a sense of normality, we'll remember him this way of course, a good life well lived. With Patrick it's different and I'm sat writing, fighting with unforgiving words, terrified he'll be forgotten.

I suppose it's a gut reaction that the only way I could make any sense of Patrick dying was to take every positive that he gave us, to treat his life as a gift for us to use, to make the very most of our lives as a consequence.

Hey, we have to celebrate what we did have rather than what we don't, it's better to have loved and lost, live everyday as if it's your last, don't go to sleep with grudges and all that. Every bloody day. While simultaneously trying to move on, looking backwards without going backwards. Going forwards. It's a difficult balance, but there's literally no choice.

And perhaps that's why I've written this story: to look backwards, to ensure that as long as one copy survives somewhere, Patrick (and Dad too) can not be forgotten. Their lives and stories and joys can be remembered and celebrated, and discovered maybe by people who never knew them. And that I, in some sense, can then go forwards.

And that while I'm at it, don't pause, don't stop, don't think, don't moan, just go on and on and on being positive, productive, cheerful and pretending, because I'm so fearful of what will happen, what might crash down if I hesitate or doubt for an extra second.

Do you understand that?

No?

See, I said the words were fighting me.

***

Patrick's first anniversary has passed and those tree decorations remain a loving source of energy, some cherished sparkle in the bare winter garden. I am so thankful for each one and ignore the cold and biting wind to touch them, read them, feel them and be humble and grateful for the time and thought spent creating them. Each of those decorations took a unique twist on Patrick, on what he meant to them, and how they remembered him now. Some of them are beautifully crafted works of art, some of them are simple, they each mean the same to me. The winter has started to take its toll, and they are now returning to a more natural wooden state, albeit blurred by ink and tears. When darkness comes, a little later into the grey afternoons now, if I'm feeling OK, the tree lights up, sparkling its truth as if saying *this is Patrick. I am here. I am with you.* There are days when I'm not OK, and I can't see the tree. The lights don't shine, it's remote, just out there in the neverending darkness somewhere, nowhere.

Somehow, amid the turmoil of the past year, Niamh has completed her Masters degree and graduated. She's lost her brother and Grampy, been locked down, straddled lives in Sheffield and home and only scored herself a bloody distinction. So if you've yearned to know more about the Belfast punk scene between 1977 and 1982, Niamh's your go-to expert. With Covid getting in the way of ceremonies, her graduation pictures are a little unusual. Our friend Paul from Fat Lils was embarking on a photography project where he took domestic pictures from friends' gardens, at nightime. Very literally, from the outside looking in. So that's why he was shuffling around in the dark, while we, dressed in fineries and clinking champagne flutes, chatted away pretending that this was a usual Monday evening in the Walsh stead. I loved the results as I loved what Niamh had achieved, and completed, during such a tumultuous time.

As the first signs of daffodils appear and as buds begin to form, the decorations hang from the tree, entwined with the lights, part of the tree, part of the story, a precious part of us and of Patrick and his ashes in the stone pot just inches below.

When they come, the waves of grief are still so all-consuming and overwhelming. I literally want everything to stop. I cannot go on. It is utterly impossible to describe how much I miss Patrick, his noise, touch, his sense, his just being. Swindon have won, fortuitously and thankfully, it's a Saturday and the house should see into the evening with joy and laughter. I can almost feel him celebrating. Yes, it was only Crewe. Yes, I still daren't look at the dismal league table. I have to go on because I can't take any steps backwards. If I even contemplate it, what else will crumble and envelop me. So again, I can go on, because I have to.

Swindon proved capable of losing to just about everyone: Shrewsbury, Portsmouth, Sunderland, Oxford, Accrington, Gillingham in despairingly quick succession. The team is crumbling and hurtling through ignominious defeat after defeat. If promotion (even with an asterisk) felt like World War One in the trenches, with every single point chiselled out of perseverance and endeavour, then this impending relegation is like a nuclear explosion. A flash, and we're vapourised. There are question marks over the future of the club and chairman Lee Power pops up to spread a doom and gloom message, fuelling fears that losing six games in as many weeks is the least of our problems.

***

The rugby's on the telly. This in itself is something of a novelty, in that I've possibly watched more televised football during lockdown than in the rest of my life put together. Football, stripped bare of pomp and fans, is barely recognisable. Jock Stein knew: Football without fans is nothing. But that nothing is still our nothing, our football. And now it's rugby's blue riband, the Six Nations and there's no one there, and literally, what is the point?

More poignantly, Dad's not here to make these remarks to, so what is the point? He would not agree. We'd have had about three pints, warming up on a cold winter's eve. The pub would be quieter now, those sporting England, Ireland, Scotland or Wales colours would be or should be heading for home. They've had a good day, a couple of Six Nations games offering companionship, identity, history, rules they don't understand, and a lot of drinking. Unsteady, swaying now, and boring drunk, I try to avoid engaging with them and talk to Dad, and I'd say, *rugby, what is the point?* As football has become ever sharper, more skilful and artistic, professional rugby has headed the opposite way, towards science not art.

I'd say it's relentlessly dull: bigger and bigger blokes repeatedly smashing into each other until one lot capitulates. It's as turgid and slow as one of those World War One battles, and as pointless too. I'm being provocative now, grinning as I take another sip, slipping away from the opinion of someone who watches five games of rugby a season (World Cup not included) and has had twelve pints, moaning about the intricacies of an England line-out. Dad will offer balance and remind me about the great days we've had watching rugby together.

I'll remember that he cared enough about rugby to name one of his fish O'Driscoll after that mesmerising hat-trick of tries in Paris. And then we'll have another drink and we'll remember our days, occasional days following Munster or London Irish. Of Peter 'The Claw' Clohessy and Big Bob Casey. And what I remember, is what I'll always remember, is that rugby doesn't really matter. It may not be pointless, but it doesn't matter. It's not football.

We'll remember those four Munster European Cup finals. Dad did each of them between 2000 and 2008 and I learned a life lesson: don't ever let work get in the way of stuff that really, properly matters.

We had tickets for Munster's first European final at Twickenham, against Northampton in 2000. I was working on a heady and demanding work proposal with European partners; a business-transforming opportunity delivering long-term shared destiny, strategic relationships and profitability or something. Unfortunately, I just had to be in a meeting on the Saturday of the final. And so it was. Mum had my ticket and accompanied Dad for a day out on the train, wearing a silly jesters hat, treated to an enthralling match. I was holed up in strategic, destiny-building self-importance in a hotel across town in Heathrow. When I saw their glow, heard their stories, tasted the disappointment, and laughed at the hat, I knew I'd made the wrong call. Sure, it was only rugby, but it should have been me there with Dad, enjoying the atmosphere along the Thames, the tension at Twickers, bristling at the indignity of narrow and preventable defeat.

The work project was soon dead, abandoned within a couple of weeks.

Some mistakes we make again, some we don't. Munster made a rather fortunate habit of reaching European finals played at the Millennium Stadium in Cardiff, the greatest of venues in the most fabulous location.

Dad and I were always keen to pay our glory hunting dues and before the Leicester final we particularly enjoyed the pre-match opportunity to mingle, socialise, and take in the atmosphere. Even so, sat way up in the heavens at the back of the top tier, and not understanding the peculiarities of the rules, we could still spot Neil Back's dastardly sleight of hand in the scrum which literally handed glory to Leicester. Even as part-time supporters, it was a tough one to take, only soothed slightly by a further stop or two on St Mary Street, before taking the train home.

The time we did see Munster win together, in 2008, was entirely wonderful. We took a minibus from the local pub, organised by our amiable landlord Nick, and parked near the University in Cardiff. It was an area I was happily familiar with, wide avenues, and sturdy Georgian stone buildings. The buildings of a confident, compact and at ease capital city. Cardiff does these days so well. The castle sits unobtrusively yet undoubtedly still dominating. Years later, I'd be back with Euan and Patrick, sampling the atmosphere, the day before Real Madrid walloped Juventus in the Champions League final. Together, we revelled amongst the tourists, took a boat along the Taff, grabbed freebies by the handful, desperately wished we had tickets for the match, posed for pictures by the dozen, watched washed-up has-beens showing that actually, actually, they'd still got it in the legends beach football at the fan zone down at Cardiff Bay. We were part of it. We laughed, and smiled our way through it all. And through it all, we checked our phones for any news of Swindon's next manager.

This day though, was a Munster day, with barely any fans from Toulouse. Munster men and women of every county swarmed the city streets. Fifty, sixty, seventy thousand? It was extraordinary, an incredible support. And if that was outside, inside the stadium, this fabulous, fabulous sporting arena, the fervour, with the roof closed too, was utterly intense. A red heat, and thousands upon thousands of beating red hearts, an exhilarating coming together of sporting hope and desperation. It was pulsating, a privilege to be there, and for me, to be there with my Dad.

The intensity and emotion of the occasion was punctured somewhat by the spectator next to me, a genuine and intelligent neutral rugby fan. Warming to my own red Munster jersey, he completely mistook me for an actual living breathing Munster fan. And to be fair, sure why shouldn't he? Now he was asking me about players who were injured, or some of the provincial games, or, or something else. I didn't know. It was as embarrassing as it was chastening: I pretended to be too drunk to understand him, and then, once defeated, withdrew and ignored him.

Glory supporters, we're all the same.

Munster won, as far as I could tell, by shoving the ball up someone else's red jersey and hiding it for about twenty minutes. Nobody cared about that, and nobody who cared less for Munster could begrudge this moment. There was an astonishing outpouring of elation and catharsis, of Fields and Fields and Fields of Athenry, of tears and pauses to remember all those who weren't here with us. I hugged Dad like everyone else was hugging each other, and jumped up and down and sang and shouted in all the right places. We were part of it, and those moments, for those moments, rugby mattered.

Mum has kept Dad's old Munster shirt. It's still hung up in the wardrobe. It's keeping safe and savouring those memories. I can almost smell and feel them, and those late night pub provocations too. They absolutely mattered to him. It's too big for me.

It'll always be too big for me.

***

Dealing with the sudden and unexplained death of a child isn't just hard for the rather obvious reason that Patrick isn't here anymore.

But why isn't he here? And if he can die suddenly, well what about Niamh or Euan or Kate.

Or me.

It's a scenario Bruce Springsteen has only gone and opened his latest album with.

Footsteps cracklin' on a gravel road
Stars vanish in a sky as black as stone
One minute you're here
Next minute you're gone

It's tender, understated, heartfelt, creaking with sorrow and magnificent. Oh Bruce, why do you do this?

One minute you're here
Next minute you're gone

What about me?

There is the ever-present fear that because we don't have a reason, we are powerless to stop it from happening again. It seems impossible that in this day and age science is unable to give us an answer.

There is a feeling that it might be easier — or at least enable a focus or direction — to have something or someone to blame. Instead, there is constant looking back and wondering if we missed anything. Did Patrick make complaints we didn't hear? Did he feel pain he didn't share? For us, nothing. Just nothing.

So we'll take meaning in white feathers and robins and mystical signs. Or a cereal bowl in a documentary, or when Euan's door keeps closing mysteriously, or orbs on photos, or a Christmas decoration smashing randomly, or Regan's picture falling down, or Alexa joining in at bizarre 'Patrick' moments. Or when a picture of Patrick crashes down while we're watching Swindon toiling against Bristol Rovers and I bring that picture to sit with us on the sofa and we win 1-0. Or every ginger cat.

The angels took him for their own. We'll take meaning in anything to give us something.

Patrick's initial post-mortem was inconclusive and after further tests, including toxicology, no reason could be found and that his death was categorised as SADS (Sudden Arrhythmogenic Death Syndrome) was just a different way of saying nothing. His heart stopped working but we don't know why.

It's just one of those things, I suppose.

It took six long months to get an appointment at the Inherited Cardiac Condition clinic at the John Radcliffe Hospital in Oxford. We all attended together and quietly took turns to go in and be poked, prodded, measured, assessed and judged. Of course, they had already meticulously worked through our family tree and full medical histories. The NHS professionals were genuinely, scientifically interested and as with other appointments, we were taken aback at how rare our case was. How fervently we hope and wish that some learning comes from our experience, and even one fewer family has to hear what we heard, and walk out of a hospital with a plastic carrier bag full of photocopied leaflets instead of their child. As several members of my family had died prematurely, I think we all thought that if anything untoward was found it would be with me. We were taken together to a room with no windows, multiple computers, serious faces and hard chairs and as we were presented with our results, one by interminable one, we heard a new surprise.

Liam, it's not you.

Kate was diagnosed with a heart condition, dilated cardiomyopathy, that was most likely linked to Patrick's death. We all struggled to take it in while wearing masks, gulping for air and desperately trying not to cry. The cardiologist said that they needed to see Kate again, took some further blood tests and sent us home.

Most likely.

What on earth does that mean? The entirely unexpected and shattering feeling that Kate was struck with, that she may have been a cause in Patrick's dying was an impossibly awful one. Beyond the emotions soon came a practicality and need to wrestle with adapting to a life that immediately involved daily medication. Oh, and Google is most definitely not the place to spend idle time wondering after such a diagnosis.

Some months later, Kate received a phone call from the genetic counsellor to tell her that after testing the fifty-two genes known to be responsible for heart conditions there was no evidence that either her heart condition or Patrick's death were caused by a faulty gene. So, cue immediate relief that there was no link, or 'cause', or in Kate's mind, 'blame'. However, that relief was twinned with a sinking realisation that there was nowhere else to go with testing. They will keep the samples (stored at a hospital in London at our request thanks to advice from SUDC UK) for future research and maybe in five, ten, twenty years, science will have moved on and something, anything could be found. It's that or the angels again.

Meanwhile, Kate continued to have cardiac check-ups and follow the advice to reduce alcohol consumption, cut out caffeine and avoid strenuous exercise. Niamh and Euan are tested annually and we are reassured that their tests are all clear. But then, at another appointment Kate asked the consultant if they would have found anything if Patrick had had these tests. She is told no, nothing would have been found.

Again, we know nothing and there's nowhere to go. In that case, any future reassurance about the future, and what ifs, disappears.

Kate turned again to the ever-supportive SUDC UK and was told about a research project happening at New York University that we could be part of. We signed up after phone calls with Laura, the inspirational founder of SUDC and herself a bereaved mother. We have had our blood samples taken and shipped off to America in an insulated box, with colourful labels. In comparison to the fifty-two genes tested here they will test the whole exome sequencing. It all sounds fabulously clever and incredibly scientific, but it's too late for Patrick. Eventually, we will get a report for Kate and I that tells us all our genetic information, including any markers for cancers and dementia, and just maybe, a hint or clue or something about why he died.

It's a long process and we are still waiting for the report.

March

March, my favourite month, remember, ticked around again.

With no end in sight to lockdown, no spring at the end of this longest winter, there was no Cheltenham Festival to look forward to attending either. Even so, it proved a compelling, dramatic theatre to follow on television. Somehow it had never felt so personal. The television coverage was sensational. With the roar of the crowd silenced, the humanity and dignity of the jockeys, the grooms and the stable staff was amplified. The brilliance of their stories was not only exemplified by Irish dominance, it was an extraordinary Waterford-led triumph. Henry de Bromhead produced probably the greatest individual training performance ever by saddling six winners including the Champion Hurdle, the Champion Chase and the Gold Cup. As the week unfolded, I gasped at how overjoyed Dad would have been. When Ruby Walsh's analysis lauded the influence of one of uncle Maurice's old trainers and Dungarvan legend John Kiely, I turned to say to Dad — *did you hear that?*

But he didn't hear that because he wasn't there.

Dad wasn't there, but of course he was there. I had felt him beside me, within me, every step and triumph and breath of this oddest of festivals.

***

Meanwhile, Swindon Town were imploding on and off the pitch. It was also a special awareness month for SUDC, and I embarked on a typically over ambitious, almost wilfully complicated social media project. In recognition of Patrick's favourite board game 'Touring England' I shared daily, very short stories of our real travels around the country, usually watching our beloved Swindon Town. I compounded it by including a parallel Strava art element. This necessitated a small army of precious athletes throughout West Oxfordshire joining in by running or walking in planned directions to create 'letters', for example, running around Welch Way roundabout to produce an 'O'. Take a short jog down Corn Street too, and hey, you have a 'P'.

I started the tour, our stories, closest to home. We then travelled up the eastern side of the country, and back down the west. With a couple of sojourns to Scotland and then Italy, Spain and Portugal thrown in, it became an intense whirlwind of memories with forty-plus destinations, and once started, it was a bittersweet commitment to share each day in the month.

Each away day had its stories and the feedback I had from sharing them was heart-warming, although some grounds were more sourly endured.

It's a grand stadium at MK, but wasted on this awful franchise club. Each year, we say 'never again' and each year we're back; money might buy plush seats but it can't buy class. Speaking of which, last year we met up pre-match with Andy and Jill in a dilapidated pub in Bletchley, before grabbing a quick KFC at the stadium. I know which Patrick preferred!

"We suffered a freezing night over Christmas there a few years ago, survived a scarily foggy journey home ... then had a slightly worse for wear cyclist ride up the wrong side of the road and straight into the car on Newland. Luckily she was fine, but I'm not sure about the bike.

Along with the Strava art that started out as fun, I soon regretted it. It was emotionally draining.

In late 2018, Patrick was taking his first solo train journey, from Sheffield to East Midlands Parkway, and I waited a little anxiously, desperate for him to arrive. He soon appeared, bouncing and grinning, another rite of teenage passage ticked off. We parked on the banks of the River Trent, watched some squirrels playing in the autumn leaves and wandered in the rain around Trent Bridge cricket ground and Forest's stadium. Teams of rowers were bringing the river to life, as we found our way back over the bridge to Notts County. Our team could kindly be described as inconsistent, stirring discontent as they predictably fell behind. Funny old game though, and as we snatched a barely deserved win, the celebrations were as surprised as they were joyous.

I regretted it much further when Kate and Niamh pointed out that all these lovely jaunts and ditties were about boys' days out: where were they? Where were the precious memories that we'd all created together? The holidays on every sandy beach in western France, the magic green gate on the Isle of Wight, the days out exploring in London, the parks we'd picnicked in and New Year's Eve quizzes. Just how many calories could there be in an apple?

And how right they were.

I reflected. It was so conflicting. I'd started off writing about Patrick and Dad a year ago through the prism of football — and that's just how it had continued. The more I wrote, the more it felt that this could become more than an accumulation of stories: there was a possibility that I could turn these words into a football-focused book. What greater act of devotion to Patrick and Dad's passions could there be, than a permanent, written memorial? Yes, there were detours into cricket, and hurling and horse racing and music, but this was essentially a football story. It wasn't a comprehensive family history. Still, called out, with motivation drained and feeling guilty and selfish, I wished the month away, counting down the days until I could abandon my vanity project and stop writing.

A whole book was a fanciful idea anyway.

But I had committed to completing the month's tour.

***

It was ever more difficult to write, some days more than others. I cheated by including two grounds Patrick never saw.

He didn't make it to Celtic, and he didn't make it to Hibernian.

Celtic were always part of Patrick's identity. He wore their shirts from a young age, and their songs often filled our house. Whenever working in Scotland I'd bring the boys back a Celtic souvenir and one day we'd have visited together for sure.

The green and white segued into Hibernian in Edinburgh after Patrick was mesmerised by videos of their fans singing 'Sunshine On Leith' at Hampden Park.

And so began the whole Hibs story that culminated in singing that song at his memorial service. Kate, Niamh, Euan and I visited Edinburgh and the ground in August. It was both tough and uplifting at the same time, but we left stickers at the docks in Leith and at the turnstiles on Easter Road, wishing everything was different.

We saved a line from 'Sunshine On Leith' — I Will Be With You — for Patrick's stone in the Windrush cemetery.

It was on the neck of our bespoke Patrick's Place football shirts as well.

It was fun too, to include our European travels.

We were in Milan after a family holiday in Lake Como. Kate was supposed to be getting tickets for the Last Supper, but somehow we all ended up at the San Siro instead. For those of us of a particular Italia '90 vintage, it's one of the most iconic stadiums in the world.

Breathtaking and awesome, just being there was better than the game — Inter, inspired by Icardi, routinely beat Fiorentina. We were excited that we could buy beer from our seats, less excited when they ripped us off ... there certainly wasn't one left for Patrick.

Bucket list ticked, back on the tram to the beautiful city, smiles all round.

We're not that big on family heirlooms, but used to joke that the closest we got was the Barcelona cufflinks that Dad passed on to me on account of him never wearing proper shirts. He'd visited the Nou Camp with Mum in 1964, and now, our journey follows their steps for ground tours there in 2013 and 2019.

I can remember how excited I was, so goodness knows how Patrick felt a few days away from his ninth birthday. The museum, the tour, the stadium are all absolutely awe-inspiring, never mind the megastore! No trip was complete without Patrick buying a Messi 10 shirt. The history and soul of the place is simply enchanting. Pictures paint a thousand happy words and memories.

We'd have loved to have seen a game there, but it's a privilege to have been. Last time, we left Kate and Niamh waiting in the sun while we savoured every last minute. It could be a while before we're back for Swindon's Champions League visit.

Our break from Touring England found us weaving down the coast of Spain, and to Valencia.

Patrick and I left Kate to go shopping for shoes or something in this most fabulous of cities, and went to explore the Mestalla. It was another ground tour and another wonderful experience. For such a famous club, it felt welcoming, friendly and very, very proud. I'd love to go back before they move into a shiny stadium, where they'll struggle to replicate the soul and steepling splendour of this one.

We spent even more in the club shop than Kate did on shoes.

Our last day on our Iberian tour before getting the plane back to complete Touring England took us to Lisbon. Patrick worked so hard to get fit for the Henry Box sports tour in spring 2019. He absolutely loved it, spending time with friends old and new, playing a full part. They visited the Benfica ground, where funnily enough, he bought a football shirt. We'd done the same on holiday a few years earlier, another ground to half tick off.

One we did manage properly in Lisbon was Belenenses — how thrilled we were to discover they had a Europa League qualifying round against Gothenburg to play. It was leafy and low key, pre-season perfection, watching the fans, sometimes the game and enjoying the summer breeze ...

Soon, we were back in England, remembering Crawley, QPR, Fulham, Wimbledon, Brentford, Millwall and Charlton in London.

Three days to go on tour, and staying in London, from one majestic stadium to another, from the Olympic Stadium to ... Wealdstone. We parked here, sampled the pre-match atmosphere, met the world famous Wealdstone

Raider and heard his "do you want some?" battlecry ... oh and then we went to Wembley.

Patrick was lucky enough to see Swindon play three times here, unlucky enough to see us lose each one, without scoring. Imagine all that expectation, then familiar, crushing disappointment. He saw several England games, a Community Shield, an Olympic Games match between South Korea and Gabon, the vast ground packed to the rafters on a Tuesday afternoon (we missed the first twenty minutes as Kate had the tickets, unfortunately in the Tate in central London), even a non-league finals day.

He did ok, didn't he? He did love a big day out, and there's not much better than walking down Wembley Way, with hope in your heart.

There was one more London visit to come.

On 14th January, 2020, Patrick went to watch Tottenham with his brother Euan, and never came home.

I saved the best until last.

Patrick first went to the County Ground, Swindon when he was aged two. He was so scared by the Rockin' Robin mascot, that it was a wonder he ever went back, never mind another 243 times. There were wonderful times — a miraculous 5-5 draw with Sheffield United which took us to Wembley, Di Canio's ferocious winners, occasional cup victories. There were plenty of mundane times that lower-league football fans whether following red or yellow or whoever, will recognise so well. There were miserable times, seemingly stretching months without a goal, when we only went to spend family time together. But none were so happy or so optimistic as his final few months, we had our Swindon back, albeit temporarily it turned out.

Somehow the Strava art project had maintained its momentum. The engagement throughout the month was massively appreciated and inspiring. Among other phrases, we were able to use our 'letters' to raise awareness for SUDC.

And with our memories shared, our tour completed, I implored my social media friends to please remember the 'Sudden' in SUDC ... all those journeys through Burford, Lechlade, Highworth, parking in the same place, walking along Shrivenham

Road, sometimes re-enacting winning goals, meeting friends and relations, grumbling or cheering. All those things we thought would last forever. We took them, including the grumbles and the misery, and the hope that next week it might be better, for granted.

And for me, football stories dutifully and somewhat painfully shared, I could now abandon any notion of writing a book. I could stop tapping the keyboard after conjuring memories late at night and focus attention elsewhere instead.

April

I stare and stare at the football map of the world on the wall. It's hung in a simple black frame above the screen for the PlayStation in Patrick's Place. I can feel everything around me. My senses are on alert. I'm awake and imagining, willing, every nuance on call for presence, for a smell or a sign. It's always like this in here.

Today, I'm drawn and drawn again to the map. It tells me that Thomas Ravelli is the most capped Swedish player (143 appearances), that Theodore Whitmore became such a Jamaican legend after scoring two goals at the 1998 World Cup in France that he had an apple named after him, and that Angola's national stadium shares a name with Niamh's birthday. Who knew!

I love maps, am intrigued by them, their endless possibilities, how much there is to find, to learn. I thought Patrick would love this present too ... a map! About football! But no, he never mentioned it, never shared a single thing he learned from it.

Now it's just here, for moments such as this when I need to stare and stare and disappear. A world with so much within it; continents and context, history and possibilities. But mainly, just blue, the sea.

Perhaps that's how this grief feels too, a world around me containing islands, connections, masses of flavour, happenings, details, context, colour, vibrancy. But mainly blue. Mainly sea.

Mainly never-ending nothing. Deep trenches and interminable stretches of water, grief, pain, solitude, hostile waves, hidden creatures, soul crushing cold, gasping for breath, drowning, going under. Oceans, literally oceans of the stuff.

Two-thirds of footballs worldwide are manufactured in Sialkot, Pakistan. That's over forty million balls a year. Souleyman Mamam played a World Cup qualifier for Togo at the tender age of just thirteen.

Oceans of the stuff.

***

Over the course of the last year, Kate and I have attended a support group for parents facilitated by two wonderful counsellors from Helen & Douglas House — the Oxford-based charity providing support for terminally ill children and their families. It extends, fortunately for us, beyond that too, and is the world's first children's hospice to care for bereaved parents. It says everything about the society that we have collectively chosen to create, that they must fight and scrap and compete against other magnificent charities every day to find and fund the £4m required to survive each year.

Kate has had a weekly walk throughout lockdown with 'Switzerland', her care worker/guardian angel/therapy saint and very possibly friend too. The time came for that to be extended into a network with other parents, and, unable to meet face to face, our monthly sessions were all online. The first meeting was beset with anxiety, emotion and IT issues, as each family wrestled with coming to terms with yet another virtual platform. And there we were, introducing ourselves to strangers, talking about our babies and children dying. Each tale was in itself, uniformly sad and profoundly unfair and each told by stoic, heroic, loving parents. Our children ranged in age from a young baby, to Patrick, fifteen summers old, but our stories all had the same endings. We had an immediate bond, unwilling members of and participants in the Sad Parents Club.

After the first Saturday morning meeting, we were encouraged to reflect, to allow our emotions to settle and to take it easy for the weekend. Sage advice, but too late! I was meeting my precious friend Jimmy for a walk in twenty minutes and had a packed agenda to follow. For me, it wasn't perhaps the most sensible introduction, but one to learn from for the next month. As the months passed, the group bonded beyond the headline reason we were there, and offered each other valued and tender guidance and support. We became invested in one another's journeys, recognised our differences, and had each other's backs. We became a club.

One session ended in utter misery, when the intent was the absolute opposite: for us to leave with a smile. We were each encouraged to share a happy memory of our child, a reasonable enough suggestion. However, one by one, the recollection of sweet times, unburdened by what was to follow, dissolved us into tears — and once started there was little chance of that abating. We resolved, after that, to find gentler and emotionally safer ways of ending our meetings. Once that big red button in the corner of the screen was tapped, we were out of our kind Helen & Douglas House cocoon and immediately back in the real world. There was ironing to do and a late delivery from a reputable company to chase on an unhelpful online app.

In those sessions, we addressed issues and dark questions and existential motivations. We talked about navigating family and friend reactions and behaviours, about tackling anniversaries and Christmas and Mother's Day and about how we had changed, how we coped with our feelings. We shared as honestly and articulately as we possibly could, and respected our sad clubmates for it.

In the very last session, we discussed what kept us going, what drove us on, what we wanted. One of our bereaved mums, heartbroken to the bone, said:

"I just love being alive. I just love life."

It was one of the most beautiful, humble, meaningful sentences I've ever heard.

***

It had been six months since Euan and I had spent that afternoon
in a pub deep in rarest Bristol. I was mainly sipping tea, Euan
was talking to the Patrick he'd just met whose sister Lauren had
also suddenly died. All the while, they were being filmed, guided
delicately by Lindsay and Aodh from Storyvault. Now, Sudden
Death: My Sister's Silent Killer was about to be screened on
BBC1. It was a sensitive, non-sensationalist story, and an absolute
sobfest. It was probably easiest that we each watched our preview
copy privately, and were able to reflect and gather thoughts before
sharing and talking. What struck me was that while Lauren's story
was so individual, there was so much in common with our family's
grief. Little things, small nuances. It was, too, a story with football
at its heart and soul: the club who'd suffered multiple sudden death
cases, routine testing at Italian clubs, Patrick's own release through
playing, and Fabrice Muamba.

On 17th March, 2012, Muamba, playing for Bolton
Wanderers against Tottenham at White Hart Lane, suffered a
cardiac arrest. His heart stopped for seventy-eight minutes.
Muamba recovered sufficiently to be released from hospital one
month later. And here he was, back at Tottenham's stadium
nine years beyond, the miracle who lived to tell the tale to the
documentary's Patrick. I was proud and in awe of how his family
had been filmed as the central characters in the film, and proud
of Euan for being himself. His short part was lauded by all who
commented, those Bristol pub scenes of two heartbroken boys were
candid and maybe even cathartic.

***

It's just a domestic garden, but being at home I can see so much
there's so much life here — not all at once, but there's life. Every day
of this spring, I notice a little more green in the garden. The silver
birch tree cut back in the autumn is coming to life. Daffodils have
bloomed. The apple and pear trees planted for the children are

beginning to stir. The plants that Kate has tendered are spreading roots, the wild flowers brightening by the day. The grass grows lush and demands more and more attention. The sturdy holly and Patrick's tree with decorations, weathered into its being now. Life goes on. Frogs, oblivious to the pond having long disappeared. On summer evenings to come, there'll be busy hedgehogs too. A watchful red kite, circles, surveying it all. The residents and daily visitors, the pigeons, chaffinches, mice and squirrels go about their daily routines as we do ours. At dusk, it'll be the bats and when nightime comes, we hear the piercing cry of foxes. We are grateful to see occasional tourists, a buzzard, an heron and each is part of this new spring.

At the heart of the garden, our garden, our spring, are the robins.

Life goes on.

May

Alan McLoughlin, Macca, hero of Wembley, Belfast, Genoa, hero of mine, had posted that he was ill with cancer. I was sad, but heartened by the huge banner placed on the empty Stratton Bank for the Pompey game. I was gladdened further by the charity game for Prospect House that was arranged: the footballing community was pulling together. I wanted to share something that I'd written about him, for him to know how special he was and thought it would be a companion piece to the game, a gentle reflection while he recovered. I'd add my two penn'orth to the pot and hopefully help him to smile.

Life got in the way and, deterred by that weekend's social media blackout, I held off finishing it.

He was still my hero, he could wait.

In what was left of the real world, Swindon Town's season had indeed fallen apart. From consistently dreadful on the pitch, to utterly rotten off it, it was hard to know which was worse: the embarrassment and immediacy of weekly thrashings; or the longer-term fear for the future survival of the club. Lee Power's characteristic cheeriness had long given way to a foreboding chill. Our best player and only genuine asset had been sold to pay the bills the next month. We had more than being stuffed by fellow strugglers Wimbledon to worry about. If there was one solace, it was that the spectacular reversal of last season's fortunes was still being played out in front of empty stadiums; the toxicity and stench of a club being run aground was steaming enough online. John Sheridan resigned as manager with relegation confirmed, his tenure as disastrous as many predicted, only to be temporarily replaced by his hapless accomplice, Tommy Wright. With the season shattered, insider accounts soon exposed the depth of the shambles.

There was no manager, assistant manager or indeed, even anyone able to professionally manage the departure of out of contract players, most of whom couldn't get away quickly enough. Rumblings around the ownership of the club were exacerbated by the silence of Lee Power. He, along with previous partners Michael Standing and Gareth Barry, along with the club itself, were charged by the FA with breaching funding and ownership regulations. Power also failed to overturn an injunction preventing him from selling the club to an obscure American company for an improbable-sounding £7.5 million. Wright was charged by the FA in relation to earlier convictions for bribery while he was at Barnsley. The groundsman was convicted of drink driving. There was minimal dialogue with fans — our goodwill in waiving refunds for season tickets had of course funded the club through the season — never mind there being any season tickets available for the next season. More gory speculation suggested sponsors were abandoning the club, and that kit and other suppliers wouldn't touch us with the proverbial bargepole.

Indeed, if there was a bargepole, it could have played centre half. It could have improved the team, it could have propped the club up.

There was no bargepole. Swindon Town was falling down, falling down. Bye, bye Swindon.

***

On 4th May, Alan McLoughlin died of cancer, aged fifty-four.

***

On 27th May, it was Patrick's seventeenth birthday. Despite ongoing Covid restrictions, we were determined to do something, anything to be with our community. We were keen to be social and to show off our survival, resilience, perhaps some defiance. By we, I mean Kate and I. As a family, dealing with our grief is often a draining, individual experience. We will rarely feel the same things at the same time, hence one person's need to reach out and be social will conflict with another's need to be private and reflective. It means agreeing on and organising the smallest thing can be fraught and tense.

Patrick's birthday isn't a small thing.

Kate and I plough on with arranging an open house for the afternoon, and wish upon lucky stars for a sunny day. Hey, we want to see people, we want to say thank you for your support, we want to share homemade chocolate cake and make endless cups of tea.

Mostly, really, we're saying: don't forget us, don't forget Patrick.

It is a calm, suitably sunny spring day. There is a freshly mown lawn and the garden blossoms with the optimism of spring and hints that this year the trees will bear fruit and sumptuous order will prevail. We have balloons in many colours and cakes in different shapes and SUDC posters and carefully crafted signs with our Patrick's Place heart logo. The kettle is soon humming and visitors come and come. Old connections are renewed and new ones are established. Every chair in the garden is taken, and there is a poignant, cherished buzz as people catch up. Mindful of being restricted to thirty visitors, my heart flutters on counting twenty-nine — but that's the maximum we get to. We hover around that number and later count more than sixty dear friends and family who've visited through the afternoon. We've waited so long to do this. Cakes are appreciated and devoured. I hear talk of recipes and hopes of summer holidays. There's no respite for the kettle.

Front and centre are Patrick's friends, sat together on the lawn. At first, a semi-circle of boys and a semi-circle of girls.

Soon, just a circle.

A circle of Patrick's dearest, with the dog enjoying unexpected attention right in the middle of it all. They are sharing iced buns, his favourite. He would have been in his element. For us, this simple sight is the most welcome and beautiful one imaginable.

To all intents and purposes, it's been a glorious occasion, a celebratory get together and an opportunity to look forward as summer and possibility beckon. It's been delicately stage managed and carefully crafted. Our last guests are nudged on their way.

Kate, Niamh, Euan and I hide the reality.

We're exhausted, shattered, divided on whether we should have done it and how. We're overloaded on sugar and caffeine and no-one wants to walk the dog.

Hey, *happy birthday Patrick*.

We're here and Patrick isn't.

Euan and I ended the evening sitting on the edge of the road, crying in each other's arms at 2am. It took us an hour and a half to walk half a mile back from the pub we'd taken evening refuge in.

Summer

I'd already discovered that the best way of keeping Patrick's memory alive was to write about him. To create something that I could read in twenty years, and to relive and cherish him. The feedback on the writing I'd shared had been uplifting and motivational for me. And if it would be football and sport-focused and not a fully inclusive or representative family history, then so be it. Kate and Niamh understood that, and if they didn't, I would stop. So I resolved to start writing again.

At least it was something. What else could I do?

In between arranging lockdown-compliant nights out and occasional running companionship, Rupert was also undertaking a daunting writing mission. As novices, we provoked and inspired each other in turns towards our very, very distant and optimistic seventy to ninety thousand-word targets. Did cul-de-sac count as three words, or just one? He asked what my 'book' was called and I had no idea. Soon after, I heard Nena's song on the radio and '99 Red Balloons' became more than an earworm. I felt a belonging I didn't quite understand. It made me think of vapour trails and connections and Wembley finals and a sense of loss. Curious to this emotional pull as the very words twisted around my head and tugged at my heartstrings, I wondered if they did actually mean anything.

I found a definition: *Red Balloons can signify how fragile love and happiness can be — especially the ease with which it is burst.*

My resolution was confirmed.

I was writing a book.

It had to be called 'Red Balloons'.

***

It's been a tortuous summer on Planet Swindon Town Football Club. If there is a club of course. As far as we can tell, Lee Power seems to have left the building. If there is a building. It's left to fans groups to stitch together what's going on, and even more improbably, to galvanise some fight and hope in what's left of the fanbase. There was a new manager, John McGreal, for a week or two, but he scarpered. The court shenanigans rumble interminably on. The sun is sometimes shining, the pubs and restaurants are open, and there's a semblance of normality in the rest of existence.

If I can't be bothered to properly try to understand what's going on, I know that in all likelihood, precious few will be.

And those that actually have the motivation, inclination and determination to tangibly do something about it, well they're going to be even more precious still. There are occasional glimmers of hope, and keen rumours as a minor investor with major plans, Clem Morfuni, issues a battle cry, a manifesto, a load of promises. From Australia. While this is encouraging, to weary old cynics like me, saying the right things is rather different to doing them. Sure, it's easy for Mr Morfuni, with no discernible link or motives to so desperately wish to pour millions of his own hard-earned Aussie dollars into the STFC black hole, to talk of community and sustainability and sunlit uplands.

It's easy for him to say that, I thought, as it's not his club hurtling towards oblivion. Once this implodes, he'll be out of town and back on the beach in Sydney before the *Swindon Advertiser* memorial special mourning the liquidation of Swindon Town Football Club has hit the shelves.

Equally, the supporters' trust team at TrustSTFC did a magnificent job of distilling the complexities and sharing concise updates, rallying and growing its membership in the process. However, the timebomb was ticking. Every other club was parading new signings, fine tuning their systems, enjoying that sense of summer optimism, even selling season tickets. Our one remaining asset, Scott Twine, signed for that loathsome franchise in Milton Keynes, and another footballing part of me died.

Do you know what footballing oblivion looks like? Maybe it's being less than three weeks away from the start of the football league season with six professionals, no manager, no coaching team, no kit, no financial management, no discernible chairman, no income and no bloody hope. The remaining staff aren't being paid.

It's when your pre-season schedule has been binned, with fixtures against supportive local non-leagues sides fulfilled by playing the youth team. It's a once proud fanbase, now anxious, divided, unsure and in the utter absence of certainty or development or news turning in on itself on increasingly rancorous social media outlets. There are published fixtures, starting with Scunthorpe United away, followed by Carlisle United at home, but no likelihood that we'll fulfil them, never mind a means of buying tickets to actually watch them. Clem Morfuni is surely our only hope.

It's thinking, *I'm glad Dad's not here to see this.*

It's thinking, *this would be breaking Patrick's heart.*

That's my oblivion.

On 11th July, Mike Spearman died. Mike had lived until he was ninety-two and had been a popular chairman and president of the club. He'd signed Jan Åge Fjørtoft, and was still actively following the Town, still championing the Academy teams, until his late eighties. Late eighties! Each of us will have our own arc of support, a journey that might last a few games, a few hundred perhaps. But thousands! For most, there comes a time, a life change, a circumstance, boredom, a crooked owner, a frustration, and we drift quietly away, still checking the scores, drifting, drifting, drifting, checking out.

Mike never checked out.

More personally, as a fellow Witney resident, he made sure I checked in. With crowds dipping below two thousand in the miserable 83/84 season, he'd pick me up in his impossibly glamorous white Mercedes, and deposit me safely in the North Stand. When going to away matches, Mike, immaculately dressed, usually with a pipe on the go, always knew that a better pub was just around the next corner. Over the next decades, he wore his disdain for some of the boardroom charlatans who succeeded him well. He'd divulge just enough gossip to avoid being aloof, and he supported his club, our club, through every occasional strain of thick and an awful lot of thin.

***

It's the afternoon of 20th July. Tonight, a Swindon XI, any old eleven I guess, are due to play the annual pre-season friendly at Swindon Supermarine.

After an interminable period of scepticism, doom-mongering, and desperation too, news breaks suddenly and jubilantly that Clem Morfuni has been confirmed as the new owner of Swindon Town Football Club.

I'm working, of course I am, but verify the news through reading the press statement on every available platform across every outlet. On Twitter, on the Town End forum, there is joy unconfined. There are metaphorical jubilees and hypothetical open-topped bus tours, this is the real deal and this is what sheer waves of relief actually means.

I don't cry, because I do enough of that anyway. But if I did, I'd surf those tears of joy all the way to Supermarine.

Even so, even without the tears and the surfing, it's a contemplative, emotional drive down the A361. I'm alone, and that in itself, is very much not right. I'm positive, hopeful too —

I can't change the past and what I've lost — but I have to find ways of looking forward. Suddenly, I can be a football fan, and dream again. I can imagine glory-filled evenings, last-minute winners, a charge towards promotion. I can temper all that, and quietly wish for a self-sufficient, sustainable, community-based club. Just like Clem's promised. That would do.

I park, pretty atrociously, on the verge, and there's no one there to chide me for it. I straighten the car, straighten myself and head for the ground. Inside, there's no Red Arrow flypast, no fireworks, no red balloons. There is, though, an excitable murmur of friends catching up and sharing the good news, smiling. This is what optimism looks like. As a mixture of the loyal professionals, Academy players and a smattering of trialists take to the field, there is special, heartfelt recognition of Steve Mildenhall. Our erstwhile goalkeeping coach has fulfilled a multitude of roles through the summer, most certainly not in the job description, and clearly deserves the immense credit he's receiving. It's a touching moment.

I've found a quiet bit of barrier to observe from, and lean on. In front of me, the press photographer is stationed, painstakingly piecing his craft together between sporadic bursts of action. The murmur grows and gentle applause ripples, Mexican Wave style around the ground. It's evident that the rumours are true: not only is Mr Clem Morfuni in the country, he's here at Swindon Supermarine, now. He's making his way slowly around the perimeter of the pitch, acknowledging well-wishers with smiles and waves as he goes.

He's coming my way.

Good luck Clem, I say, when it's my turn, and shake his hand. When scrolling through Twitter the next day, I see that the handshake moment was hazily captured by an onlooker, and there, I think, that's what optimism looks like. On the pitch, our scratched together team scrub up fairly well. Anthony Grant, the spiritual leader of our asterisked championship winning team makes a popular and surprise appearance, and I quite like the look of a quirky goalscoring trialist called Harry McKirdy. Of course there are other trialists I'd happily drive back to their non-league resting places, and we barely see or hear of them again.

At last though, at last, we can look forward to cheering on or occasionally moaning at a team of footballers in red doing their best on a rectangle of green. We just need a few more of them, but that can wait a day or two, although not too many please.

The league season starts in two weeks.

The following Tuesday was Mike Spearman's funeral. Sat next to my uncle Jasper, listening intently to Mike's son Paul's eulogy, hearing new stories while knowing there were a million more too, I'm struck by the sheer homeliness, friendliness; the heart and soul of this club. Mike has embodied these qualities over many years. We have a genuinely small, warm football community to treasure.

It's not just results and league tables and lists and nefarious owners. It's friends, family, adventures, stories, memories, it's us. It's a funeral after all, so of course I feel reflective, but what a life lived, and what a humble honour to represent Swindon Town so vividly, so actually. After the service, we're sheltering ourselves from the July drizzle, and I find myself standing with Clem, and Rob Angus, his new CEO. A CEO who's a fan — and not just a fan, but one coming straight from helping steer TrustSTFC so magnificently through this crisis. We're admiring the flowers, the deep red of the roses, the summer white lilies, waiting for one of the fantastic new home shirts to adorn Mike's coffin. I say something ham-fisted and earnest to Clem about this new privilege bestowed on him. About this opportunity he has to now embody our community, to build a Swindon Town that we deserve. We talk for a few minutes while the untimely shower blows through. He smiles, he's engaging and humble and he smells nice, but I'm not entirely sure he gets it.

A couple of weeks later, he's driving a branded Swindon Town van around the area, imploring locals to support us, he's pulling pints in the County Ground Hotel watering hole, he's selling season tickets in the club shop, he's posing for pictures with puppies, he's sitting with the away fans and savouring the attention at Scunthorpe, and you know what?

I think he gets it.

***

Two years on from that suitcase-packing excuse for missing the first game and oddly we're away to Scunthorpe again. Is this a portent that the season will allow us to remove the asterisk from Champions*? Points per game or not, the message this year is of rebuild, pure survival. Of defiance. So Euan and I take that first day M1, M18 journey to Scunthorpe.

This time, there's no spectacular murmuration of starlings, no misery of being four down at half-time, there's no Patrick. It's heartbreaking.

It's heartbreaking to be starting a new season, with hope swelling in hearts, with bellowing *we've got our Swindon back* alongside nine hundred desperate other travelling fans, but without Patrick. We win, a comfortable 3-1 and it's glorious and it's delirious and vibrant and *allez allez oooh* and it's heartbreaking.

It's heartbreaking to do everything without Patrick.

But it's especially heartbreaking to live these moments that he'd have loved, and to be without him.

The next Saturday, it's Carlisle at home and it feels as if we're preparing to celebrate the rebirth of our club. There's so much anticipation, so much to look forward to. If I was more accustomed to this feeling, I'd be able to recognise it as 'hype'. I rather like it. Euan and I spend the week checking online ticket sales, watching blue dots turn grey — and sold — on the interactive seating plan.

Have you had a little look lately?

Yeah, D6U is flying and there's only singles left in A4L.

Up and up we revise our crowd estimates. Eight thousand? Eight and half? Pushing nine?

The club have also confirmed that they'll be holding a roll call of all those we've lost over the past two seasons. Of course, this is such soothing news for us, and a direct reminder of that Swindon Advertiser front page from 18th April last year, and the public remembrance we never had for Patrick and Dad. I read back through comments made by our then manager Richie Wellens, *I would love nothing more than to invite you and your family to our next home game*, and Eoin Doyle, *Next time I have the privilege to pull on the Town shirt, I'll be thinking of Patrick and Mick*, and Keshi Anderson and messages from other players, from comedian Ivo Graham, from so many people we didn't know, but now knew of us. Those messages we cherished, they nourished and warmed us.

That though, was a different world and a different Swindon and of course Richie wasn't around when the fans came back, and Eoin had the privilege of pulling on another club's shirt instead.

I worry a little about the roll call.

Will they have got it right? What if I'm on it as my name was on the simple survey sent through in April? What if Patrick and Dad get missed off?

Andrew, doing an incredible job on the club's social media platforms, emailed me at 1am on the day of the game to confirm they had the right details.

I sleep soundly.

I dream of the roll call of the dead ahead.

I hear Macca's name and I think of his dancing through Watford's defence, of his Wembley roar in celebration, of Genoa and a wild night in Ruislip celebrating a man from Manchester scoring a goal in Belfast to send Ireland to America. I hear Mike Spearman's name and I think of his familiar warm greeting, his urgency, his sniffing out a different pub when there was trouble at Northampton. I think of him picking me up one Sunday in 1984 and driving me to the County Ground to watch Mansfield with barely two thousand others. Since that day when we barely managed a team sheet, never mind a programme, our club has suffered some horrendous times and enjoyed some phenomenal ones. I think of him telling me to open the batting for my cricket team by playing only between mid-on and mid-off to settle my innings and I think of a man who lived for our Swindon Town community, a man who'd be desperately proud to be here today, witnessing the rebirth of our club.

The names fly by, each with their own stories and memories and just before the end there's Dad, and there's Patrick.

And in that dream, it's 2:55pm, and there's a cacophony of applause in the sunshine followed by a raucous, guttural roar to greet the players. It's nearly time to kick off. Season number one hundred and twenty five on this same proud, treasured rectangle of green. Let's do this.

Nearly ten thousand of us have got our Swindon back, even if we don't have everyone back who made our Swindon.

That was the dream, anyway.

With the benefit of decades of build up and anti-climax, I had so enjoyed the almost hysterical excitement of the days until the game, while being wary of a sting in the tail. Maybe the game will be a damp squib, maybe excitement we'll give way to anxiety and frustration. Maybe the emotion and the gratitude will simply give way to more mundane disappointment of mediocre fourth division football. Maybe we'll realise that these new signings are not yet world beaters bestowed on us by the sympathetic footballing gods, maybe they're merely journeymen, thrown together at incredible haste doing their honest, toiling best for us and themselves. Maybe the crash will be today, maybe on Tuesday against Tranmere, surely sometime.

Now though, is a rare chance to reflect, and just to be.

The reality is an incredibly harsh one, not foreseen with 970-odd games of experience.

We've taken Mum, as she deserves to hear and feel and applaud the roll call too, and we're in the ground unusually early, supping in the tension and excitement in the Don Rogers concourse. We get a drink, looking out for familiar faces to earnestly discuss the new team with. We're all trying hard to contain our expectations.

There's a real hubbub, there's anticipatory chatter, the odd chant, and the atmosphere is bubbling. It's helped that the PA in the concourse is barely working, not drowning us out with the more forced and communal build up.

That becomes more of an issue at around 2:35pm, when I detect the possibility that there's a list of names being read out.

Surely not?

I dash to the nearest entrance to the stand and up the steps, straining to hear, gasping for breath. I still can't hear much, but I know this much.

They're reading the roll call out to the few hundred fans already in their seats, and to even fewer who can hear them.

It ends, just a list of names as if it were a shopping list. Try as I desperately do, I heard nothing of Patrick or Dad, just more muffle. There's a ripple of applause from those who have heard, the players are mid warm-up, practising shooting scenarios. The stadium announcer plays the next song.

It's a crippling, crushing disappointment. I'm furious, frustrated and want to go home. Normally it's the first wayward shot that has me feeling like this, but there's still twenty minutes to kick-off and first, I have to tell Mum what she's missed.

We crumple in our seats, crestfallen.

***

The football itself lives down to modest expectations, and a fitter, more streetwise and stronger Carlisle team deserve their 2-1 win.

However, the crowd of close to ten thousand is the highest opening day home support for many years, which rather validates Clem's positivity and the publicity overdrive. We've got our Swindon back, and the possibilities, quite suddenly, are endless.

There is constructive feedback following the roll call debacle and the club resolve to repeat it at the next game.

To their credit, they do. They do repeat it.

They repeat just about everything they got wrong.

This time I'm rueful and resigned.

Sometimes, even when your club is progressive and fan-focused and engaging and generally doing everything else right in the most trying of circumstances, they'll somehow still find a way to fuck it up.

***

I'd wanted to go back to Tottenham since 15th January, 2020. I'd wanted to go back there before of course, to gasp at the billion-pound spaceship that had landed just off the High Road. I'd had Dad pangs of envy that Euan and Patrick were going without me. Dad concerns that they weren't wearing appropriate coats for Storm Brendan. Now I just felt a need to be in the place where Patrick had spent his last, happy hours.

I'd first been to White Hart Lane almost forty years before, and enjoyed so many other glory glory games there, your Bayern Munichs, your Barcelonas and your Derby Countys. My Spurs connection felt real enough. What's more, given Fabrice Muamba's participation in the Sudden Death documentary, the Storyvault team gave me the details of the Spurs media team. I'd half hoped the club might invite us to meet Fabrice maybe, to see a game, but really, I just needed them to acknowledge, somehow, that give or take a tube ride, that Patrick's magical, beautiful life had concluded at their magical, beautiful stadium.

They didn't reply. And they didn't reply when I politely chased them either.

Even so, an UEFA Europa Conference League play-off round against Paços de Ferreira presented an opportunity to get some tickets simply enough. It might have been a half-arsed competition against Portuguese opponents I'd never heard of, but that wasn't really the point. As usual, I'd deliberated more over how Euan and I should get there, than what we would do when we indeed got there. Wherever 'there' is, as London is a big place. A significant proportion of that deliberation was this: Marylebone or not?

Were we prepared to effectively re-trace the post-match steps and aim for that fateful train just after 11pm?

It was without particular plan or purpose, but with time in hand that we alighted at Marylebone. It was still summer, but less absolutely, with the first chimes of autumn not far away. As had become custom, we left flowers on the railings at Gloucester Place, and stood lost, as has also been custom, for what felt like ages. In reality, it was the time for a young family to approach, fumble and find the right keys, enter and disappear beyond the forbidding black door. I pondered for a second about their lives, where they'd been, what they'd do tomorrow, everything they didn't know about Patrick, whether the blue lights and the panic had woken them that night, and whether they ever wondered of it.

We took the Central Line to Liverpool Street, and walked. We were content enough in ourselves, buried in observing the buildings and vibrancy, dodging traffic, enjoying just being. On we walked, Bishopsgate, St Botolph's and memories for me there of productive, collaborative work meetings. Then Aldgate and north towards Spitalfields and the market. Euan introduced me to Brick Lane and on, on we walked to Shoreditch. This wasn't football-territory, it was an enchanting, independent, backstreet London. We really should have stopped to eat and drink but we were in the zone now, sharing our own in-jokes and discovering new places.

An hour or so later, via a deserved pint and watching a test match batting collapse in a garish pub at Highbury, we were wide-eyed on Tottenham High Road. The club shop itself was the size of a small village and even if the ground was to be half-full, there was an expectant match day buzz and busyness. I could feel how much Patrick would have loved this. Inside the stadium, the concourses were more like the food court of a modern shopping centre — a craft ale bar here, noodles stall there, Mediterranean street food too. I didn't see any roasted peanuts though. There were nods to the club's fine heritage, and winks to its space age present.

Goodness me, I could get used to this, I thought. It was mighty grand, if not quite the County Ground.

Our seats were plush and spacious and Tottenham made predictably light work of overcoming a first leg deficit to comfortably progress. To be fair, Swindon would probably have beaten Paços de Ferreira too, but still, the athleticism, technique and verve of an essentially second-string Spurs, albeit including Harry Kane, Lucas Moura and Eric Dier, were exceptional. The lights felt too bright though, the sound was loud and obtrusive and too many of the crowd were curious daytrippers like ourselves. It was a most modern experience, even if tonight, lacking a dash of passion and tension. The thrill of the chase was completed with a couple of deft Kane finishes early doors. But it was football, there was still a rectangle of green, and I bet this place is awesome when it's full and there are three points at stake.

Euan and I didn't talk much on the drag back into central London on the tube. We didn't need to. We'd done what we needed to.

We comfortably made the last train from Marylebone, and possibly exorcised a demon or two in the process.

***

Post-Patrick, as if there was a life before, and less of a life since, I've thought more and more about Nick, my Swansea uni friend who'd been shot dead in the Brazilian rainforest. More specifically, I've thought about what he left behind, how his family coped, how they knew how much we cared.

And in my case, they'll never have known, because I never said a word.

And why, as a friendship group, had we drifted so completely apart?

I wanted to understand, to put things right, make amends, and start afresh. Maybe too, it could offer a neat conclusion to this story. Swindon playing Salford away in August offered such opportunities.

Unfortunately, my attempts to trace Nick's family drew blanks — I'd have loved to visit and say: *sorry, I have sincerely cared all these years.*

It's taken the death of my own son for me to see how much you needed that.

I had better fortune in making contact with three of my dear friends from the time — Andy, Mark and Jackie. But it just wasn't logistically possible to get together and answer our own questions — and maybe, for the first time, nearly thirty years late, to laugh and cry and remember Nick.

That's how it was: me and Euan, just the two of us again, on another journey to find Nick's grave, another journey to Salford. We left early, for us, at 9:30am with an old Swindon scarf draped from the rear passenger window. Patrick would have insisted and he would have put up with the repeated thud of the scarf against the window. It's a grubby red now, having seen action the length and breadth of our motorway system, with the old chevron 'S' badge, and suddenly this simple polyester emblem carries with it a life load of significance.

It was raining and the traffic was backed up on the A40 before we'd even made it to Eynsham.

It didn't get any better. Holds ups on the M40. Roadworks on the M6. Euan dozed and that rush of early excitement waned. We couldn't agree on what to listen to. Time was getting tight. We ran for a comfort break at Knutsford Services, but there was no time for food.

We had to find Nick.

It was a minute to 2pm when I pulled up on the slip road opposite Manchester's Southern Cemetery. There was a row of shops — funeral directors, flower shops, a carpet store, a Persian Grill. We had an hour to find Nick, get back to the car, drive across the city to Salford, park and get in the ground.

This time I had flowers.

This time I had a letter to leave, in the hope that someone, anyone finds it.

I've written:

Dear family of Nick,

I'd love to think this message finds you fit and well. Many many years ago now, I was a friend of Nick's at Swansea University. While I wasn't his closest friend, everyone was his best friend. That's how he made people feel. Together we'd laugh, drink, dream, debate and laugh some more. His grin is unforgettable.

I want you to know that I care and have cared all these years, although I'm sorry that I've been hopeless at telling you that. Of course a little of Nick will have lived on in each of us — that smile, his determination to enjoy life, his sense of adventure, his gentle caring nature — I'm so grateful for how he was the best of friends, in the best of times.

I'd like you to know that I've often thought about Nick, sometimes visited his grave here, watched his tree grow strong in the sea breeze at Swansea University. I've thought about you too, and how desperate your journey must have been without him.

I appreciate now how lonely that must have been, as my own son Patrick died suddenly, aged fifteen last year. I know now your pain and your devastation and your loneliness. I sincerely hope that somehow, through all these years, that you're here and reading this and have carried Nick's beautiful light with you.

Take care and best regards,

Liam x

Facebook: Patrick's Place

I took the time to gather myself, breathe, fiddle with an extra layer, pull the scarf in from the window. It had been a shocking journey. I had printed pictures of Nick's tree at Swansea, folded with the letter in a simple plastic container and wrapped with a green bow. It was the best this boy could do. That, and hope.

Moment of calm over, we dashed over the road and through Morrissey's celebrated cemetery gates. The place was enormous and absolutely daunting. It must have been more than ten years since I was last here and surely it had doubled in size and grown arms and legs. I recognise pretty much nothing.

Euan remembered nothing of his visit before that Stockport game in 2007. Except:

Dad it was raining then, and it's raining now.

He was a boy then, he's a man now.

We strode purposefully in a direction, as if the haste we approach the task in will make it more effective. This was colossal, there must be millions, millions of people buried here. We weren't even remotely close to needle in haystack territory.

It was hopeless.

I summon a Pogues lyric, and while 'Galway Races' may have been written in a different context, I could really do with inducing fresh acquaintance with Nick's grave right then.

There was half a million people there
Of all denominations
The Catholic, the Protestant, the Jew, the Presbyterian
Yet there was no animosity
No matter what persuasion
But fáilte hospitality
Inducing fresh acquaintance

At least there was a method to our haste, I worked north to south, Euan west to east. Occasionally we criss-crossed and had to say *Found anything?* as if the answer would be *oh yeah, just back that way but I forgot to tell you.*

I had such a range of emotions — mainly bemoaning the frustration of the moment, the futility of our search, the feeling of letting Nick down, the lack of pre-planning and nearly forgetting … the football. Salford! It was forty-five minutes to kick-off.

We won't miss the kick-off.

There's surely no chance?

It had to be quick.

Poles, there were hundreds of Poles buried. Surely the Irish can't be far away?

I don't think it works like that Dad.

We found the grave of Sir Matt Busby's wife, but it was not happening.

It was really not happening.

It was half past two when we got back in the car. Disconsolate, without time for being disconsolate.

I didn't even leave the flowers.

***

Game heads on, we headed for the heart of Manchester and knowing we'd be lucky to make the kick-off at Salford. I took accidentally clever detours through Hulme and Moss Side, without convincing Euan that I knew Manchester like the back of my hand. I couldn't even find a grave.

I smiled the most wry and most reluctant of wry smiles as I saw a sign for that vast Catholic Church where Nick's service was held. I think of the rushed arrival then, and even more bad parking on the verge and of the dizziness and overwhelming pain of the occasion. At the same time, Euan was trying to tell me the team news and we were discussing potential permutations and formations and I was trying to navigate four lanes of traffic and conflicting advice from the satnav and Google on the phone and in my head I was thirty years away and sat in a pub in Rusholme.

Twenty-three minutes until kick-off.

It was five and a bit hours since we'd left home. We were starving, and on the wrong side of a big city. Euan said:

What do you think the most hungry you've ever been in your life is?

And we had a beautiful, bizarre discussion, wondering whether we might get a set of delightfully presented downloaded data on our deathbeds, answering our questions, informing us when we'd most needed a wee, of the biggest sandwich we'd ever eaten, which words we'd said the most, the nearest the moon we'd been … and so on. After all, we said, we'd then have eternal time to analyse it.

I weaved across the carriageway and soon we were passing the turning for Salford Lads Club. That Smiths pilgrimage, followed by the Classic Football Shirts shop and Patrick becoming the retro Hibee, felt an eternal time itself away. It was less than two years ago.

Silly conversations aside, we really were hungry and at 2:45pm we ran into a garage beside the A576, the sort of garage where I had to pay to take some cash out. However starving we were, however limp and unappealing and pitiful the sandwich fare was, we needed this. Beggars can't be, and all that, so Euan had a chicken tikka masala sandwich with a pickled onion monster munch side and a cold mocha and I had a chicken and bacon sandwich, a brave packet of very beefy crisps and a bottle of water.

We weren't far from Salford City's Peninsula Stadium now, but it was permit-only parking everywhere and fans were scurrying towards the ground, anxious in case they missed the first precious moments of a new game. I couldn't find anywhere to park.

Every game starts the same, with the promise that anything could happen. This could be that day.

They won't miss the kick-off.

We ended up parking in exactly the same place as our previous visit, and at least half a mile from the stadium. It was 2:54pm and I ensured I was parked legally and decently, deliberated unnecessarily over layers, hid away anything that could be attractive, and readied myself to eat my sandwich on the go.

Two mouthfuls and twenty paces in, and we saw a ginger cat.

For me, it had already been a whirlwind day: tortuous journey, failing Nick, neglecting nutrition and basic care, dealing with swirling emotions. The cat made me pause. I felt Patrick's presence so strongly with us — ahhh, what a day we had here before, what a day.

And then our world exploded.

Two more houses and remarkably, there was another ginger cat and it's moments like this that carry me and nourish me and sustain me. When it feels like friends have stopped messaging, invites stopped landing and that the world is too cruel a place — a ginger cat at the right time and the right place and on I shall go.

We were rushing now, I barely registered the extra strong flavour of the crisps and could hear match day cranking into life, with the Swindon fans in fine voice in the distance.

We rushed on, not far now.

What's the most you've missed the kick-off by Dad?

Last time we went to Wycombe, we were 2-1 down by the time I made it, and once I saw the last ten minutes of Leeds against Oxford. That was a weird weekend.

Today, we did miss the kick-off, but not by so much. We took our place on the terrace, in the same place as before and breathed, we were here. The game, without being pulsating or particularly high quality, zipped along and it was half time before we knew it. We looked sloppy and shaky, with some square pegs in round holes. In the second half we pinched a goal, which later proved to have been marginally offside, and scrapped and game managed and fluked ourselves to a 1-0 win. Any victories are special, but this one, this fortuitously, after this day, felt more special than many others.

We've got our Swindon back.

The journey home was, thankfully, a relative breeze. We were tired, yet content, and looking forward to the next game.

I opened the front door and said to Kate:

Here, I've bought you some flowers.

Sorry Nick, one day.

***

Have I avoided thinking much about Patrick's last evening? How much of a contrast it was to Dad's most tranquil passing? Dad died so gently, in peace and at peace, soothed by Christy Moore's gorgeous songs. Patrick will have been consumed by the football, Tottenham's remarkable stadium, Mourinho's pacing and histrionics, I know that much. But what about the tube journey back to central London and then the walk towards Marylebone? He'll have been tired, I know that much too. A day at school, the excitement of getting to and across London, the grins and gasps at this new White Hart Lane, a dash back to Seven Sisters. Of course, he'd have been tired as he sat down, maybe felt his eyelids softly closing, comfortable with the brother he adored beside him. Did he feel any pain? Any twinges? Anything at all other than satisfaction of another beautiful evening and a longing to be back home in his bed? I know too that he knew he was loved by those not beside him, his sister, mum, dad and grandparents and wider family. His friends were incredibly precious to him too. He'd have been as desperate to tell them about his adventure at school the next morning as I was to tell of Ardiles and Hoddle and roasted peanuts nearly forty years before.

And what else went through his mind in his fateful last minutes? Storm Brendan had wreaked its havoc, its impact limited to debris strewn on streets, while a personal hurricane was about to blow our lives apart. Sucked into the vortex and spinning, spinning, spinning until we were catapulted out into a world we no longer recognised or much cared for.

Was he purely living in the moment, concentrating on dodging puddles, crossing roads, smiling at the sights and sounds of late-night London? Surely he wasn't worrying about his Maths homework being shoddy or late? Was there a bolt of pain, a knowing of his fate? Did his life flash before him? One last burst of 'What Shall We Do With The Drunken Sailor' rising through him perhaps? A last goal? A last cheeky impression? A last feeling of overwhelming, natural love and blinding lights?

For me, to have to even consider these questions is still unbearable, and to write and share them is simply heartbreaking. I don't have any answers and I never will have. My only comfort is that Euan was with him. However, at least I have considered, written and shared them, and maybe that's progress.

***

There's more progress to share. That painful and unique arm cancer that haunted my nights before a flight to Dubai has been cured. It's a wonder what a few months of physiotherapy, a realignment of work desk configuration and a whoopee cushion to improve sitting posture can do.

December

Wembley Way. It's cold, the stunning arch of the new stadium shimmers white, dramatically before me. High above, plane passengers peer through tiny windows, scanning the London skyline for any glimpse of the iconic landmark.

In my mind though, as my eyes close, are the two huge twin towers of the old stadium. We're in the vastest car park, the size of our town. There are fans scurrying towards the stadium, there are flags, scarves, rosettes, and programme sellers. There is a sensory overload of sights and sounds. There are roasted peanuts for sale. I want a flag.

I'm eight years old.

There's my Dad.

I'm eight years old and I want a flag.

I breathe, open my eyes and walk on.

This time, Patrick is nearly eight years old. Swindon have just lost to Chesterfield in the Football League Trophy final at Wembley. He pulls his Paolo di Canio mask over his face to hide his freckled face of tears. A giant, polyester flag lies crumpled beside him. The anticipation, excitement and emotion of the past few weeks — we scraped past Barnet over two legs to get here you know — come pouring out.

That's football, son. It comes in many shapes and sizes.

That's life, Patrick. He has a lifetime, his brief beautiful lifetime ahead of him, to grow accustomed to snatching improbable defeats. To walk with hope up Wembley Way, and disconsolately back down it.

You need not wear a mask, my son.

I breathe and walk on, hope in my heart.

Tonight, I reach for Niamh's hand and tell her about all the times we came to this place. Once a dark, forbidding, grim palace fading fast, now a giant, too big for its boots cavernous, corporate bowl. But always with a special place in our dreams, in our dreams. All the times watching England, or supporting Ireland against them, the highs of Swindon in the old stadium, our woes in the new, the easy times as a neutral.

As a father, as a son.

The time I forgot the tickets for an Olympic game, the time Patrick was waving an Arsenal flag at a Community Shield, the time we were home before our friends had finished queuing at Wembley Stadium station.

I know I'll never walk alone.

We're nearly at the steps now, the Bobby Moore statue ahead of us. We pause and I glance back, once that vast car park, now a collection of gleaming skyscrapers.

Don't look back, Liam, keep moving.

I do look back, and am overwhelmed by a million memories. I tighten my grip on my daughter's hand. This evening, we turn right and head for Wembley Arena. Oddly, of the hundreds of gigs I've ever been to, I reckon I've been here just twice before, and hey Niamh, how special they were.

The Pogues, Christmas 1988. All the times I went with Dad to see the Pogues at Brixton Academy, and he didn't come on this raucous night of fairytales. But it wasn't Brixton.

Then a huge gap to see Frank Turner supported by Billy Bragg with Kate. All the times we'd seen Billy. I pull at my collar and muse wistfully:

When the world falls apart, some things stay in place

All the venues up and down the Cowley Road in Oxford we'd adored Frank. And here they were, together, playing *Wembley*.

Now, tonight, Niamh and I reach the entrance, in neon letters the size of our house it says Manic Street Preachers. And I stop moving and look back again. I look back to Swansea, to rejecting these outlandish valley boy upstarts of 1990, to my old mate Nick and to all that I had then, and appreciate all that I've gained since. And the Manics, like Swindon Town Football Club, have remained constant in my life.

It's my first arena gig for a long, long time and I'm taken aback at how emotional the light show, the immense sound and the melancholic sweep of just being here makes me feel. And the songs. The songs and the memories and the room glistens with rich, evocative meaning. The sense of how much time has passed, and also how little. Five of these songs are about thirty years old.

The Manics *know*. They play 'La Tristesse Durera': the sadness will last forever. They play 'Afterending':

We enter a night of nothingness
Even your shadow disappears
Reality becomes an apology
And waking up the catastrophe
Sail into the abyss with me
After ending, and after belief"

The sadness will last forever. I'm quite overcome.

However, *yma o hyd*: we're still here.

With majestic and dramatic inevitability, James leads thousands into bellowing 'libraries gave us power ...' and I tell Niamh that the Manics don't do encores, that this is it.

'A Design For Life'.

The Manics don't do encores.

I take Niamh's hand.

Life, *life* doesn't do encores, I breathe.

This is it.

***

Outside, there are stars, of course. There's a sensation of cold air kissing our faces and a blur as we accustom ourselves to being out of the noise, emotion and escape and back into this world.

I think of Dad, of his train trips from Bampton, of a rural Irish boy marvelling at the sight of Wembley stadium, pre-floodlights, for afternoon England games. Of him in March 1969, skipping down Wembley Way with the widest grin. Of his gentle, beautiful humility.

I think of Patrick — soaked for Millwall, in tears after Chesterfield, utter dejection after Preston. Those were his ultimately miserable childhood Wembley days supporting Swindon. Of everything we did together, the love we had, and not regretting a single thing. Of his own gentle, beautiful nature, and what he's left us with.

So I think of our journey since late night, 14th January, 2020 and Storm Brendan.

The love and support, the loneliness, the anxiety, the longing, and the sheer bloody pain. Kate, Niamh, Euan and I have shared the positives and are proud of these, of every step we've taken. I'm so proud of each of them, and Mum, for each one of those steps. We've not really publicly shared too much of that pain, or the immense emotional and physical effort to just be, to carry on.

Every day since Patrick died is a day further away from the connection we had and every day his old friends are a day further into their own journeys without him. The idea that who he was gets loosened, lost or forgotten is unbearable for me.

The air outside is sharper now. High above a lone plane traces across the sky. I can't help but wonder where from, where to. Connections, connections. I can't help but wonder that for all of us too, where from and where to? Where to?

The words the Manic Street Preachers left the stage to are etched within me. This time it's not 1983 and Nena singing about red balloons, it's 2021.

There's a time for departure, even when there's no certain place to go.
(Tennessee Williams)

Epilogue

2022

27th May

It's Patrick's eighteenth birthday.

This week, I dreamt vividly about Patrick. He's playing football. He's busy, tidy, utterly consumed by the game, living the moment.

Later, he'll talk about it endlessly, analysing each touch, pass, and exaggerating each intervention. Until the next game. There's always a next game. He's in his place.

This morning, Kate and I visited his stone at the cemetery. We left flowers, left homemade cupcakes with too much icing on and ran together. We ran over the fields towards South Leigh, back up and over the hill at High Cogges. We appreciated nature, today for its resilience and endurance as much as its wonder and beauty, and dug deep for our own. A kestrel circled high above, tugging briefly at our attention.

This afternoon, as a family, we walked again up White Horse Hill, watched a train meander from east to west and breathed in gulps of the fresh ancient ridgeway air. The sun, knowing we were on a mission, shone valiantly for us. We could see the clump of trees above Burford to the north and the shape of the Chilterns way to the east. We ate Kate's delicious Guinness cakes and watched planes trace across the sky. I couldn't help but check their journeys: London to New York, Frankfurt to Toronto, Paris to Boston, and wonder about the lives within; the loves and dreams, and anxieties and concerns thirty-five thousand feet above me. Their connections. For a moment, just a minute or two, as I lay back on the sharp hilltop grass, close my eyes and feel the sun kiss my face; things feel ok.

This evening, we cracked open the bottle of champagne that Patrick won at the Witney Mills Cricket Club quiz five years ago. We promised then that we'd save it for his 18th.

Patrick, my love, we did.

A few weeks ago, we'd stopped in an unfamiliar town, hungry strangers seeking swift sustenance before continuing our journey. A group of five teenage boys came out of a Sainsbury's Local giggling, relaxed, full of the joys of spring and youth. How familiar this looked to a lost world of ours. Saturday mates without a care in the world. One of them was a little shorter than the rest, his hair was a subtle red and his face was sprinkled with freckles. He reached for his bag and pulled out a packet of iced buns to share with his friends, oblivious to us observers.

It was heartbreaking and comforting and normal and ridiculous all at once. Waves of emotion crashed through me, while Kate's tears flowed as she stood open-mouthed and motionless.

Two years on, I don't know what this tells us about our grief. I do know though that grief won't go away, or get better, or to expect healing. Rather, our lives will continue to grow around the grief. I do know that when the waves hit, they hit. I know too that whenever there is calm and peace or sometimes fun and laughter, then that's ok. The grief is still with me, a scratch or photo or comment or song away. It is so much a fundamental part of me, and always will be.

Patrick's friends have gone out to celebrate his birthday and we cherish them dearly. In the last few weeks, they've invited us to share in their pre-prom pictures and with A-Levels imminent for many, planted a tree at Henry Box School in Patrick's memory. Although both events were heart-wrenchingly difficult for Kate and I to attend, they were beautiful, sensitive and unforgettable.

We shared iced buns together, and asked them to take a little of Patrick with them on their exciting adventures ahead and to know that he'd be so proud of every step they take.

It has seemed like destiny for months that Swindon Town's remarkable season would end in a playoff victory at Wembley tomorrow. After the travails of last summer, our humble, magnificent football club has been reborn. From impossible beginnings it has been an extraordinary year. We've got our Swindon back.

And with the denouement scheduled for the day after Patrick's 18th? What abundantly obvious triumph awaits!

With Niamh living literally in the shadow of Wembley Stadium, we'll take flowers to Gloucester Place, take Dad and Patrick in our hearts, seal promotion and mark his eighteenth in a very special way.

Swindon's playoff journey took us to the Potteries, optimistic and expectant. One last step before Wembley. When Port Vale missed two of their first three penalties in the semi-final shootout last Thursday, Euan turned to me and whispered *Dad, we're nearly there.*

I couldn't watch.

For sixteen penalties, I stared at my trainers and thought of Patrick, his lifetime flashing before me, and what he'd give to be sharing this glorious agony with us. Of Dad, and all the glorious agonies we shared together. I depended on the reactions; the sighs and the roars of the crowd around me. I anticipated Wembley with and without them ahead.

Somehow, incredibly, we lost.

Defeat, most improbably snatched.

The season was over.

Minutes later, we were traipsing out, silent and broken, into the now chill Burslem air.

Football comes in many shapes and sizes, I thought, *but it doesn't do fairytales.*

Or maybe, for some, it does. Just half an hour up the M6, Stockport County were revelling in their own promotion and a return to the Football League that had appeared entirely unlikely a few short long years ago. So at last they can look forward to stuffing us 3-0 again. And I'll look forward to finding Nick's grave again and leaving a note in the hope his family finds it, and know how much I've thought of him all this time.

I'll leave some flowers too.

Three days after Swindon's ordeal, Waterford's hurling season ended with a crushing defeat to Clare. Despite beginning the Munster Championship on a wave of optimism and second favourites for the All-Ireland on the back of a National League victory, early promise disintegrated.

It's now sixty-three summers since Waterford last won an All-Ireland Senior Hurling Championship.

Yesterday, I met Paul for a most civilised cup of tea in what passes for a bustling rush hour in Clanfield. By chance, it was exactly two years since we'd run together, jogging past the attention-seeking roses and the frankly ridiculously splendid houses of Eastleach, the day before I did ten thousand steps for the 1,000th consecutive day.

The day before Patrick's sixteenth birthday.

We chatted through so many things that day, and now this one too. We planned designing a bespoke kit for Patrick's forthcoming memorial football match half a mile up the road, and Patrick's Place sponsoring a kit for the South African football academy half a world away. Paul brimmed with pride telling me that they were now expanding into another Cape Town site and offering education and life coaching to the township teams too.

I grinned as I said I like neat endings and connections that wrap and make sense.

This would wrap the story of Paul and I, since the best of days he left that message when I was three quarters of the way up a hill or maybe a mountain in Knockeengancan, Waterford, Ireland. Niamh admired the horse. The bloodstained farmer halted calving. He kindly showed us the remarkable remains of my grandmother's family home. Then Paul phoned to say that he might, he might just have tickets to the All-Ireland Senior Hurling Final. Dad was happy.

This would wrap that perfect story with the most colourful luxurious paper and the prettiest, most extravagant bow.

Paul did a better grin, and said:

No, this isn't an ending, this can be a beginning

He said that the guys in Cape Town are really keen and love the idea. We shared more ideas and part of me could already see myself joining him on a forthcoming trip one day.

I've now managed 1,730 consecutive days of ten thousand steps, since the headiness of the Guinness and the excitement of those tickets inadvertently prolonged my evening in Whelans Bar, Stradbally beyond midnight.

So much has happened along those 25,517,463 steps since. Those steps have come in many shapes and sizes, I think, and while many of them have been unbearably tough, there have been fairytales too.

I know that I, and Kate and Niamh and Euan, do not walk alone.

I know that I do not walk alone because I have cherished friends like Rupert and Leggy who today sent a picture from their Champions League Final weekend in Paris. They'd left one of Patrick's Sunshine On Leith stickers in a Parisian bar. The bar, of course, was called Patrick's, and now they're the ones grinning, toasting it with a beer with his name too.

***

So it's been some week.

And on Saturday, my gorgeous friend Graham died by suicide.

***

At his funeral in a couple of weeks, we'll be implored to respect his choice.

We'll hear 'Vapour Trail' by our local favourites Ride and be asked to think of those trails in the bright blue sky above as our memories of him and a beautiful life warmly lived. I summon another sad wry smile reflecting on my own fondness for staring at vapour trails and wondering, wondering. And now, Graham, *this*.

Graham and I have been friends since primary school. He has been there for me, smiling in a million photos, enjoying a thousand nights out, supportive over life's twists and turns for forty years. Our families became friends too. That's why I'd picked him to run the first leg of that half marathon with me: he was literally my first choice. He'd recently run his own first half marathon, while injured, to honour those who'd sponsored him. I was beyond proud of him. Last Saturday, we ran the first half of Witney parkrun together. We chatted cheerfully about football, about gigs, about his recent cycle ride across south Wales.

About plans. About the future.

We were running through our sumptuous tree-lined avenues. I knew every bump and protruding root, each low-hanging branch. The rain in the week had given fresh and accelerated growth to leaves, bushes, clumps of grass, and stinging nettles in awkward places. The sense and spring scents of green felt extravagant, this wholesomeness of May abound with the certainties of nature and life.

Perhaps sensing I was impatient to run a little quicker, Graham said:

Mate, you go on.

I will.

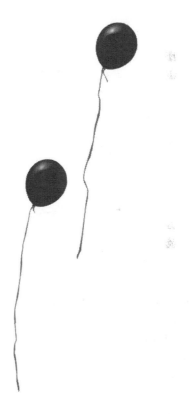

Acknowledgements

22nd April, 2023

I'm writing this update and these acknowledgements en route to watching Swindon Town play away at Wimbledon. While the end of a largely underwhelming and dispiriting season is nigh, at least the club now jointly own the County Ground with TrustSTFC, and perhaps the next years will be better than the last ones. We'll leave a Sunshine On Leith sticker at Gloucester Place in Marylebone, and think of Patrick. We'll have a pint close to the ground in The Castle at Tooting Broadway and raise a glass to Dad, imagining him at twenty-six springs young as Swindon won the League Cup, and he was three days away from becoming the best father.

As one season ends, so another begins. Tomorrow, Waterford's hurling championship season starts against Limerick, the All-Ireland champions. Expectations are modest, but you know what, who knows? That wait, since 1959, surely it has to end some time?

It's what football does to you; it's what hurling does to you.

Yesterday, I met up with Paul, and he was right. Maybe it still is the beginning for us with the We Love Football Academy in Cape Town. Today, there are players there running around in Patrick's Place kit, and tomorrow? Well, now we have fresh ideas …

Next month, we will remember Graham as we run around Blenheim Palace on the first anniversary of his death. We're raising money for CALM — the Campaign Against Living Miserably charity (thecalmzone.net) — and maybe there'll be vapour trails to gaze at too.

It's now 2,061 consecutive days of ten thousand steps since that late night giddiness in Stradbally. Each step — and I'm a day away from thirty million in that time — very literally, counts.

***

I am humbled to share *Red Balloons* and delighted to be able to thank some of those who've made it happen.

Little do they know it, but when Faye Carrick and Brigid Greaney sat on our sofa drinking tea imploring me to *do it, do it*, a vague idea became an actual possibility. It was an otherwise innocuous moment that I returned to time after time to re-energise and focus.

The greatest supporter of my writing, over many years, has been Anthony Bunn (@DUCKmagstoke on Twitter). If you have a yearning to delve into Stoke City Football Club's last decade, I heartily recommend his seventy-eight splendid issues of *Duck* magazine. Thanks too to the wider footballing community, particularly Chris O'Keeffe of the fantastic *Turnstiles* magazine (@turnstilesmag). The extraordinary, unofficial, online encyclopedia swindon-town-fc.co.uk is what the internet was invented for. Thank you to Rob Angus and Dave Wrixton at Swindon Town Football Club.

Once I'd written ninety thousand words and was nervously ready to share them, I needed someone to actually read them. Gretta Whelan was bravely the first to complete that initial draft, and although I was too scared to read her feedback for three days, her response was so heart-warming and encouraging that I was ready for more. Andrew Cannons offered much valued insight, sharp pencil suggestions and caring support in equal measure, while Alan Frost confirmed its emotional impact.

Together with Alan, the likes of Steve Harris, Rupert Macfarlane, Lee McGuinness and Peter Osborne offered not only treasured companionship through shivering nights in socially-distanced beer gardens, but genuine interest and encouragement.

Kudos to all in the Witney Roadrunners and the Witney parkrun communities: each of your personal journeys inspire me so much, and who knows, maybe someday there's a story in that …

As if they'd been hiding around the corner waiting for me to cry *what next?*, Adam Bushby and Rob MacDonald at Halcyon Publishing materialised at exactly the right time. Their guidance and desire to make *Red Balloons* real means the world to me. They have been sensitive and welcoming, and I can't thank them enough. As well their other books, check out the Halcyon Podcast too. Steve Leard's beautiful cover design has achieved heartfelt and unanimous praise from all directions; visit your local bookshop and you'll see his excellent work looking at you from all directions. Thank you to Graham Holland for his stunning and patient photography. Thanks too to Halcyon's right-hand woman Lizzie Fee, who gave so much of her time and vital experience to bringing our story to the attention of so many people. Massive thanks to everyone at the Art Of The Possible Agency and Caoimhe Hale in particular.

We're really grateful for Halcyon Publishing's support of SUDC UK (sudc.org.uk) too. Thank you to all at SUDC UK and the SUDC Foundation in the USA, and most particularly to the inspirational Nikki Speed and Laura Gould, for their ongoing support.

Nikki led the SUDC UK contribution to the National Child Mortality Database's Programme Thematic Report published in 2022 on Sudden and Unexpected Deaths in Infancy and Childhood. From that, we now know that Patrick is one of just ten children aged 5-17 whose 2020 death remains 'unexplained'. Our experience with the Coroner's Service is captured in a 'Poor communication and information sharing' section. SUDC was consequently debated in the House of Parliament in January 2023 and it felt a critical step forward in awareness, understanding and towards preventing future occurrences. Meanwhile, we have now received our results from the genetic testing in the USA: the SUDC Registry and Research Collaborative provided a Family Genetics Analysis Report and its findings are that no clinically significant variants were identified. This means that there are still no genetic clues, but as science progresses it might be that we learn more at some point in the future.

Other charities too have supported our steps. They are staffed by amazing people doing extraordinary things. Kate is now one of them, working part-time as a facilitator in London with SLOW.

Thank you in particular to all at:

- Helen & Douglas House (support for terminally ill children and bereaved families): helenanddouglas.org.uk
- SeeSaw (grief support for children and young people in Oxfordshire): seesaw.org.uk
- SLOW (Surviving the Loss of your World — support for bereaved parents and siblings): slowgroup.co.uk
- Cry (Cardiac Risk in the Young): c-r-y.org.uk
- HASAG (Asbestos Disease Support): hasag.co.uk
- SADS (Sudden Arrhythmic Death): sadsuk.org.uk
- Compassionate Friends (supporting bereaved parents and families): tcf.org.uk

Whether you're part of *Red Balloons*, barely mentioned or not at all, thank you to everyone who has supported us through the last three years: every message, hug, bunch of flowers, cup of tea, walk, or whatever, is sincerely appreciated.

The story and arc of *Red Balloons* itself soon took on a particularly sports-centred and above all, male focus. It is not a comprehensive family history, and the adventures and special memories created with Kate, Niamh and Mum, for example, are hugely under-represented here. I thank them enormously for their love and understanding, and Euan for his, in that the opposite may be true and that there's too much of him. I am so proud of them all; while keeping their hearts full of memories, they're able to look forward and embrace their own new challenges and adventures. Each has their own beautiful perspective and story to tell. Niamh especially has also provided wonderful editorial and sage input throughout, and, of course, ensured that horses are fairly represented.

Last month, I was back in county Waterford, gathered with wider family descendants to commemorate the life of John Walsh, aged twenty-three when he was killed in the Irish Civil War exactly a hundred years ago. As we shared old photographs, tall tales and hand-written family trees, we smiled and pondered at the fates that had brought us back together. More than anything, we thought, it was storytelling, and a natural, instinctive yearning to evoke and to keep our shared belongings and history alive.

It was a timely and tender realisation for me too.

Of course!

This is precisely what I've intended for Patrick, and for Dad.

If I could find a souvenir
Just to prove the world was here ...